175
High-Impact
Resumes

175 HIGH-IMPACT RESUMES
SECOND EDITION

Richard H. Beatty

John Wiley & Sons, Inc.

New York • Chichester • Weinheim • Brisbane • Singapore • Toronto

Copyright © 1999 by Richard H. Beatty. All rights reserved.
Published by John Wiley & Sons, Inc.
Published simultaneously in Canada.

No part of this publication may be reproduced, stored in a retrieval system or transmitted in any form or by any means, electronic, mechanical, photocopying, recording, scanning or otherwise, except as permitted under Sections 107 or 108 of the 1976 United States Copyright Act, without either the prior written permission of the Publisher, or authorization through payment of the appropriate per-copy fee to the Copyright Clearance Center, 222 Rosewood Drive, Danvers, MA 01923, (978) 750-8400, fax (978) 750-4744. Requests to the Publisher for permission should be addressed to the Permissions Department, John Wiley & Sons, Inc., 605 Third Avenue, New York, NY 10158-0012, (212) 850-6011, fax (212) 850-6008, E-Mail: PERMREQ@WILEY.COM..

This publication is designed to provide accurate and authoritative information in regard to the subject matter covered. It is sold with the understanding that the publisher is not engaged in rendering professional services. If professional advice or other expert assistance is required, the services of a competent professional person should be sought.

Library of Congress Cataloging-in-Publication Data:

Beatty, Richard H., 1939–
       175 high-impact resumes / Richard H. Beatty. — 2nd ed.
          p.   cm.
       Includes index.
       ISBN 0-471-31476-5 (cloth : alk. paper).
       1. Resumes (Employment)   I. Title.
    HF5383.B324   1999
    808'.06665—dc21   98-24356

Printed in the United States of America

10   9   8   7   6   5   4   3   2   1

To Michele Brown and Ann Sheara, my competent, motivated, and ever efficient office managers, who played a major role in helping me to pull this project together.

Preface

This book gets quickly to the heart of the target—what is important to preparing a "high-impact" resume—one that will command the attention of prospective employers and stack the employment deck in your favor. There is much you can do to improve the overall effectiveness and impact of your employment resume, and the benefits of such improvement to your job-hunting campaign are countless!

This book is divided into three chapters. The first of these chapters provides a complete blueprint and step-by-step instructions for preparing a "high-impact" resume, including a sample resume that can be used to model your own resume.

To facilitate learning, the key elements of the model resume are numbered on the face of the resume sample itself. As the chapter proceeds, each of these components is then systematically described in detail, so there is a clear understanding of its design, content, and overall importance to resume effectiveness.

By following this step-by-step process and using the model resume and chapter instructions, the reader should be able to easily prepare a highly effective resume.

New to this Second Edition, in Chapter 1, is a brief section on the electronic resume. This section provides guidelines for preparing a resume document that is computer scannable, and includes a sample of such a resume for your reference.

Chapter 2 contains 125 high-impact resumes. They represent the resumes of experienced persons who, in many cases, have several years of work experience. They are "actual" resumes that have been hand-picked from more than 25,000 resumes received by the author's company over a five-year period. As such, they represent a broad cross-section of resume samples, and were chosen for inclusion in this book on the basis of their overall strength and impact. Although these are authentic resumes, minor alterations have been made in the interests of protecting the privacy and confidentiality of the candidates.

In Chapter 3, you will find 50 high-impact resumes of recent college graduates who have little if any professional work experience. Many are seeking their first full-time, entry-level professional job in their chosen field. As with the resumes of experienced personnel in Chapter 2, these college resumes are actual resumes that have been carefully selected and have been somewhat altered to protect the identity and confidentiality of the individual.

The collection of resumes contained in this book is intended to stimulate your thinking on how to improve the effectiveness and impact of your resume. By reviewing what others have done to create good resumes, you will come across some helpful ideas and techniques that will serve to increase the overall impact and forcefulness of your own resume document.

To facilitate the use of Chapters 2 and 3, you will want to refer to the Contents. You will discover that like resumes (i.e., resumes of persons working in the same fields or occupational areas) have been grouped together throughout the book. This will help you to identify those resume samples that most closely correspond to your areas of occupational interest and personal need.

It is believed that by following the step-by-step resume instructions in Chapter 1, and then using the resume samples contained in the subsequent chapters to further upgrade and strengthen your initial resume draft, you will end up creating a highly effective resume that will serve you well throughout your entire job-hunting campaign.

I wish you great success in your pursuit of a meaningful and satisfying career, and I hope that, through this book, I might somehow help you to achieve what you are capable of becoming. Best wishes for career success!

RICHARD H. BEATTY

West Chester, Pennsylvania

Contents

1

The High-Impact Resume

Having a hard-hitting, high-impact resume can do wonders for the effectiveness of your job search. The validity of this statement becomes particularly evident when you examine the many ways this document is used by employers in deciding which employment candidate to hire. Let's take a moment to consider various uses and their impact on the employer's hiring decision.

- **Communications Document**

Your resume is first and foremost a communications document. Its purpose is to communicate clearly and succinctly to employers your work-related skills and abilities. If your resume communicates effectively, employers will be able to easily understand and assess your qualifications for current openings. If your resume is poorly organized and sloppily written, communication will be impeded and employers will likely move on to the next resume on the pile, never giving yours a second thought.

- **Marketing Document**

Your resume is also a marketing document that can persuade employers of your value for the type of work for which you are applying. Your resume must do a solid job of convincing employers of your "unique value" when compared to the many other employment candidates with whom you are competing. Failure to quickly and effectively establish this value will relegate your resume to the reject pile. If you get a reply at all, it's likely to be a "no interest" letter.

- **Interview Road Map**

Frequently, a resume serves as a kind of interview road map. As such, it can have significant impact on interview results.

How many times have you participated in or observed an interview process where the interviewer uses the resume as the basis for guiding the interview discussion? In doing so, the interviewer generally goes through the resume line by line, asking appropriate probing questions along the way.

A poorly organized and badly written resume can create confusion and waste valuable interview time while the employer seeks clarification. Additionally, if poorly prepared, your resume may guide the interviewer down some side roads and back alleys that you may not wish to traverse (i.e., focusing discussions on your shortcomings and failures).

Conversely, if well written and thoughtfully organized, your resume is likely to keep the interviewer on the main highway and focused on your strengths and successes. The choice is yours. Either way, your resume is bound to have significant impact on the outcome of your interviews.

- **Post-Interview Comparison Document**

Following the interview process, when the interview team meets to make a decision among candidates, your resume may be used as the basis for comparing you with other candidates. If the comparison is to be favorable, your resume must be well designed, causing your qualifications to make you stand out from the others. A thoughtful, well-constructed resume can go a long way toward shifting the hiring decision in your favor. A poor resume, on the other hand, almost guarantees that you will not make the cut.

As you can see, your employment resume is in many ways the focal point or keystone of your job-hunting process. Taking the time and effort to prepare a thoughtful, well-organized resume is sure to have major payoff for your job search efforts.

THE HIGH-IMPACT RESUME

What is a *high-impact resume?* What does it look like? What are the important elements that contribute to its effectiveness? How do you prepare such a resume? These are the key questions that are answered in this chapter.

Two primary factors contribute to resume effectiveness: *format* and *content*. Both are critical to resume performance, and they must be carefully balanced to construct a high-impact resume. Neither can be sacrificed in favor of the other if you are to create a resume document that will have maximum impact.

The format is the physical layout of the information on the resume. It is the way the information is displayed on the paper. To be effective, the resume format must be simple, neat, well organized, and visually pleasing. It must offer little reader resistance and should, in fact, greatly enhance readability of the document. To be effective, design your resume for quick reading and easy identification of your key qualifications for the position in question.

The format used in the sample resume (pp. 3–4) is a good example of a neat, clean, and uncluttered layout. You can see how easy it is to read this document quickly and to extract the key qualifications and accomplishments with little or

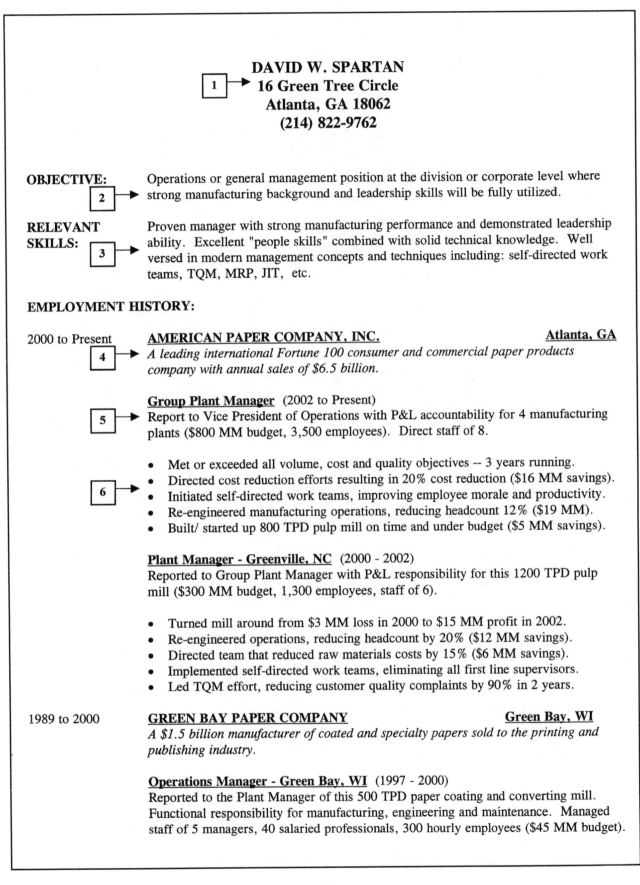

DAVID W. SPARTAN
1 16 Green Tree Circle
Atlanta, GA 18062
(214) 822-9762

OBJECTIVE:
2 Operations or general management position at the division or corporate level where strong manufacturing background and leadership skills will be fully utilized.

RELEVANT SKILLS:
3 Proven manager with strong manufacturing performance and demonstrated leadership ability. Excellent "people skills" combined with solid technical knowledge. Well versed in modern management concepts and techniques including: self-directed work teams, TQM, MRP, JIT, etc.

EMPLOYMENT HISTORY:

2000 to Present **AMERICAN PAPER COMPANY, INC.**   <u>Atlanta, GA</u>
4 *A leading international Fortune 100 consumer and commercial paper products company with annual sales of $6.5 billion.*

<u>**Group Plant Manager**</u> (2002 to Present)
5 Report to Vice President of Operations with P&L accountability for 4 manufacturing plants ($800 MM budget, 3,500 employees). Direct staff of 8.

6
- Met or exceeded all volume, cost and quality objectives -- 3 years running.
- Directed cost reduction efforts resulting in 20% cost reduction ($16 MM savings).
- Initiated self-directed work teams, improving employee morale and productivity.
- Re-engineered manufacturing operations, reducing headcount 12% ($19 MM).
- Built/ started up 800 TPD pulp mill on time and under budget ($5 MM savings).

<u>**Plant Manager - Greenville, NC**</u> (2000 - 2002)
Reported to Group Plant Manager with P&L responsibility for this 1200 TPD pulp mill ($300 MM budget, 1,300 employees, staff of 6).

- Turned mill around from $3 MM loss in 2000 to $15 MM profit in 2002.
- Re-engineered operations, reducing headcount by 20% ($12 MM savings).
- Directed team that reduced raw materials costs by 15% ($6 MM savings).
- Implemented self-directed work teams, eliminating all first line supervisors.
- Led TQM effort, reducing customer quality complaints by 90% in 2 years.

1989 to 2000 **GREEN BAY PAPER COMPANY**   <u>Green Bay, WI</u>
A $1.5 billion manufacturer of coated and specialty papers sold to the printing and publishing industry.

<u>**Operations Manager - Green Bay, WI**</u> (1997 - 2000)
Reported to the Plant Manager of this 500 TPD paper coating and converting mill. Functional responsibility for manufacturing, engineering and maintenance. Managed staff of 5 managers, 40 salaried professionals, 300 hourly employees ($45 MM budget).

- Reduced headcount 10% with simultaneous 20% increase in plant productivity.
- Led successful start up of $40 MM coating operation -- completed 3 months early and $1.5 MM under budget.
- Trained entire operation (345 employees) in SPC/Total Quality with resultant first year quality improvement of 80% ($5 MM annual savings).

Department Manager - Coating (1993 - 1997)
Reported to Operations Manager with accountability for running a 120 employee, fine paper coating operation ($18 MM budget).

- Saved $2.5 MM annually through implementation of raw materials JIT program.
- Redesign of mix room reduced operating labor by 20% ($1 MM annual savings).
- Improved employee morale and productivity through more participation in key department decision-making.

Senior Process Engineer - Coating (1990 - 1993)
Reported to Department Manager - Coating. Provided engineering support to department through the design, installation and start up of new coating equipment ($ 3 MM annual capital budget). Also provided engineering trouble-shooting support on major coating problems. Managed 2 Process Engineers.

- Installed $3 MM billblade coater on time and 20% under budget (saved $600,000).
- Redesigned reel section, improving coater output by 15% (1 year payback).
- Provided critical technical support to highly successful start up of # 9 coating machine (achieved first year's production goals in only 7 months).

7 → **Process Engineer - Coating** (1989-1990)

Associate Process Engineer - Coating (1989)

EDUCATION:
8 → B.S., Mechanical Engineering
Bucknell University, 1989
Cum Laude
Tau Beta Psi

PROFESSIONAL:
9 → Professional Engineer, State of Wisconsin, 1991
President, TAPPI (Green Bay Chapter), 1994
Vice President, TAPPI (Green Bay Chapter), 1992 & 1991
Member, ASME, 1988 to Present

2 U.S. Patents

no effort. Notice also how the use of tools such as white space, bold type, underlining, capitalization, italics, and bullets creates good visual separation of the material presented, greatly enhancing the ease with which this resume can be read.

Resume content, on the other hand, refers to the actual information presented in the resume (i.e., employers, dates of employment, positions held, key responsibilities, major accomplishments, and the like). Good format enhances resume readability, while it is resume content that actually makes the sale! To understand what content is important and how it should be presented in the resume, you must ask yourself two questions:

- What is it that the employer needs to know about me and my qualifications to make a good employment decision?
- What is the logical order or sequence in which to present this information to facilitate the employer's decision?

Good answers to both of these questions are essential to creating an effective employment resume that will motivate the employer to pursue your employment candidacy. The following instructions for preparing a high-impact resume will provide meaningful answers to these important questions.

PREPARING YOUR RESUME

The balance of this chapter is dedicated to providing you with step-by-step instructions for preparing a high-impact resume. To facilitate this process, I have included a sample high-impact resume (see pp. 3–4), and have numbered each of the key resume components for your easy reference. To assist you in the preparation of your resume, I will systematically present each of the numbered resume components in the order in which they appear on the resume document with a thorough explanation of each. If you follow this approach carefully, by the time we reach the end of the chapter, you should have what it takes to prepare a highly professional resume that will serve you well throughout your job-hunting campaign.

☐ 1 Resume Heading

As can be seen on the sample resume, the resume heading (see item #1) contains three pieces of information: your name, address, and telephone number. Where appropriate, you may also want to include your office number, fax number, and/or e-mail address.

The heading is normally presented in bold type using two type sizes larger than the balance of the resume text. In the sample resume, I have used 14 point type for the heading, with the balance of the resume text displayed in 12 point type. Note the use of all capital letters, which sets the candidate's name apart from the rest of the resume heading.

The resume heading is typically separated from the next major resume component (Objective) by three lines of white space.

2 Objective

Candidates who fail to include a well-defined job search objective on their resume are placing themselves at a great competitive disadvantage. In such cases, since the employer is now uncertain of the type of position sought, it will require that the employer call the candidate for clarification. Most won't bother.

In this day of downsized organizations, spartan staffs, and crushing workloads, most employers lack the time, resources, and desire to make frivolous phone calls of this type. Don't place yourself at a competitive disadvantage by excluding this important information from your resume.

When writing your objective statement, be sure not to use too narrow an objective. Doing so may cause the employer to screen you out from positions in which you may have an interest. On the other hand, don't be too vague. An objective statement that is too broad or too vague will make it unclear as to the type of position you are seeking. This would again require the employer to call you for clarification, an unnecessary step that most will be unwilling to take!

As you can see from our model resume, a well-constructed objective statement normally includes two basic elements: job level and functional area(s). In our sample, job level is defined by David as a "management position at the division or corporate level." Functional areas are defined by David as "operations or general management." In combination, these convey a clear understanding of David's objective to the employer and, as stated, are not unusually narrow or restrictive in scope.

3 Relevant Skills

The inclusion of a relevant skills area on the employment resume is a fairly recent phenomenon that has exploded in both usage and popularity. Today, an estimated 95 percent of all resumes include this component. Although used by the great majority of job seekers, there seems to be little uniformity in the title used for this section of the resume. Alternate titles include:

- Summary
- Executive Summary
- Key Qualifications
- Qualifications Summary
- Key Skills
- Skills Summary
- Highlights
- Qualifications Highlights
- Skills Highlights

Whatever the title, this section has one primary purpose: to motivate the employer to read the rest of the resume. The relevant skills section provides a brief three- or four-line summary highlighting what the candidate considers to be his or her most salient skills and qualifications for the position sought (i.e., the job search objective).

4 **Company Name and Description**

In preparing the employment history section of your resume, note that "company" employment dates are positioned at the left margin of the resume. Dates during which a given position was held with that employer (i.e., "job" dates), by contrast, are placed in parentheses to the immediate right of the title of the position. This approach provides good visual separation between employment dates and job dates, and avoids the general confusion that frequently results when the employment candidate positions both dates at the same margin. (Note, for example, how easy it is to distinguish between company employment dates and job dates in the sample resume. There can be no confusion here!)

Additionally, by placing company dates at the left margin next to the name of the employer, you provide better visual compartmentization of the resume, enhancing the ease of reading. Company names visually stand out from job titles, which are then presented as a logical subset under the company name at which these jobs were performed.

To further enhance the visual separation, company names are presented in bold type and underlined with *all* letters of the name set in capitals. Additionally, location of the company's corporate headquarters is positioned at the right margin in line with the company's name.

Job titles (see 5 on the sample resume), on the other hand, are set in bold type using both capital and lowercase letters. This again serves to visually separate company names from job titles and enhances overall resume readability.

As 4 illustrates, company name is followed by a brief description of the company. This normally includes such information as organization size, products manufactured (or services provided), and annual sales volume. Notice how this company description is set in italics, further reinforcing the visual separation between employer information and job information.

Prospective employers want to know what size and type company you worked for so that they can make some reasonable deductions about your probable fit with their own organization. An employer who is a widget manufacturer, for example, is going to want to know whether you have had any exposure to the manufacture of widgets. If this information is not provided, the employer may well pass on your resume in favor of another candidate who has had experience in that employer's industry and/or product line.

Don't just automatically assume that the new prospective employer is going to be familiar with the companies for whom you have worked. This may not be the case, and by failing to present this information in the resume you may well be placing yourself at a competitive disadvantage when compared to those who have furnished this information to the employer. There is a natural tendency for employers to prefer candidates who are familiar with their industry and product lines. This cuts down on training time and in most cases ensures that the candidate will "hit the ground running" rather than requiring an extensive industry and product orientation period.

5 Job Description

The next section of the resume presents the job title of the position held as well as a brief description of that position (see 5 on the sample resume). There are five key elements to include when constructing this portion of your resume. These are as follows:

1. Job Title
2. Job Dates (i.e., dates employed in that position)
3. Reporting Relationship (i.e., title of the person to whom you reported)
4. Size and Scope of Position Held (described in quantitative terms)
5. Functional Responsibility (specific functions you were accountable for performing or managing)

Job titles, as illustrated on the sample resume, are set in bold print, are underlined, and make use of both capital and lower case letters. This helps to clearly distinguish them from employer names and visually separates and subordinates this information from information describing the employer. This is fitting treatment, since descriptions of positions held are really a kind of information subset and offer further information about the kind of work performed for that employer.

A final word about job titles: If the job title of the position you held does not effectively communicate the nature of the work performed, and there is a generic job title that better communicates this information to the outside world, by all means use the generic title. Since a key purpose of the resume document is to effectively communicate your qualifications to others in a way that will be clearly understood, don't handicap yourself by using the actual job title. This is especially true today since many organizations have created unusual job titles that have internal meaning but have little or no meaning to the outside world.

For example, if your job title is Technology Enabler, but you really are a Research Project Engineer, by all means use the title Research Project Engineer. No one on the outside will understand the meaning of Technology Enabler, but most will have a pretty clear understanding of the term Research Project Engineer. Likewise, if your internal job title is Director of Technology Enabling, but you really are serving in the capacity of Director of Research & Development, by all means use the title Director of Research & Development on your resume.

You have a certain amount of poetic license and flexibility in the resume that you will not have in the formal employment application. Since a key purpose of the resume is to clearly convey a good understanding of your qualifications, use of generic rather than actual titles can often make the job easier and help you to accomplish your goal. Be sure not to gild the lily, however, by calling yourself a vice president when your actual position level was that of a director or manager. This will not sit well with the prospective employer since it is a clear attempt at misrepresenting your credentials.

In the case of the employment application, it is strongly recommended that you use exact job titles rather than the generic ones used in the resume. Since this is a formal, legal document, you will want to make sure that all information presented is accurate and precise. You should not assume that you have the same latitude that you have with the resume, where there is far greater flexibility.

If the job was located at a site other than the corporate headquarters, you may want to make this fact evident by showing the location of the position immediately to the right of the job title. Notice how this is accomplished on the sample resume.

Job dates (i.e., dates during which you were employed in a given job) are best positioned immediately to the right of the job title and are enclosed in parentheses. As discussed earlier, this serves to make the distinction between job date and employer dates very clear and will eliminate any possibility of confusion. To list both of these dates in the same margin of the resume can confuse the prospective employer and, if the resume is being read quickly (which is usually the case during its initial scan by the employer), the reader may misinterpret the dates as dates of employment with *different* employers and conclude that you lack employment stability. So, be sure to distinguish between these two dates by positioning employment dates with a given employer at the left margin of the resume (as shown in the sample resume), with job dates positioned in parentheses to the immediate right of the job title.

Following the job title and dates, you will need to provide a brief description of the position held. Employers need to know how closely the positions you have held resemble the position they have to offer. Information such as reporting relationship, job size and scope, and functional responsibilities are essential to the employer's ability to make such an assessment. Take a moment or two to study the brief job description shown at ⑤ on the sample resume.

Start the job description by describing your reporting relationship. Starting this statement with the words "report to" or "reported to" and then following this with your boss' title makes this a simple task.

Next, provide a brief description of your key functional responsibilities—the key things you are responsible for doing. If you are a manager, cite the various business functions for which you are accountable. For example, "Functional responsibility includes business planning, corporate finance, money and banking, and international finance." On the other hand, if you are an entry level clerk, describe the key functions you are accountable for performing. For example, "Functionally responsible for mail delivery, filing of correspondence, assistance in filing monthly financial reports, arranging executive travel schedules, and meeting setup and coordination."

Prospective employers need to have a clear understanding of your functional job responsibilities to determine if you have performed the same or similar work to the position they are offering. This will infer to employers that you have the requisite skills and abilities essential to successful performance of the position which they must fill.

When describing the positions you have held on your resume, it is also important to provide a quantitative description of your work. This gives the prospective employer a clearer understanding of the size, scope, and complexity of the job you were performing. The employer is looking for evidence that you have successfully handled positions of similar scope and complexity to the open position, thus giving the employer a warm feeling about your ability to handle the position in question.

Besides describing the breadth of your functional responsibility, which we previously discussed, one of the best ways to clearly convey the scope and complexity of the positions held is to include "quantitative" descriptions of the work you have preferred. If you are a manager, indicating the size of your staff, budget size, sales volume, and the like will get this critical information across. If, on the other hand, you are an administrative assistant, your quantitative description could include the number of bosses served, the volume of correspondence typed, the volume of records processed, and the like. Such quantitative descriptions will effectively communicate the size, complexity, and demands of your job, providing the prospective employer with important information for assessing your match with the current opening.

In the sample resume, you can see how effectively quantitative descriptions are used to get across the size, scope, and complexity of each of the positions held by David Spartan. Note how succinctly and concisely this information is presented. There are no wasted words, and yet the employer should be able to come away with a very clear understanding of the important elements: reporting relationship, functional responsibilities, and size and scope of the position. This is all important information that the employer needs to make a reasonable decision about your qualifications and fit with the current position.

⑥ Key Accomplishments

Of all the elements of the resume, this section of the document is perhaps the most important to "making the sale." In years past, it was sufficient for the resume to provide the prospective employer with a simple job description showing functional responsibilities and scope of your position. This is no longer the case!

In the current work environment there is great pressure to accomplish far more with considerably fewer resources; managers feel a strong urgency to be sure that they are hiring hard-working, productive employees. For the most part, they need to hire persons who require little or no hand-holding, who are well-motivated, and who will produce a high volume of work with excellent quality.

As a result, employers are paying far more attention to the key accomplishments section of the resume. They want to know, "What is it that you have done? What significant contributions have you made to current or past employers for whom you have worked?" A record of continuous accomplishments and significant results in each position held goes a long way toward convincing the employer that you have what it takes to be successful in the position they have to offer. Perhaps no other single component of the resume will do more to affect your job-hunting success than the key accomplishments section. It is important, therefore, that you put considerable thought and effort into developing this section of the resume.

To do this, list each of the positions you have held on a separate sheet of paper. Below each job title, list a minimum of three to five major accomplishments or improvements that you brought about while in each position. Copies of old performance evaluations and salary reviews may prove particularly helpful in identifying these key results.

If you get stuck in performing this exercise, here is something that has proven helpful to many who have experienced difficulty in remembering past accomplishments. Think about the condition of the job when you first entered it. What were the key problems that existed? What did you do to resolve these issues? What were the results of your efforts? It is important in each case to identify three to five major improvements for each of the positions you have held. Once identified, reorder these accomplishments with regard to the type of position you are seeking. List the most important accomplishment first, the second most important accomplishment second, and so on. This should then be the same order in which these accomplishment statements are presented on the resume document.

When writing each of these accomplishment statements, start with a verb. This will force you to be concise. Note how this is done on the sample resume. Follow the verb with the thing or area you acted on, then follow this with a "quantitative" end result. Taking time now to study a few of these accomplishment statements on the sample resume will quickly get this point across.

The use of quantitative results conveys to the resume reader the degree of improvement you brought. For example, simply stating that you "increased sales" has little meaning. Stating, however, that you "increased sales 50% in the first year" gives a much stronger message that is likely to grab the employer's attention. Where possible, express your key accomplishments in quantitative terms that highlight the extent or degree of improvement. This is a key part of making sure that your resume will be high-impact, and that it will maximize your chances for employment.

Should you have difficulty recalling exact percentages or numbers, use the words *approximately* or *about* as long as you know that you are in the ballpark. So, for example, you could state "annual savings approximately $1 MM," rather than simply indicating that there were savings (without citing the magnitude).

Note in reviewing the sample resume that each major accomplishment has been preceded by a bullet to help highlight it. Additionally each key accomplishment section of the resume has been separated from its corresponding job description by two lines of white space. This causes the key accomplishments to stand out from the balance of the resume text, drawing the reader's attention to them.

If these accomplishment statements have been thoughtfully prepared, you will likely realize the benefits of this preparation during the course of the employment interview. Since the employer frequently uses the resume as a kind of interview road map when conducting the employment interview, and since the special highlighting used in the resume will tend to draw focus to your key accomplishments, there is a good likelihood that much of the employment interview will be focused on these accomplishments. Much of the interview will tend to examine these accomplishments in greater detail, allowing you the opportunity to showcase your key strengths and capabilities.

If done particularly well, this section of the resume will do much of the selling for you. If thoughtfully prepared, showing three to five significant accomplishments for each of the positions you have held, the resume will show a solid history of hard work and accomplishment, suggesting to the interviewer that you are well-motivated, hard-working, dedicated, and productive. These are key attributes that most employers find highly desirable.

7 Earlier Positions

It is not necessary to provide much detail on positions held early in your career. Your recent job experience is usually far more germane to your current job search objective than positions held earlier in your career. In fact, most earlier positions (see 7 on sample resume) should simply show job title and dates, with no job description or key accomplishments cited. In this way, you will conserve resume space, allowing you to devote far more space to current positions and qualifications rather than using valuable space to describe early positions that will probably have little bearing on the outcome of your employment candidacy.

If age is a potential barrier to your employment candidacy, you may want to consider dropping some of your early positions off the resume entirely. This action can be justified to the prospective employer, should you be queried as to why this was done, on the basis that there was limited space on the resume and you felt it more important to cite current qualifications than to devote valuable resume space to earlier career positions that have little or no bearing on the level or type of position you are seeking.

If the employer demands further explanation or suggests that you have violated some ethical standard, tell the employer that you were also concerned about the potential for age discrimination and wished not to be judged unfairly. Such explanation is likely to cause the issue to evaporate quickly!

To further disguise your age, simply leave graduation dates off your resume when presenting your educational credentials.

8 Education

As illustrated on the sample resume, the education section lists the degree and major on the first line, followed by the name of the school and date of graduation on the second line. The third and fourth lines, where appropriate, are devoted to listing academic honors. Education is normally positioned after employment history for an experienced candidate. However, it is usually listed right after the relevant skills section of the resume, for relatively recent graduates who have little or no professional experience. Such positioning would be most appropriate, since the recent graduate's education is likely to be the most important qualification that they have to offer.

If you have advanced degrees, list the highest level degree attained as the first entry. This is then followed by listing the next highest degree followed by the undergraduate degree.

9 Professional

List your professional qualifications next. As shown on the sample resume, this normally includes professional certifications received, offices and memberships held in professional and trade association, and other appropriate items lending testimony to your qualifications as a professional in your field.

This section of the resume can also be used to cite patents held, publications written, speeches and lectures presented, special recognitions and awards received, or other evidence of your professional skills and competencies. Don't overdo this section, however, and stick to those items that have some reasonably significant bearing on your qualifications for the position sought.

Miscellaneous

The modern resume presents only job-relevant information. Topics that are not relevant to your ability to perform the targeted job should be excluded from the resume entirely. For this reason, most resumes today purposely exclude nonrelevant topics such as hobbies and extracurricular activities. Also excluded is all personal information such as age, height, weight, health, and marital status. None of these topics have much if anything to do with your ability to perform the job, and are therefore best left off the resume.

Writing Tricks and Techniques

Careful review of the sample resume will show that certain writing tricks and techniques were employed to make this resume a brief, concise, and relatively forceful document. Note how these techniques were used in the resume sample and employ them when writing your own resume. You should find the following writing tricks and techniques particularly beneficial in improving the overall quality and impact of your resume:

- Use of articles (e.g., a, an, and the) is unnecessary and should, for the most part, be eliminated from the resume. They usually add no meaning or clarity to the resume.

- Eliminate the use of personal pronouns (e.g., I, me, you, they, them, us). Such pronouns are unnecessary in a resume and tend to distract from its impact and forcefulness.

- Avoid complete sentences when writing an effective resume. Highly descriptive clauses and phrases can communicate quite forcefully.

- Be concise. Eliminate all unnecessary words from the resume that do not enhance its meaning or impact. To do this, carefully read each word of the finalized resume, and ask yourself the following question, "If I eliminate this word, will I change the meaning or impact of this statement?" If removal of the word does not change the meaning or impact of the statement, then remove it! It serves no particular purpose!

- Begin most resume sentences or statements with a *verb*. Doing so will almost automatically force you to be brief and concise. Try it! Review the sample resume in this chapter and observe the high percentage of statements contained in the resume that begin with a verb. Most of them.

By now you should have a clear understanding of what is important in preparing a high-impact resume, one that will be viewed favorably by the employer and provide you with the competitive advantage that you will need to come up on the winning side of the employment equation. Perhaps no other element of your job search is more important than your resume. So make the most of this opportunity to prepare a good one!

THE ELECTRONIC RESUME

When sending your resume to a specific functional manager (and this is always preferable to sending it to the human resources department), use the resume format illustrated on pages 3 and 4. In those cases where you are forced to send your resume to the human resources department (such as when responding to an employment advertisement in a newspaper or professional journal), however, you will want to use a resume format that is computer scannable. This format is commonly referred to as the *electronic resume* format.

Here are some basic guidelines for creating an electronic resume that can be easily scanned by today's automated resume scanning systems:

- Use standard 8½" × 11" white or off-white paper (avoid using darker colors).

- Use common typefaces such as Times, Courier, Helvetica, or Palatino (avoid out-of-the-ordinary fonts).

- Provide original copy using high-quality printing that is crisp and neat (preferably a laser printed or typewritten original). Use of a high-quality photocopy, although acceptable, is not preferred.

- Use 12 point type size, although 10 and 14 point are normally acceptable.

- Minimize use of bold highlighting and underlining. Always avoid unusual effects such as shadows and reverse typeset (i.e., white type on dark background).
- Keep it simple—stick to text only and avoid using graphics, tables, charts, and the like.
- Follow standard resume formats employing common resume section headings (as already described in detail earlier in this chapter).
- Describe qualifications and skills in specific, concrete terms (avoiding vague or broad-sweeping statements).
- Use standard terminology when describing your field, specialty, type of work performed, and skills.
- Scan your resume carefully to make sure you have made effective use of key words that will most likely be used to identify candidates for the type of position you are seeking.

The following resume of David Spartan (previously presented in this chapter using a standard recommended format) has been modified to reflect an acceptable electronic, scannable version. Due to the growing use of resume scanning by many companies, you may wish to adopt this approach when directing your resume to the human resources department. When mailing your resume directly to the manager or director of your job-search targeted business function, however, it is strongly recommended that you use the standard format presented earlier in this chapter.

DAVID W. SPARTAN
16 Green Tree Circle
Atlanta, GA 18062
(214) 822-9762

OBJECTIVE: Operations or general management position at the division or corporate level where strong manufacturing background and leadership skills will be fully utilized.

RELEVANT SKILLS: Proven manager with strong manufacturing performance and demonstrated leadership ability. Excellent "people skills" combined with solid technical knowledge. Well versed in modern management concepts and techniques including: self-directed work teams, TQM, MRP, JIT, etc.

EMPLOYMENT HISTORY:

2000 to Present **AMERICAN PAPER COMPANY, INC.**   Atlanta, GA
A leading international Fortune 100 consumer and commercial paper products company with annual sales of $6.5 billion.

Group Plant Manager (2002 to Present)
Report to Vice President of Operations with P&L accountability for 4 manufacturing plants ($800 MM budget, 3,500 employees). Direct staff of 8.

- Met or exceeded all volume, cost and quality objectives -- 3 years running.
- Directed cost reduction efforts resulting in 20% cost reduction ($16 MM savings).
- Initiated self-directed work teams, improving employee morale and productivity.
- Re-engineered manufacturing operations, reducing headcount 12% ($19 MM).
- Built/ started up 800 TPD pulp mill on time and under budget ($5 MM savings).

Plant Manager - Greenville, NC (2000 - 2002)
Reported to Group Plant Manager with P&L responsibility for this 1200 TPD pulp mill ($300 MM budget, 1,300 employees, staff of 6).

- Turned mill around from $3 MM loss in 2000 to $15 MM profit in 2002.
- Re-engineered operations, reducing headcount by 20% ($12 MM savings).
- Directed team that reduced raw materials costs by 15% ($6 MM savings).
- Implemented self-directed work teams, eliminating all first line supervisors.
- Led TQM effort, reducing customer quality complaints by 90% in 2 years.

1989 to 2000 **GREEN BAY PAPER COMPANY**   Green Bay, WI
A $1.5 billion manufacturer of coated and specialty papers sold to the printing and publishing industry.

Operations Manager - Green Bay, WI (1997 - 2000)
Reported to the Plant Manager of this 500 TPD paper coating and converting mill. Functional responsibility for manufacturing, engineering and maintenance. Managed staff of 5 managers, 40 salaried professionals, 300 hourly employees ($45 MM budget).

- Reduced headcount 10% with simultaneous 20% increase in plant productivity.
- Led successful start up of $40 MM coating operation -- completed 3 months early and $1.5 MM under budget.
- Trained entire operation (345 employees) in SPC/Total Quality with resultant first year quality improvement of 80% ($5 MM annual savings).

Department Manager - Coating (1993 - 1997)
Reported to Operations Manager with accountability for running a 120 employee, fine paper coating operation ($18 MM budget).

- Saved $2.5 MM annually through implementation of raw materials JIT program.
- Redesign of mix room reduced operating labor by 20% ($1 MM annual savings).
- Improved employee morale and productivity through more participation in key department decision-making.

Senior Process Engineer - Coating (1990 - 1993)
Reported to Department Manager - Coating. Provided engineering support to department through the design, installation and start up of new coating equipment ($ 3 MM annual capital budget). Also provided engineering trouble-shooting support on major coating problems. Managed 2 Process Engineers.

- Installed $3 MM billblade coater on time and 20% under budget (saved $600,000).
- Redesigned reel section, improving coater output by 15% (1 year payback).
- Provided critical technical support to highly successful start up of # 9 coating machine (achieved first year's production goals in only 7 months).

Process Engineer - Coating (1989-1990)

Associate Process Engineer - Coating (1989)

EDUCATION: B.S., Mechanical Engineering
                Bucknell University, 1989
                Cum Laude
                Tau Beta Psi

PROFESSIONAL: Professional Engineer, State of Wisconsin, 1991
                President, TAPPI (Green Bay Chapter), 1994
                Vice President, TAPPI (Green Bay Chapter), 1992 & 1991
                Member, ASME, 1988 to Present

                2 U.S. Patents

2

Sample Resumes—
For Experienced Persons

This chapter contains a total of 125 carefully-chosen resume samples covering 30 different occupational areas. These are *actual resumes* that have been carefully selected and hand-picked from a large group of well over 25,000 resumes received by my firm over a five-year period. As such, they represent a broad cross-section of resume samples and were chosen for inclusion in this book on the basis of their overall strength and impact.

Although these are actual resumes, they have been altered to protect the identity of their author. These alterations include names, addresses, phone numbers, names of employers, dates of employment, and so on. This was done to protect the privacy and confidentiality of each employment candidate. Other than these superficial changes, however, these resumes are authentic. The format and basic content of each resume remain as originally submitted.

Although the format and content of the high-impact resume contained in Chapter 1 of this book are *strongly recommended* as a model for tailoring your own resume, looking at actual samples of other strong resumes should serve to stimulate your thinking on how to further strengthen your resume document.

To facilitate use of this section of the book, I suggest that you see the Contents contained on page ix. You will discover that these resume samples have been grouped into similar categories by occupational area and page numbers have been provided. Thus, all sample accounting resumes are grouped together in one section of the book, marketing in another, technical in another, and so on. Use of this Contents should prove helpful to you in locating those resume samples that most closely correspond to your own occupational area and employment objective.

ALAN KEYES

902 Chestnut Street
Woodbridge, NJ 08854
908 – 932-7512

Fourteen years P&L and Balance Sheet responsibility as Division President, domestically and internationally, in manufacturing environments.

Strong record of achievement in re-engineering companies while building sales, market share, people and profit, and adding significant value in marketing, operations and finance functions. Personal strength in business development and team building.

BUSINESS HISTORY:	**FEDDERS CORPORATION**	**1986 - Present**

A leading manufacturer of air conditioning units serving the commercial, industrial, retail, and institutional markets with facilities in the United States, Canada and Mexico with revenues of $320 million.

President - Residential Division, Woodbridge, NJ   1998 - Present

Asked by Board of Directors to turnaround break-even business of $65 million consisting of three brands: Quiet Kool, Air-Max and Kool Pro. These were sold through retail, wholesale and specialty channels. Responsible for P&L and balance sheet, two manufacturing facilities (USA, Mexico), sales, marketing, finance, engineering, HR and 450 employees.

Reviewed and reduced product lines, re-engineered operations for profitability, and relocated one facility to improve costs and customer service.

Results:
- Reduced manufacturing overhead by $3.8 million.
- Improved customer service from 8 days to 56 hours with 98 percent line item fill.
- Planned and implemented a real-time warehouse management system.
- Planned and executed a complete facility relocation.
- Overall ... positioned the business to grow over the next five years ahead of projected market growth.

Vice President, Marketing, Hartford, CT   1996 - 1998

Recruited by President to manage sales and marketing of $300 million multi-brand organization.

Results:
- Developed strategic sales plan.
- Grew sales by 20% in falling new commercial construction market.

President - Lighting & Controls, Piscataway, NJ   1992 - 1996

Full P&L and balance sheet responsibility for a $19 million manufacturing operation of lighting and controls for the commercial and industrial markets. Functional responsibility for sales, marketing, finance, engineering, HR, and operations with 135 employees.

Results:
- Grew market share from 5 percent to 20 percent.
- Increased profits from breakeven to 17 percent.
- Planned and executed the consolidation of two companies into one viable operation.

Sales Manager - Lighting & Controls, Piscataway, NJ   1986 - 1992

Results:
- Grew sales an average of 16 percent per year.
- Developed territorial sales and distribution capabilities.

EDUCATION: B.A., Business (Marketing)   1986
Princeton University

Center for Creative Leadership   1995

JENNIFER GORDON

17683 Hot Springs Road
Houston, TX 77503

office: (713) 323-7841
home: (713) 977-3586
fax: (713) 323-7842

CHIEF EXECUTIVE/OPERATING OFFICER

Seasoned and effective CEO/COO general manager. Strong track record managing turnarounds, new ventures and high growth business. Good crisis manager. High energy, aggressive. Results-focused team leader. Effective organization builder. Solid leadership, strategy and analytical skills.

EXPERIENCE

PRESIDENT/CEO   **1999-Present**
OWEN HEALTHCARE, INC.
Houston, Texas

Owens Healthcare integrates proprietary electronic technology and outcomes management systems with specialized nursing and pharmacy expertise to reduce cost of care and to improve clinical and quality-of-life outcomes. The company has created and set the standard for a new, $2.5 billion potential niche market. Company valuation increased from $4.2 million to $17 million during the period.

· Created and implemented the company's vision and business strategy.

· Ramped annualized revenues from $500,000 to $2.5 million in three years (500%); turned around beta site operating income from -30% to +25%; exceeded corporate net income plan.

· Managed Medicare reimbursement to obtain coverage, establish policy, increase reimbursement rates. Increased Medicare patient margins from 18% to over 45%.

· Raised $9.5 million in operating capital through stock sale.

· Conceived and directed development of a patient data base and management/acuity systems to prospectively manage patient outcomes. Positioned Owens Healthcare to capitalize on managed care opportunities with risk management and at-risk strategies.

· Installed and upgraded organization and infrastructure; expanded from 90 employees at four sites to 400 employees at nine sites.

· Conceived and directed a national clinical study (and local studies) with leading health care centers and thought leaders which defined the clinical and cost value of the company's patient care.

PARTNER   **1994-1999**
MEDFIT OF AMERICA, INC.
Teaneck, New Jersey

A consulting firm for CEOs, COOs, sales/marketing executives and investors. Client firms included both start-up and established health care companies and home care providers. Assignments dealt with strategic and operational issues involving high growth, turn around or corporate change.

· New business, new product, acquisition programs. Opportunity and risk assessment, due diligence, strategy development, business plan, marketing/organization plans. Implementation.

· Weak/failing business situations. Problem analysis, options assessment, strategy development. Assisted implementation of corrective actions.

- Interim management. Temporary senior manager to run the business, put new programs and organizations into place, deliver results until permanent executive is installed.

- Organization development. Programs to strengthen the effectiveness of senior management, sales, marketing and customer service organizations.

EXECUTIVE VICE PRESIDENT, MARKETING   1991-1994
BIOMET, INC.
Warsaw, Indiana

Directed worldwide sales, marketing and business development for this $200 million company with core businesses in electronic imaging and medical instrumentation technologies.

- Achieved 35% sales increase, improved margin and marketing productivity despite unfavorable international currency movements, and severe product quality, development and regulatory problems.

- Built an aggressive sales/marketing team for U.S. and international markets through management style, reorganization, personnel changes, management systems and personal development.

VICE PRESIDENT/GENERAL MANAGER   1989-1991
UNITED MEDICAL CORPORATION
Haddonfield, New Jersey

Led this $43 million entrepreneurial manufacturer of artificial heart pumps through a period of transition and high growth, following acquisition and consolidation by a multinational and the departure of the founder.

- Increased sales and pre-tax profits 25% and 20% respectively; inventory turns up 18%; receivables (DSO) down 5%.

- Installed organization and systems infrastructure to manage the size and rapid growth of the business, the new competitive and regulatory pressure, and the needs of the multinational parent company: recruited CFO, VP Operations and finance, engineering, manufacturing and marketing Directors; installed Standard Cost, Inventory Control, Forecasting/MRP, Labor Standards, MBO and Information systems.

DIRECTOR OF MARKETING   1982-1989
CAP GEMINI AMERICA INC.
New York, New York

Reporting to the president of this start-up venture, set up marketing and distribution, developed all marketing and product plans, managed the development and launch of the first products, established policies. Captured 15% market share with $9 million sales.

Prior assignments with B&R included International Marketing Manager, New Product Development Program Manager, Sales Representative.

EDUCATION

MBA (Marketing), 1982, Barnard College
BME (Mechanical Engineering), 1980, Cornell University
Pi Tau Sigma Engineering Honorary Society
Various AMA courses and management seminars

CASSANDRA RUSSELL
78 Pinehurst Drive
Southfield, MI 48034

Home: (313) 903-4578
Fax: (313) 903-4580

SUMMARY

Proven record in executive management (P&L), operations management, program management, engineering and marketing. Demonstrated ability to develop and manage multiple projects in a fast paced environment. Extensive hands-on experience in virtually every area from business development to final production and delivery. Strong executive presence coupled with excellent presentation skills. Entrepreneurial spirit, team motivator with keen sense of urgency.

WORK HISTORY

BRASS-CRAFT MANUFACTURING COMPANY, Southfield, MI   **2000 - Present**

Executive Vice President/General Manager Operations

Responsible for the turnaround of non-performing divisions of this $200 million company that manufactures and sells specialty fasteners to the aircraft and aerospace industries. Answer to the President of the Structures Group.

- Restored one $65 million division to profitability within four (4) months that had been losing over $4.3 million per year and currently managing a second $40 million division that will become profitable by January 1 by replacing key management, right-sizing and instituting strict cost controls.

- Restored customer confidence by settling outstanding warranty claims and implementing corrective action to improve overall product quality and eliminate warranty returns.

DELMAR AVIONICS, Irvine, CA   **1995 - 2000**

President and Chief Executive Officer

Full P&L responsibility for this $20 million 250 employee company that designs and manufactures aircraft instrumentation and control systems. Delmar Avionics was a major turnaround situation.

- Implemented company-wide cost reduction/right-sizing.

- Rebuilt customer confidence by reducing delinquencies by 78%.

- Upgraded skills via training and selective hiring. Completely rebuilt the Quality Staff.

- Fostered open communications by practicing management by walking around.

Cassandra Russell   Page 2

THE AEROSPACE CORPORATION, Los Angeles, CA   1990 - 1995

Vice President, Operations

Operating Officer for this $3.5 million company that overhauls and repairs gas turbine engines and provides maintenance services to military and commercial aircraft.   Answered to the President and CEO.

- Accomplished a major improvement in customer satisfaction by significantly reducing engine overhaul turn time from well over 100 days to under 30 days.

- Maintained divisional profit levels while reducing overhaul and repair prices which further improved customer satisfaction.

- Expanded market share in a shrinking market by more than 25% in less than three years.

- Negotiated exclusive agreement for an indicated production of turboshaft engine used by leading U.S. commercial helicopter manufacturer.

THE BOEING COMPANY, Seattle, WA   1984 - 1990

Program Manager   (1988 – 1990)

Department Manager   (1986 – 1988)

Project Engineer   (1984 – 1986)

EDUCATION

Rochester Institute of Technology, MSME   1984

Rochester Institute of Technology, BSME   1982

ANDREA MALAS
467 Baylor Avenue
St. Louis, MO 63225
Home: 314-233-5435   Office: 314-432-7844

PROFILE:

Results-driven executive with strong background in general management, sales, marketing and distribution. Strong experience in consumer products and electronics. Trained in markets at Monsanto Company. People-oriented leader who builds strong corporate culture. Decisive strategic operator driving revenues and managing rapid growth.

EXPERIENCE:

BELL ATLANTIC MOBILE   2000 to Present

President & General Manager
One of the largest cellular phone operating companies in the United States. Responsible for all company operations, including customer service, sales and marketing, engineering, regulatory and legal affairs.

- Grew revenue, subscribers, and profits from $35M to $125M in six years. Excellent gross margins.
- Built enlightened corporate culture during rapid growth (from 55 to 825 employees).
- Reduced turnover from 32% to 12%; improved customer satisfaction from 70% to 92%.
- Positioned company against larger, better-known competitor as the quality provider.
- Ramped-up operations (from 70 to over 200 cell sites) and managed one transition to digital transmission.
- Despite record profits, successfully lobbied Missouri legislature and public utilities commission thwarting additional regulation.

SONY CORPORATION OF AMERICA   1991 to 2000

Vice President & General Manager, Television Products (1995 – 2000)
Managed United States operations for all television products (including direct television).

- Increased profitability of T.V. Division by 13%.
- Increased revenue 27%.
- Introduced new direct T.V. line.
- Launched large screen projection T.V. product line.

Director, Marketing (1993 – 1995)
Responsible for developing and implementing product line marketing strategy for all television products.

- Planned and launched Sony *Thin Line* television business.
- Developed new market channels through enlarged dealer network.
- Initiated first Sony partnerships with Sears, Circuit City, Silo, Wards and Home Depot.

Director, National Accounts (1991 – 1993)
Responsible for Sony Consumer Product sales to national accounts.

- Developed national accounts program, increasing sales from $62MM to $175MM.
- Obtained/increased distribution for Sony products at Wal-Mart, K mart, Sears, Wards, Circuit City, Silo, Target, Best Products and Service Merchandise.

MONSANTO COMPANY   1985 to 1991

Regional Sales Manager   (1987 – 1991)

District Sales Manager   (1986 – 1987)

Marketing Representative   (1985 – 1986)

Sales Representative   (1985)

EDUCATION:

M.B.A., George Washington University, 1985

B.A., Business Administration, Michigan State University, 1983

COMMUNITY INVOLVEMENT:

- Director, St. Louis National Bank
- Executive Director, United Fund Drive (Greater St. Louis)
- Member, Missouri Council of Female Executives

DENNIS FIELD

234 Lakeshore Drive   (415) 654-3400 (Business)
San Francisco, CA 98131   (415) 368-1473   (Home)

SUMMARY:

Over twenty years of progressive experience in general management and marketing within consumer products industry, with a track record of achieving results in highly competitive product categories. Consistently increased market share and profit through strategic focus, team orientation and solid execution.

EXPERIENCE:

NESTLE USA, INC., Glendale, CA   **1990-Present**

Vice President and General Manager   2000-Present
Full P&L responsibility for a $415MM business unit which includes recent acquisition of Stouffer Foods. Direct ten manufacturing locations with total organization of 1,500.

· Led acquisition team and managed integration including development of organizational structure and staffing plans and site consolidations. Reduced costs by $7.5MM.
· Exceeded monthly sales/volume goals by 5.5% since acquisition.
· Increased operating income for frozen dinner line by 14%.

Vice President of Marketing and Sales, Frozen Foods   1998-2000
Directed marketing and sales functions for this $1.9 billion frozen foods business which resulted from the consolidation of Frozen Vegetables and Frozen Dinners Divisions. Portfolio included brands such as Lean Cuisine, Hungry Man, and Hanover distributed through retail channels. Managed marketing staff of 85 and field sales force of 360 with advertising/promotion budget of $70MM and trade promotion program budget of $350MM.

· Initiated five-year strategic development effort and directed implementation achieving:
  - Volume gain of 5MM cases and share gains on all major brands within 12 months.
  - Product improvement on Hanover brands which increased volume 15% since introduction.
  - Introduced large size products which have generated $75MM+ in sales with 75% ACV distribution.
· Introduced recycled packaging to meet environmental needs. Test markets currently 50% ahead of volume goals with 100% ACV distribution.
· Increased frozen vegetable volume 2.5MM cases (10%) despite entry of new major competitor.
· Identified/corrected major product packaging problem. Volume increased as a result, reversing 7% decline in prior nine months.

Vice President and General Manager - Confections Group   1995-1998
Vice President of Marketing and Sales - Confections Group   1991-1995
Vice President of Marketing - Confections Group   1990-1991

Assumed increasing marketing and sales responsibility leading to general management assignment with full P&L responsibility for this $400MM business. Managed marketing staff of 50 people, sales department of 80 and four manufacturing locations with 670 hourly employees.

- Strategically refocused business on growth opportunities and restaffed/upgraded marketing and sales organization. Grew volume $152MM to $400MM in sales, while growing profits from 4% to 12.5% with an ROA that exceeded 25%. Specific achievements included:

  - Identified need for and introduced three new products which now account for $70MM in sales.
  - Revitalized Crunch brand resulting in sales increase of over $50MM through design upgrades, strengthened copy and EDLP approach to list price.
  - Introduced licensed characters on Nestle Mini Cakes which now account for more than $38MM in sales. Led negotiations with licensor and developed creative executions.
  - Identified pre-measurement concept/opportunity and developed it into a national business with sales of $15MM and potential of $45MM.
  - Created and implemented profit-based sales incentive plan.

STAR-KIST FOODS, INC., Long Beach, CA   **1984-1990**

Director of Marketing   1989-1990
Responsible for all brand management activities for this $1.5 billion company. Brands included Star-Kist Tuna, Salmon and Chicken. Managed 35 employees with A&P budget of $135MM.

- Led development and introduction of Star-Kist's new advertising campaign, which is still on air. Exceeded category norms and improved awareness by five percentage points.
- Developed Olympic sponsorship program and related incentive program which increased sales 7%.
- Introduced Star-Kist Seafood as a national brand. Grew cases by 1.5MM units.

Director - Canning Business   1987-1989
Led multi-functional business team of six managers in development and commercialization of a new canning process with capital budget of $125MM.

- Led Midwest roll-out of "Star-Kist's Best". Achieved 7% share.
- Recommended and obtained approval for application of process for replacement alternatives which developed into $25MM business. Business now earns 23%+ ROA.

Brand Management   1984-1987
Progressive marketing assignments within the Seafood Products group, from Assistant Product Manager to Group Product Manager within four years. Managed Star-Kist's Seafood conversion which provided quality performance and enabled brand to break 10% share level for the first time, and to eventually reach its current number two position in the marketplace.

QUAKER OATS COMPANY, Chicago, IL   **1983-1984**

Brand Assistant, Quick & Hearty
Managed two national promotion events and introduced packaging change.

MILITARY: U.S. Army, 1974 - 1976

EDUCATION: M.B.A., Marketing, Northwestern University, 1983
                 B.A., Business, Northwestern University, 1981

THOMAS L. POOLE

323 Fieldpointe Drive
Arlington, VA 22340
(703) 248-4000

OBJECTIVE:

To join an organization in an executive capacity where I can apply my leadership and management skills toward improving the firm's growth and long term viability as a successful business concern.

EXPERIENCE:

Orion Group (1996 to Present)

Vice President and General Manager
Management of all divisional resources toward accomplishment of the division's long and short term goals. Responsibilities include direction of all Product Management/Marketing, Customer Service, Engineering, Production, Quality Assurance, Material Control, and Human Resource functions toward company goals.

Specific Accomplishments:
- Personally cultivated business relationships with several major domestic and international OEM clients.
- Doubled overall manufacturing labor efficiency during four year period.
- Increased sales per employee by 125% during five year period.
- Sales growth of tooling products of 250% during five year period.
- Established Systems Division with average annual sales growth of 45% during six year period.
- Improved response time on customer shipments from 21 days on average of 0.6 days for tooling products.
- Earned Excellence Award for achievement of 97.5%+ inventory accuracy with less than 1% financial error.
- Installation of AMAPS MRPII system for material planning and control.
- Reduction of "out of box" product quality problems by 76% during four year period.
- Improved product reliability on mainline products by two to seven fold.
- Earned numerous Preferred Supplier Awards from customer for superior quality (0 PPM defects) and delivery.
- Initiated program to obtain regulatory agency approvals for primary products to improve sales in international markets.
- Transformed manufacturing environment via capital investment program to upgrade machining equipment and develop in-house capabilities for critical processes.
- Preparations for ISO 9000 audit in early 1998.

THOMAS L. POOLE, Page Two

Gannett Corporation   **(1984 to 1996)**

Director, Research and Engineering   (1993-1996)
Responsible for R&D and product development of new printing, duplicating, copying and record processing products, and full complement of ancillary products.

Manager, Manufacturing Engineering   (1990-1993)

Manager, Advanced Manufacturing and Producibility Engineering (1989-1990)

Manager, Manufacturing Engineering - Assembly Operations   (1986-1989)

Manufacturing Engineer   (1985-1986)

Quality Assurance Engineer   (1984-1985)

EDUCATION:

James Madison University
B.S., Major - Operation Management, Minor - Marketing, 1982
M.B.A., Major - Operations Management, 1984

University of Virginia, currently enrolled toward M.A. in Organizational Development

Ohio State Scholarship Recipient, 1974

DENNIS ESPOSITO
431 Lords Highway
Weston, Connecticut 06987

Home: 206-437-1264   Office: 206-784-2300

OBJECTIVE

Executive position offering P&L responsibility for division/group of large company. Alternative would be significant operating responsibility with smaller company where equity is included.

SUMMARY OF QUALIFICATIONS

Proven track record in diverse businesses, domestic and international, across all major business functions, most recently as division president. Company experience includes manufacturing, engineering, sales and distribution of industrial boilers and utilities. Annual sales ranged from $5.5 million to $130 million in recent years.

EXPERIENCE

CONNECTICUT GENERAL POWER, Richfield, CT   1999 - Present
President and CEO

$155 million power and utility manufacturing and engineering firm. Hired by new owners to streamline operations and improve profitability.

- Increased profitability and cash flow throughout management transition period.
- Directed the consolidation of three manufacturing facilities into single location.
- Planned and managed the consolidation/relocation of 45,000 SKU inventory valued in excess of $32 million.
- Streamlined distribution sales network.
- Initiated actions to begin ISO 9000 quality certification.
- Established and managed newly reorganized corporation to acquire additional products/companies to complement existing products.
- Evaluated foreign companies for possible acquisition.

BOILERMAKER CORPORATION, Greenwich, CT   1994 - 1999
President - Industrial Division

Managed $101 million plus (sales) industrial boiler business with 8 facilities and 12,000 employees. Autonomous division with complete P&L responsibility.

- Directed company growth from $23 million to over $101 million in sales, restoring profitability.

DENNIS ESPOSITO   PAGE TWO

- Led sales and marketing efforts with major domestic and international customers and distributors.
- Negotiated domestic and international distribution and license agreements with Asian and European companies.
- Directed the administrative and marketing activities that led to the sale of the business to Connecticut General Power in 1999.
- Initiated Total Quality Management.
- Renegotiated and directed $35 million military power boiler (U.S. Navy) program.
- Converted ships' boiler manufacturing facility, equipment, and staff to industrial boiler production.
- Consolidated four boiler divisions into one, reducing overhead by $3.4 million.
- Saved over $6 million by closing two of three manufacturing divisions.
- Instituted team building, empowerment, and employee training, improving productivity, reducing cost and decreasing turnover.
- Managed non-union and union facilities.

IMPERIAL METAL CORPORATION, Stamford, CT   **1992 - 1994**
President - Annual sales $9.5 - $14 million.
Precision metal formed boiler plating components.

FRAMATECH ENGINEERING, Farmville, VA   **1986 - 1992**
VP-Controller - Annual sales $6 - $11 million.
Engineering and start-up industrial boilers and utilities for the pulp and paper industry.

AMERICAN ELECTRONICS, Richmond, VA   **1982 - 1986**
Accounting Manager
Cost Accountant

EDUCATION

BS, Accounting/Business, Northeastern University, 1982

LEONARD SPARKS, CPA
807 Hot Springs Lane
Cleveland, OH 45385
(412) 794-8936 (H) • (412) 652-5200 (O)

OBJECTIVE: Senior level position in Financial Management.

PROFESSIONAL EXPERIENCE:

**1990 to
Present**

ARDEN GROUP, LTD. – Brussels, Belgium
A $1.5 billion diversified holding company based in Europe.

Ecogen Chemicals
A Division of Arden Group (Cleveland, OH)
Ecogen is a $90 million producer of specialty chemicals for the pulp and paper industry, manufacturing in three U.S. facilities.
Vice President of Finance & Administration (1999 - Present)
Responsible for accounting, data processing, and personnel with four managers reporting to me and a staff of 25.

- Improved the financial forecasting procedures allowing us to issue accurate and timely forecast of sales and profits to local and corporate management.
- Promoted the data processing department's effectiveness by improving its timeliness, accuracy and responsiveness to its internal customers.
- Transformed Ecogen's budgeting process by establishing a program that included functional managers in the budgets' preparation and focused them on their role in achieving budgeted results.
- Controlled annual audit costs allowing no increase in fees for the third year in a row.
- Identified cost saving opportunities decreasing losses at a troubled manufacturing facility by $500,000 per year.
- Developed alternatives to dispose of two years accumulation of excess inventory.
- Participated in development of incentive compensation programs for personnel in sales, marketing, purchasing, manufacturing and distribution which were paid from cost savings and sales increases.
- Key person on project to identify a data processing system that would incorporate all Ecogen businesses.
- Coordinated a division-wide review of suppliers with goal of consolidating purchasing of $100 million of raw materials.

Ecogen Graphics
A Division of Arden Group (Portland, OR)
Ecogen Graphics is a $45 million producer of graphic arts supplies produced in three domestic plants and sold through a world-wide distribution system.
Director of Accounting (1994 - 1999)
Responsible for accounting, data processing, personnel and purchasing departments. Supervised four managers and a staff of 16.

- Oversaw operations of two subsidiary companies, including the development of budgets, operations reviews and capital project reviews.
- Participated in negotiations for establishment of joint venture with Australian company including preparation of operating forecasts and capital requirements.

LEONARD SPARKS, CPA   **Page 2**

Director of Accounting (continued)

- Prepared worldwide sales forecasts for $40 million graphic arts supplier coordinating with U.K., European and Australian sales companies.
- Performed due diligence for acquisitions identifying significant systems needs and rationalization opportunities.
- Established inventory controls that reduced inventory shrinkage from 6% to 1%.
- Developed data processing systems for production control, sales cost control and perpetual inventory tracking.
- Developed PC-based financial reporting templates to produce monthly financial reports and forecasts.
- Reduced accounts receivable days outstanding from 85 days to 45 days of sales.

Ecogen Papers
A Division of Arden Group (Seattle, WA)
Ecogen Papers is a $15 million specialty coater of papers and films.
Vice President Finance & Administration (1990 - 1994)
Responsible for accounting, data processing, and personnel with a staff of five.

- Maintained relationships with lending bank enabling company to maximize its borrowing potential.
- Established new subsidiaries, setting up accounting, personnel and information systems.
- Directed conversion of data processing system to Arden Group's system without disrupting operations.

1984 to
1990

THE BRADFORD ACCOUNTING GROUP
Audit Department Manager
Managed audit and tax engagements for real estate, manufacturing, retail, and hospitality clients of Arthur Andersen & Company.

1982 to
1984

UNITED STATES ARMY

EDUCATION:

1986   **CPA - Arizona**

1982   **Arizona State University** – Tempe, Arizona
             MS Accounting

1980   **Arizona State University** – Tempe, Arizona
             BS Accounting

PROFESSIONAL AFFILIATIONS:

- American Institute of Certified Public Accountants
- Arizona Society of Certified Public Accountants

MELISSA BIRCH

1915 Sage Street
Unionville, PA 19347
Phone: (610) 347-2804

OBJECTIVE

Challenging administrative position within professional environment providing opportunity for growth and career advancement.

PROFESSIONAL EXPERIENCE

AG TECH CORPORATION (Unionville, PA)   **1998 - Present**

Leading agricultural biotechnology company focused on development and marketing of premium, fresh and processed, branded fruits and vegetables developed through advanced biotechnological breeding, genetic engineering and other technologies.

Administrative Assistant

Report to Vice President of Business Development providing full range of administrative support services to staff of nine managers, professionals and scientists in the marketing, sales and product development functions.

- Provide domestic and international corporate travel arrangements through local travel agency
- Set up both national and international meetings
- Type and distribute all correspondence utilizing Microsoft Office '97
- Prepare presentations utilizing PowerPoint
- Compile database of business card files utilizing Alpha4 for DOS
- Work with Product Development group to provide product samples to interested parties
- Handle and sort incoming mail, responding to routine correspondence when appropriate
- Screen and field incoming phone calls for the Business Development department
- Organize and maintain Business Development files on a current basis

ELECTRONICS BOUTIQUE, INC. (Norristown, PA)   **1996 - 1998**

Major data services company providing electronic record keeping and analytical services to the automobile insurance industry and regulatory agencies.

Accounting Associate

Reported to Supervisor of Non-Sufficient Funds (NSF) within NJ-JUA (high risk automobile insurance) account.

- Researched and processed automobile insurance NSF checks using mainframe computer system
- Tested and maintained new policy procedures utilizing dBase software on personal computer
- Assisted customer service personnel in analyzing insured and producer related problems

Melissa Birch   **Page 2**

INFORMATION SYSTEMS (Philadelphia, PA)   **1995 - 1996**

<u>Clerical Assistant</u>
Assigned to Accounting Department at Information Systems to perform research assistance, data entry, billing and filing. Assignment resulted in full-time employment.

CHESTER COUNTY BOOK COMPANY (West Chester, PA)   **1992 - 1997**

<u>Bookseller</u>
Worked part-time while employed full-time and while attending school.

EDUCATION

West Chester University (West Chester, PA)
Associates Degree, Business Administration, 1996

Unionville High School (West Chester, PA)
Diploma, Business and Secretarial Studies, 1992

SKILLS

Proficient in:
- Microsoft Office '97 (Word, Excel, PowerPoint)
- Harvard Graphics (DOS and Windows)
- Microsoft Windows 6.0
- Microsoft DOS 6.2
- Alpha4

Familiar with:
- Lotus 1-2-3
- Microsoft Word for Windows
- VideoShow/Picture It

HONORS & AWARDS

- National Honor Society
- Future Business Leaders of America, Secretary
- Professional Secretaries International Scholarship
- Berkeley School Award for Outstanding Achievement in Business Education
- Katherine Gibbs Junior Leadership Award
- Porter Insurance Company Scholarship

LISA BURTON

750 South Park Avenue
Newtown Square, PA 19742
(215) 834-1981

SUMMARY

Seasoned Administrative Assistant with over ten years experience providing full range of administrative and secretarial support services to senior level executives and their staffs. Experience in finance, accounting, manufacturing and human resources. Known as a volume producer who readily adapts to rapidly changing priorities. Strong interpersonal and leadership skills.

ACCOMPLISHMENTS

Manufacturing:

- Served five years as Administrative Assistant to Vice President-Operations for Fortune 100 consumer goods manufacturer (12 plants; 7,000 employees).
- Provided full range of administrative and secretarial support services to staff of six senior managers, handling demanding workload and consistently meeting tough deadlines.
- Created, prepared, typed and distributed wide range of standard and custom manufacturing reports for distribution to senior management (including President and Board Chairman).
- Maintained highly confidential files involving salary administration, performance evaluation ratings, organizational changes and the like.
- Trained Manufacturing secretarial staff in use of the new TelStar Fast Track Manufacturing Reporting System; oversaw successful implementation of same.
- Composed sensitive letters, drafted speeches and oversaw preparation of multimedia presentations for key senior management meetings.
- Received special merit awards for outstanding performance (two years).

Human Resources:

- Served two years as Administrative Assistant to Division Vice President Human Resources - Commercial Products (three plants; 3,800 employees; staff of 12).
- Employment Assistant to Director of Corporate Staffing for three years.
- Updated, maintained and oversaw accuracy of over 3,800 personnel records (over 20,000 annual transactions).
- Screened over 6,000 applications and employment resumes annually, handling all correspondence and composing special letters where required.
- Researched and initiated purchase of Resumax, a resume scanning and tracking system resulting in $35,000 annual savings in resume handling costs.

Lisa Burton

Accounting:

- Processed over $250 million in accounts payable annually with high degree of accuracy.
- Processed salaried payroll for Corporate Staff ($45 million; 800 employees).

WORK HISTORY

1996 to Present	Nilsk Corporation (Corporate Offices)	
	Administrative Assistant to VP - Operations	(1999 - Pres.)
	Administrative Assistant to VP - Human Resources	(1996 - 1999)
1993 - 1996	Interim Employment Agency (Corporate Offices)	
	Employment Assistant to Director of Staffing	
1984 - 1993	Stanley, Inc. (Consumer Division)	
	Senior Accounts Payable Clerk	(1991 - 1993)
	Accounts Payable Clerk	(1989 - 1991)
	Payroll Clerk	(1984 - 1989)

EDUCATION

Millersville University (Millersville, PA) 1984
Associates Degree, Accounting

Winston High School (New Holland, PA) 1982
Diploma, Business Major

COMPUTER SKILLS

Windows '98	Excel
Windows '95	Lotus 1-2-3
Resumax	Harvard Graphics

VIRGINIA C. LORING

736 Sparkling Water Road
Clinton, WA 38402
(645) 972-5435

PROFESSIONAL EXPERIENCE

GREEN TREE TECHNOLOGY CORPORATION (Vinetown, WA) **1998 - Present**

Leading agricultural biotechnology company which applies a full spectrum of technologies to develop, commercialize and market premium branded fruits and vegetables.

Corporate Receptionist

- Answer, screen and route incoming phone calls for the company, its subsidiaries and joint ventures (approximately 400 calls per day).
- Sort and distribute mail for all departments, joint ventures and subsidiaries.
- Assemble and update company information packets.
- Manage mass mailings from 300 to 5,000 pieces.
- Handle routine responses to information requests from investors and customers.
- Handle and distribute incoming fax correspondence as well as send outgoing documents.
- Maintain schedule for use of conference rooms.
- Provide administrative back-up and support for various executive assistants as needed.
- Supervise relief receptionist.
- Maintain office and conference room supply inventories.
- Responsible for outgoing mail: domestic, foreign, Federal Express, etc.

WARRINGTON EDUCATION ASSOCIATION (Warrington, WA) **1996 - 1998**

Office Manager

- Responsible for a variety of administrative and secretarial duties.

OFFICE SKILLS

- Merlin phone system
- Federal Express Powership Computer System
- Pitney Bowes postage meters
- Word Processing and data entry

EDUCATION

Wilson Junior College, 1994 - 1996

TERRI FLEMING
345 Overland Street
Boston, MA 02742
Res: (203) 892-1438

OBJECTIVE

Full charge bookkeeper with growth-oriented company offering opportunity for career advancement and professional development.

EDUCATION

Boston Junior College (Boston, MA)
Associates Degree, Administrative Accounting, 1990

Charles Patton Senior High School (Boston, MA)
Diploma, Accounting & Business Major, 1988
Received Service Award, 1988

PROFESSIONAL EXPERIENCE

RELIABLE HEATING & AIR CONDITIONING (Boston, MA)   **1998 - Present**
$14 million HVAC contractor serving residential and industrial clients throughout Massachusetts, Vermont, and New Hampshire.

Full Charge Bookkeeper (2000 - Present)
Report to President/Owner with responsibility for performing all accounting functions through preparation of monthly financial systems (One Write Plus, Version 2). Accountable for quarterly payroll tax returns, W-2's, 1099's, accounts receivable, accounts payable, collections and daily cash management. Oversee day-to-day office functions including benefits administration, customer service, order entry and equipment delivery.

Key Accomplishments:

- Reformatted financial statements using "Percentage of Completion" method
- Converted to in-house payroll, eliminating external payroll service ($10,000 annual savings)
- Set up and maintained new purchase order/inventory control system
- Set up and maintained new job costing system (using Excel spreadsheets)
- Automated financial forecasting and budgeting functions
- Managed company in President's absence.

Senior Bookkeeper (1998 - 2000)

ANDERSON CONSULTING (Stow, VT)   1996 - 1998

A $5 million systems consulting firm with specialization in the design and installation of manufacturing cost control systems in the pharmaceutical industry.

Full Charge Bookkeeper

Reported to President/Owner with responsibility for all accounting functions through preparation of monthly financial statements. Prepared quarterly payroll tax returns, W-2's, 1099's and daily cash management reports.

Key Accomplishments:

- Installed and implemented new manufacturing/accounting software (i.e., Basic Four Manufacturing) using an MAI UNIX computer system.
- Assisted in preparation of computer system proposals and ordering equipment
- Provided customer support on software questions

VERMONT REFRIGERATION COMPANY (Killington, VT)   1994 - 1996

A $120 million manufacturer of industrial and commercial refrigeration equipment with distribution and installation of equipment in the Northeastern United States.

Controller's Assistant

Reported to Controller with responsibility for all accounts receivable functions including bank deposits. Handled credit/collections (350 accounts) and filled in for accounts payable/payroll personnel as needed.

METALS CORPORATION (Killington, VT)   1992 - 1994

Bookkeeper

Reported to President of this $2 million metallurgical testing laboratory. Performed all accounting functions through trial balance.

BARNES SHIPPING COMPANY (Philadelphia, PA)   1989 - 1992

Accounting Clerk

Reported to Accounting Manager of this $200 million shipping company. Processed and approved expense reports for all domestic and overseas shipping crews (850 employees) and wire transfer of funds for same. Performed bank reconciliations for domestic and international accounts.

COMPUTER SKILLS

Software: One Write Plus (Version 2), Job Track/Job Costing, Lotus 1-2-3, Basic Four Manufacturing, Microsoft Office '97

Hardware: MAI UNIX, Laser 486 Personal Computer, Various printers and peripherals

WILLIAM MAHONEY

78 Wilson Boulevard
Raleigh, NC 27354
(919) 534-7821 (Home) · (919) 682-8500 (Office)
(919) 682-8505 (Fax)

SUMMARY OF QUALIFICATIONS:

Corporate real estate and facilities director with significant experience in rapidly changing business environments. Creative and accomplished. Exceptional ability to lead others in the development and execution of visions, strategies and systems to meet individual needs and corporate objectives. Experience includes new-construction planning and development; remodelling and expansion project management, real estate leasing, acquisition and disposition; and facilities management

---

CAREER EXPERIENCE:

<u>Thomasville Furniture Industries, Inc., Thomasville, NC (1996 - Present)</u>
An $500 million manufacturer of high-end leisure furniture.

<u>Director, Corporate Real Estate and Facilities</u> (2000 - Present)

- Created the corporate real estate function, including development and implementation of cohesive strategies and policies for real estate and facilities management.

- Oversaw a domestic real estate portfolio of 2.14 million square feet, including planning, design and construction, leasing, acquisition and disposition; facilities operations and records management.

- Managed a staff of 102 and operating budget of $9.8 million. Directed capital projects up to $80 million.

- Initiated an integrated facilities management system for Georgia and North Carolina (plant and headquarters) operations.

- Led cross-company team to develop and implement corporate environmental goals and objectives.

- Achieved over $4.5 million in quality cost savings for corporate real estate and facilities operations in a three-year period.

<u>Director, Properties Development</u> (1996 - 2000)

- Led the greenfield planning, development, design and construction of $90 million, 525,000-square-foot, 225-acre headquarters campus.

- Pulled together the architectural team. Orchestrated realization of a coherent vision to meet the cultural expectations and practical needs of disparate groups; improved communication and productivity.

- Completed two-year project on budget and ahead of schedule.

- Led remodelling and consolidation of corporate administrative function for 120,000-square-foot facility in Atlanta, GA (involving the relocation of over 220 employees).

- Directed expansion of computer room facilities in Atlanta, GA facility (involving side-by-side construction work).

Blount, Inc., Montgomery, AL (1987 - 1996)
A $670 million construction and industrial equipment manufacturer.

Venture Manager, Technology Center (1993 - 1996)

- Led the planning, design and construction of a $30 million, 272,000-square-foot R&D technology center in Montgomery, AL. Completed project on schedule and under budget.

- Initiated planning study to identify space requirements in response to growth.

- Conducted site selection process; negotiated unique, highly complex land-lease agreement to indemnify company from prior environmental contamination on site.

Manager, Facility Planning (1991 - 1993)

Created and implemented a facility planning function for the company in response to business and strategic changes.

Initiated a multi-functional planning strategy that successfully integrated individual facility needs with overall company strategies.

Established office standards program; administered space allocations.

Hazardous Materials Coordinator (1987 - 1991)

Developed and administered the Hazardous Material Control Program, initiating improved procedures and training.

EDUCATION: Bachelor of Science - Biology and Chemistry (1987)
Arizona State University, Tempe, AZ

Numerous Seminars: IDRC World Congresses
Corporate Facilities Planning: American Management Association
Improving Management Skills: University of Georgia
UNIX and APICS studies

EMILY BANCROFT

1321 West Oakland Road
Perkins, IL 60342

Residence (603) 279-1265
Office (603) 279-4534

SUMMARY

Senior level executive with extensive experience reducing costs, enhancing and consolidating services, managing crises and reducing headcount.

PROFESSIONAL EXPERIENCE

PERKINS CONSULTING SERVICES, Perkins, IL   **2002-Present**
Vice President, Sales and Operations

Sell and implement expansive business management services to Fortune 500 companies (including sale of largest corporate account in company's history). Represent rapidly growing provider of corporate outsourcing services with an established annual growth rate of 20-30% (growth projected to exceed 1000% by the year 2004). Full service outsourcing and consultative services include: space planning, facilities management, mail distribution, purchasing, reception/secretarial, central files management, forms/graphics printing and copy centers.

CRANSTON & SMITH, Hartford, CT   **2000-2002**
Director of Facilities & Building Services

Managed staff of 75 and $30 million budget addressing the reorganization, automation and development of services impacting facilities and space planning, meetings and conference planning, cafeteria and catering services, purchasing, central files, mail room and security. Created more professional, cohesive groups and significantly reduced expenses.

- Directed largest Connecticut corporate move since 1978. Strategic consolidation of space and elimination of redundant and nonessential services reduced annual occupancy costs by $10 million and operational costs by $1.5 million.

- Created and implemented (previously non-existent) budget planning and tracking process across all divisions, thereby enabling accountability, stringent savings and uniform procedures.

- Introduced and implemented CAD (computer aided design) system that handled all C&S Connecticut space (500,000 sq. ft.) and provided vital information on all physical space, furniture inventory, voice and data locations as well as personnel locations. Comprehensive database enabled the automation of in-house relocations and reconfiguration with an annual savings exceeding $1.4 million.

EMILY BANCROFT   Page 2

APPLETON HEALTH CARE, Freehold, NJ   1993-2000
Vice President - Corporate Administrative Services (1997-2000)

Managed service areas including building operations, cafeteria, purchasing, duplicating services, forms and graphics, micrographics, transportation, mail, records management, corporate condominiums and space planning. Provided consulting services to agency lease administration for 49 agencies nationwide.

- "Building of the Year" award recipient in 1995 after setting up separate corporation to run operations internally (42 acres, 635,000 sq. ft.). Eliminated all outside management fees and commissions, significantly improved services and reduced operation costs by $1.50 per sq.ft. within nine months.

- Successfully managed execution of complex disaster recovery plan following weekend fire and flood (May 1995). All impacted areas and (70) employees were fully operational by 6:00 AM Monday morning (within 48 hours of mishap).

- Managed contracted insurance agreements and related files, thereby enabling the recapture of $1 million dollars in fire/flood damages.

District Administrative Manager (1993-1997)
Reorganized services negatively impacting corporate profitability.

- Implemented cost center budgets for all service areas. Managed to operate below budget ($2 million annual savings) while enhancing overall quality of services. Simultaneously managed two of the largest moves in company's history.

HENDERSON COMPANY, Princeton, NJ   1990-1993
District Administrative Manager

- Ran operations and leasing administration for nine facilities with a budget of $8 million.

- Managed seven facility moves in 11 months. Oversaw major telecommunication installation resulting in a 25% reduction in company costs and an actual capital budget attainment within 1%.

EDUCATION

B.A., Management, Lehigh University, 1990
Certified RPA (Real Property Manager)
Executive Development Program

PROFESSIONAL AFFILIATIONS

Adjunct Professor of Real Estate - Lehigh University
Building Owners and Managers Association International
Facility Management Association
Female Executives
Notary Public
Executive Women of New Jersey

RALPH COMSTOCK
591 Euclid Avenue
Cleveland, OH 44130
(216) 391-6700

Overview

Financial manager with experience in business analysis, mergers and acquisitions, budgeting, P&L responsibility, SEC reporting, treasury operations, credit, general accounting. Over 16 years of accomplishment in the entertainment, computer equipment and consumer products industries. Strong administrative, technical and organizational skills and special expertise with departmental restructuring and development. Skilled in MIS applications, personal computers, cash management, cost and general accounting systems. MBA.

Professional Experience

PREMIER INDUSTRIAL CORPORATION, Cleveland, OH   **1999 - Present**

Director of Finance
Direct all financial accounting and reporting, treasury and cash management, human resources and employee benefits, risk management and insurance and MIS activities for this $185 million production company through a staff of six controllers as well as human resources and data processing professionals.

- Restructured corporate and division financial departments to handle growing needs of business by improving management reporting and improving communications with operating departments.

- Initiated cash management and capital spending and budgeting policies resulting in tighter control of company assets and greater concentration of resources in those areas where needed most.

- Negotiated and arranged for $30 million of new financing to be used for acquisition of new company and purchase of state-of-the-art video and graphics equipment.

- Consolidated data processing centers, reduced use of outside consultants, negotiated new software purchase agreements and hardware maintenance contracts and reallocated system resources resulting in savings of $1/2 million annually.

- Saved company $1/4 million annually by reviewing operations of one of the commercial post production divisions and recommending negotiation of new utility allocations, consolidation of billing and operations areas and elimination of a messenger service contract.

CHARTER ONE FINANCIAL, Cleveland, OH   **1997 - 1999**

Management/Financial Consultant
Consulting firm specializing in expanding the capabilities and productivity of corporate financial and accounting departments, providing computer information system studies and implementation including orientation of personnel and managing financial assets using conservative investment philosophy.

- Developed client proposals specifying phase-by-phase process to maximize utilization of present system or to acquire advanced hardware and software, implement installation and initial operation of new system including orientation of personnel.

- Worked with client organizations to restructure accounting and finance functions in anticipation of changing future needs resulting in greater productivity while reducing overall personnel costs.

- Provided investment management services for $5 million portfolio achieving return on assets of 32 and 45 percent during 1997 and 1998 respectively while maintaining the fund's objective of capital preservation.

Ralph Comstock

TECHNAUTICS CORPORATION, Cleveland, OH   1993 - 1997

Corporate Controller
Controlled all financial and MIS activities for this $225 million multinational manufacturer of computer peripherals by designing and implementing the Company's manufacturing, sales and financial systems, developing cash management procedures, directing risk management, treasury operations, management reporting, budgets, credit and collections and contract administration.

- Established worldwide MIS function and directed upgrade of computer equipment by purchasing two AS400 systems and integrated software resulting in worldwide savings of $1.5 million annually.

- Restructured US and Japanese financial organizations resulting in more timely and improved management reporting.

- Initiated worldwide cash management and capital spending approval policies resulting in tighter control of company assets and greater concentration of resources in those areas where needed most.

- Developed and implemented credit approval and collection procedures resulting in collection of $920,000 of past due accounts and continued payment of current accounts in accordance with terms.

- Reduced costs of worldwide insurance program by 17% while significantly improving coverage in all areas and establishing a corporate risk management program.

MEAD CORPORATION, Dayton, OH   1991 - 1993

Manager of Corporate Accounting
Directed all accounting and reporting activities through a staff of 40 management, professional and clerical personnel. Responsible for financial systems and procedures, general accounting, accounts payable, cost and inventory accounting.

- Initiated monthly financial closings, both domestically and internationally, providing management with timely and accurate reporting.

- Automated accounting systems and streamlined work methods resulting in more efficient use of personnel and resources. Installed McCormack & Dodge General Ledger and Accounts Payable Systems.

- Recommended freight management system resulting in $275,000 annual savings.

- Implemented, as part of a team, a Data 3 MRPII inventory control system in a System 28 environment resulting in a 28% reduction in raw material inventories and an annual savings of $400,000 in carrying costs.

NCR CORPORATION, Dayton, OH   1984 - 1991

Manager of Worldwide Accounting	1989 - 1991
Supervisor of General Accounting	1988 - 1989
Senior Inventory Accountant	1987 - 1988
Inventory Accountant	1984 - 1987

Education

CASE WESTERN RESERVE UNIVERSITY, Cleveland, OH
Graduate School of Business. MBA Degree in Accounting   1984
College of Arts & Science. BA Degree in Economics and Political Science   1982

SHARON MILLER
368 FARMVILLE ROAD
RICHMOND, VIRGINIA 23291

Home: (804) 884-5376
Business: (306) 884-1000

OBJECTIVE: Top Financial Management position in the manufacturing sector.

STRENGTHS:

Business Judgement	People Development	Analytical Capability
Interpersonal Skills	International Experience	Diverse Background

EXPERIENCE:

1999 - Present

ETHYL CORPORATION
Division Controller
Specialty Chemicals, Richmond, VA

Senior Financial Executive of a diversified, $2.6 billion, international specialty chemicals business. Major businesses are located in United Kingdom, Belgium, France, Canada, and the U.S. Major accomplishments:

· Improved financial performance by divesting low return businesses and downsizing the overhead structure. Improved return on capital and return on sales by 20% and 25% respectively.
· Realigned the financial function to eliminate non value added services and strengthen the organization. Reduced total expenses and personnel by 33%.
· 2001 Chairman - Financial Improvement Awards Program. Developed corporate program to recognize and reward sustained outstanding individual performance.
· Led effort to reduce investment base and improve cash flow performance.

1995 - 1999

Director Finance
Measurement and Control Instrumentation, Alexandria, VA

Equivalent CFO position for a $180 million division. Major businesses are located in the U.S., Canada, United Kingdom, France, Belgium, Netherlands, and Singapore. Extensive international travel and personnel contact. Major accomplishments were:

· Provided leadership to improve the financial performance from a $8 million net loss to a $13 million net profit.
· Successfully completed the acquisition of Whitby Instrumentation.
· Directed the establishment of improved internal controls throughout Europe.
· Reduced fixed manufacturing costs by $2.5 million per year by consolidating two manufacturing locations into one.

1994 - 1995

JOHN BROWN, INC.
Division Controller
Pump Division, West Warwick, RI

Sharon Miller   Page 2

Directed the Financial / M.I.S. functions of a diverse, international division of John Brown, Inc. Division consisted of three autonomous operating units located in the U.S., Canada, Mexico, and United Kingdom. Total sales - $60 million; net income $4.2 million. Number of employees - 700.

· Provided financial leadership and guidance to five business unit comptrollers.
· Restructured an operating unit to return the business to profitability.
· Directed the development of strategic plans, operating plans, and monthly forecasts.

1993 - 1994   **JERRICO, INC.**
               Vice President - Finance
               Materials Handling Division, Lexington, KY

               Directed the financial function of Marketing and Distribution company with sales in excess of $300 million. Major accomplishments were:

               · Negotiated with two major German companies to establish a joint venture.
               · Designed and developed a financial organization to support the requirements of this newly formed company.

1991 - 1993   *Controller*
               Louisville Plant, Louisville, KY

               Responsible for the financial function of an $70 million, 600-employee manufacturing facility. Directly supervised 12 employees. Major accomplishments were:

               · Established controls which reduced inventory loss from $3 million to $30,000 over a two-year period. Total inventory was $30 million.

1989 - 1991   *Corporate Manager of Investment Analysis*
               Lexington, KY

               Controlled a $95 million capital budget. Presented capital plans and investment proposals to the Executive Committee of the Board of Directors. Developed new corporate policy and procedure manual for Investment Analysis. Introduced the policy through seminars presented in the U.S., Germany, France, Belgium, Brazil, and Australia.

1989   *Senior Financial Analyst*
               Lexington, KY

1988   *Financial Analyst*
               Lexington, KY

EDUCATION: 1988   **EASTERN MICHIGAN UNIVERSITY**
                          Ypsilanti, MI   M.B.A. - Finance

                  1986   **INDIANA UNIVERSITY**
                          Gary, IN   B.A. - Accounting

JANET EATON

1715 Briar Forest Drive, Louisville, KY 40329
(502) 478-3589

CAREER SUMMARY

Senior financial manager with strategic responsibility for domestic and international financial, operational, and EDP functions, most recently Group Controller with a large multinational consumer products firm. Superior leadership, organizational, and writing skills.

BUSINESS EXPERIENCE & ACCOMPLISHMENTS

GLENMORE DISTILLERIES COMPANY, Louisville, KY
A distiller and marketer of bourbon whiskey with annual sales of $3.2 billion. Operated as the worldwide center for marketing production and financial strategy.

Group Controller   2000-Present
Joined the company as Controller for USA distributor with subsequent elevations in responsibility over both domestic and international operations. Senior level financial manager, directing all finance, planning, and accounting functions. Responsible for business analysis and interpretation of trends, management reporting, cash and working capital management, financial services, and automated systems.

- Liquidated USA distribution company and managed financial aspects of major restructuring while maintaining normal operations with a 50% reduction in staff.

- Composed a strategic plan recommending consolidation of two major distributors to take advantage of natural synergies, implemented by top management.

- Created an integrated management reporting system that cut 3 days out of the monthly cycle and eliminated 10-12 hours of overtime per month.

- Created financial operations for new worldwide strategic business unit that included the establishment of a new domestic company to import into the USA, the development of work procedures, restaffing, and the installation of internal controls.

Controller - Glenmore Bourbon Division   1997-2000

- Created and implemented international financial services and cash management, eliminating capital requirements of $5.8 million, reducing inventory from 95 turn days to 55 days, and decreasing US$ exposure from $20 million to $18 million.

- Installed a foreign exchange management system, including risk quantification of $35 million, translation versus transaction budgeting, and the means to track gains and losses from contracts. Saved $120,000 in the first four months and $3.6 million in the first fiscal year.

- Developed and implemented financial controls and increased productivity through automation. This included a complete overhaul and integration of general ledger systems that reduced turnaround times by 4-5 days and eliminated 10-20 man hours per week plus a budgeting and forecasting system with an accuracy rate of better than 99%.

- Established controls over South American operations with the introduction of a direct liaise, the computerization of manual financial systems, and the development of procedures and timetables that raised the compliance rate for international consolidations to 100%.

- Successfully negotiated and documented trading arrangements, including an alternative cost transfer scheme with Scottish unit that resulted in perpetual savings of $750,000 annually.

WEYERHAEUSER COMPANY, Tacoma, Washington
A leading international consumer products company with annual sales of $6.0 billion.

Assistant Plant Controller   1994-1997
Responsible for month-end financial reporting, accounting services, and analysis. Assisted with annual budgets and various special projects.

- Developed and implemented procedures to account for the assimilation of 5-15 new hires and capital purchases of nearly $500,000 million per week.

- Eliminated emergency overtime and improved reporting compliance to 100%.

- Co-managed the installation of new mainframe financial reporting software, including planning the installation, testing the results, assisting with de-bugging and training staff.

KIMBERLY-CLARK CORPORATION, Dallas, Texas
A major Fortune 500 pulp and paper company with annual sales of $6.8 billion.

Financial Analyst   1991-1994
Performed all phases of manufacturing accounting, including financial planning, general accounting and cost accounting.

- Acted as exclusive financial advisor for a wholly-owned subsidiary with annual sales of $4.5 million, including general accounting, cost accounting and physical inventories.

- Developed comprehensive physical inventory procedures, training up to 1,800 people per year, calculating inventory adjustments up to $165,000 and defending results with internal and external auditors.

Associate Financial Analyst   1989-1991

- Developed computerized budgeting system for twelve cost centers that eliminated 5-10 man days per cycle.

- Conducted training program for other staff members in the use of LOTUS 1-2-3.

EDUCATION

M.B.A.   Texas A&M University. Honors Graduate (GPA: 3.6), 1989.
B.S.   Texas A&M University. Honors Graduate (GPA: 3.9), Phi Beta Kappa, 1987.

DAVID MASON, CPA
9023 Wheeling Road
Providence, RI 02875
(401) 345-3864 Home
(401) 345-1000 Office

OBJECTIVE: Financial Management or Controller

SUMMARY: Financial professional with 14 years of progressively responsible management positions within the Financial Services industry. Developed strong proficiencies in leadership and organization as well as special skills in:

- Accounting and Financial Analysis
- Budgeting and Planning
- Staff Selection & Development
- Project Management
- Internal Controls
- Mainframe and PC Systems

EXPERIENCE: <u>CITIZENS BANK</u>, Providence, RI   2000 - Present

Controller - City Bank of Rhode Island
City Bank is the legal entity for Citizen Bank's domestic consumer lending business ($1.8 billion in assets). Controller is responsible for all accounting, internal & external reporting, budgeting & planning, financial controls and cash management.

- Direct the Bank's regulatory and other external reporting (FDIC/Federal Reserve, rating agencies, audited financial statements). Coordinate annual FDIC and State of Rhode Island examinations.

- Prepare the annual budget and quarterly financial forecasts.

- Developed an Internal Controls program and procedures manual.

- Revised product profitability reports and implemented comprehensive ratio/trend analysis to improve the level of management reporting.

- Developed work measurement standards for the Bank's operational departments via PC modeling to improve work flows, control costs and evaluate performance.

- Implemented many financial system enhancements including a new general ledger/accounts payable system, mainframe financial reporting database and PC based applications for planning and analysis.

<u>CITIZENS FINANCIAL CORPORATION, Providence, RI</u>   1994 - 2000

Vice President, Finance - Citizens Mortgage Corporation
Directed all finance activities for Citizen's start-up mortgage banking subsidiary. Responsible for the accounting & financial reporting, planning, treasury and human resource functions.

· Prepared the annual Business Plan and Operating Budget. Also developed the five-year long range strategic plan.

· Designed and implemented a monthly management report package.

· Converted a microcomputer General Ledger/Accounts Payable system to a mainframe based accounting system.

· Obtained funding to meet daily loan requirements and administered the cash management function.

· Presented the financial results at monthly Board of Directors' meetings.

· Selected, managed and developed a staff of 25 employees.

<u>FLEET FINANCIAL GROUP, Providence, RI</u>   1989 - 1994

Accounting Officer
Supervised professional accounting staff of seven. Diversified accounting and financial reporting responsibilities included preparation of financial statements for 10 domestic companies, review and consolidation of financial statements for foreign subsidiaries, budget analysis, management, tax and regulatory reports.

EDUCATION: University of Rhode Island
Master of Business Administration, Major: Finance (1989)

University of Rhode Island
Bachelor of Science, Major: Accounting (1987)

AFFILIATIONS: American Institute of Certified Public Accountants
Rhode Island Society of Certified Public Accountants
University of Rhode Island, Business & Economics Alumni Association

WANDA D. STUART

22 Dale Avenue   Home: (802) 457-9328   Fax: (802) 457-3586

Charlotte, NC 12948   Office: (802) 457-2849   E-Mail:WDS@MSN

SUMMARY

Senior Executive with over 13 years in-depth experience in finance, treasury, accounting, strategic planning, acquisitions, divestitures and investor relations. Enthusiastic and hard-working executive with the objective of improving operating performance, profitability and business growth, by providing quality financial/administrative/operational direction.

PROFESSIONAL EXPERIENCE

MACHINE TECHNOLOGY CORPORATION   **2000 to Present**

A publicly-held international company. World leader in the development and manufacture of technologically advanced production machinery. Revenues in excess of $540 million.

As <u>Vice President - Finance & Treasurer</u>, developed financial resources for restructuring the company back to its core business. Directed worldwide staff of 27 accounting, finance and IS employees. Reported directly to the Chairman and President.

- Developed and implemented marketing plan to divest four non-core companies. Targeted 95 potential buyers resulting in the sale of three companies in separate transactions in 14 months. The $110 million received exceeded original estimates by over 14%.

- Negotiated $86 million of bank revolving credit facilities with more favorable terms. Commitment fees were reduced 40%.

- Instituted a comprehensive profit improvement program to reduce indirect expense in anticipation of cyclical decline in sales. Annualized fixed overhead expenses were reduced from $63M to $38M in 20 months.

WESTON CORPORATION   **1989 to 2000**

A publicly-held manufacturing company producing hardware and industrial fasteners. The company has revenues of approximately $115 million and 800 employees.

Vice President - Finance and Treasurer	**1998 - 2000**
Corporate Controller	**1994 - 1998**
Senior Auditor	**1992 - 1994**
Auditor	**1989 - 1992**

EDUCATION
BBA -- University of Florida -- 1989

BRADFORD DAVIS, CPA

34 Classic Street
Memphis, TN 38145

Home: (901) 375-1874
Office: (901) 457-2590
(800) 555-8300

SUMMARY

A results oriented, Senior Financial Executive with extensive experience in consumer packaged goods and OTC pharmaceutical industries, both domestic and international. Outstanding record of leadership and achievement in both line and staff positions.

Demonstrated accomplishment in:

- Asset/Liability Management
- Budgeting/Forecasting
- Controllership
- Financial Analysis
- Internal Audit

- Strategic Planning
- Acquisition Reviews
- Joint Ventures
- Organizational Structuring & Restructuring
- Management Information Systems

EXPERIENCE

ALLIED BIOSEARCH, INC.   **1994 - Present**

INTERNATIONAL DIVISION - Consumer Products
Vice President, Finance   *1999 - Present*

Directed finance and IS activities for this fast growing $700 million in revenues division which covered the world excluding the U.S. and Western Europe.

- Directed financial team which negotiated the establishment of a joint venture in Central & Eastern Europe which resulted in a $6.5 million reimbursement of start-up costs.

- Led a multi-disciplined team which developed a plan to generate hard currency foreign exchange for our joint venture in China by exporting raw materials. In addition to generating the needed FX, reduced raw material cost to our plants by 20-35% on the exported materials.

- Streamlined and automated worldwide financial reporting systems which resulted in faster, consistent, actionable results reporting.

ALLIED BIOHEALTH - USA
Vice President, Finance   *1996 - 1999*

From 1993 to 1996, this $300 million marketing and sales division absorbed a smaller division, took responsibility for manufacturing (three plants) and assumed responsibility for Mexico. By 1996 revenues had grown to $425 million.

BRADFORD DAVIS, CPA

· Led a multi-disciplined task force which recommended and then implemented a new integrated software system. This AS 400 based system which replaced a mainframe system resulted in annual software licensing and hardware operating savings of $1.8 million.

· Redesigned business processes to create a "one stop shopping" customer service department which improved customer service with a 15% decrease in headcount in the departments affected.

· Reorganized the finance department at division headquarters to participate in cross functional brand teams. This resulted in increased productivity, better communication and more efficient processes.

· Part of a three man team which managed the Division in the absence of a President for most of 1997. Overachieved budget by 109% of sales and 104% of operating profit.

· After the recall of a potentially contaminated product, compiled a list of all losses and obtained settlement from the vendor's insurance company. Received reimbursement for all out-of-pocket expenses and negotiated an additional settlement of approximately $6 million for lost business by using data obtained from the sales and market research departments.

ALLIED BIOSEARCH, INC.
Corporate Audit Manager 1995 - 1996
Audit Supervisor 1994 - 1995

· Responsible for scheduling, staffing and coordinating audit at all domestic locations. Reported to the Corporate Audit Director. Managed eight professionals.

FRANKLIN PRODUCTS, INC.
Controller, Consumer Products Division 1992 - 1994

· Conducted an audit of payments to food brokers which uncovered several instances of defalcations. The company recovered approximately $430,000 in misappropriated funds and replaced six brokers.

· Implemented annual reviews of product costs with marketing, manufacturing and finance personnel which resulted in annual cost of goods savings of approximately $1 million.

Controller Personal Products Division 1989 - 1992

· Developed a computerized tracking system for cooperative advertising payments which resulted in a 20% decrease in customer deductions and virtually eliminated over payments.

EDUCATION

Tennessee State University	MBA - Taxation	1989
Tennessee State University	BA - Accounting	1987
TN Certified Public Accountant		1990

JONATHAN A. BARTELS

Home Address: 1301 Haverford Road, Haverford, PA 19732   Home: (610) 436-0117   Work: (610) 496-3000

Work Experience:

1996 - Present   Hercules Chemical Company

International Financial Coordinator, Corporate Headquarters, Philadelphia, PA (2001 - Present)
Direct interface between company's corporate headquarters and the European/Asian International locations to ensure timely and accurate financial results and business performance data.
- Consolidation of eight companies with 1998 revenues of $750M and gross profits of $96.5M.
- Forecast and evaluate currency exposure of international operations and hedging contracts.
- Direct corporate funding process to provide working and investment capital to region.
- Annual budget preparation and monthly comparison reports and forecasts.
- Coordinate all updated policies and business procedures in accordance with US GAAP and company policy.

Sales/Marketing Services Supervisor, Specialty Chemical Division, Houston, TX (1997 - 2001)
Direct and manage staff of three handling marketing operations, international and domestic distribution, establishing production and inventory levels for manufacturing. Prepare and monitor operating and capital budgets and handle financial analysis for specialty chemical business servicing crude oil pipelines.
- Establish and maintain $4M equipment administration program tracking equipment location and costs, saving workload requirements by 20%.
- Perform economic lease/purchase evaluations of contract proposals.
- Negotiate $3M annual sales and service contracts with vendors and equipment leasing firms.
- Presented sales/marketing proposals to prospective pipeline companies.
- Implement and manage new order entry system to accommodate $80M annual sales volume.

Senior Inventory Coordinator/Analyst, Specialty Chemical Division, Houston, TX (1996 - 1997)
Monitor $3M of inventory consisting of over 250 products, generate monthly inventory level, location and bad-order reports, special studies and analysis as required.
- Volume planning and coordination.
- Set up/directed physical inventories for 21 domestic chemical stocking locations.
- Design, implement and manage reporting system for senior management identifying all bad-order domestic products.
- Eliminate unreconciled inventories backlogged for over two years, completed project independently in less than one year. Nominated and received distinguished company award.

1991 - 1996   Petroleum Products Corporation

Assistant Group Controller, Beaumont Refineries, Beaumont, TX (1992 - 1996)
Consolidate and report financial results for two refineries. Direct and monitor capital and operating budgets. Act as corporate liaison between refineries and parent company.
- Assist in design and implementation of new financial reporting and cost accounting systems.
- Develop and maintain cash management and forecasting program to maximize use of company funds.
- Successfully handled division divestitures when business units were sold to private investor groups.

Cost Accountant (1991 - 1992)
Product costing of over 200 division products and quarterly development of plant fixed overhead costs.

1988 - 1991   Lone Star Financial

Loan Analyst and Assistant Cashier, Dubuque, IA

Education: B.A., Accounting, Texas A & M, December, 1988

Computers: Symphony, Lotus, dBase, Windows '97, Freelance, AS400

CHRISTOPHER HANGE

670 Second Avenue
New York, New York 10001

Office: (212) 575-4302
Home: (212) 776-7845
Fax: (212) 776-7846

SUMMARY

Nineteen years financial management experience in a variety of businesses, ranging from equipment manufacturing to financial services, with one of the worlds largest diversified companies. Strategic thinker with excellent analytical and communication skills and strong international and M&A experience.

PROFESSIONAL EXPERIENCE

UNIVERSAL PRODUCTS COMPANY   1985 - Present
    Unistar Container Division
    White Plains, NY
    World's largest lessor of bulk liquid container systems.

<u>Vice President and Chief Financial Officer</u>   2000 - Present

- Managed the day-to-day financial operations of this $350 million business during a period in which assets grew from $500 million to $1.9 billion.

- Valued, negotiated and closed (as part of a four-person team) the $600 + million acquisition of Unistar's largest competitor, leading to the doubling of Unistar's assets and $22 million in increased earnings in the first year.

- Negotiated two cross-border leveraged leases, lowering financing costs on $100 million of new equipment to rates below comparable U.S. Treasuries and saving $750,000 in annual carrying costs.

- Established pricing guidelines and assisted Marketing in developing new or varied products to fuel continued profitable growth, resulting in over $350 million in new financing business closed in 1992.

Universal Capital Commercial Real Estate   1997 - 2000
White Plains, NY
Provider of mortgage financing on existing commercial properties located in the U.S., Canada and Europe and construction financing on U.S. residential development projects.

<u>Manager - Financial Planning and Analysis</u>

- Managed the financial, information systems and service center operations of a business whose assets grew from $1.3 billion to over $3.0 billion in three years.

- Developed comprehensive financial analysis and planning models which enabled the business to better understand and manage its growing earnings.

CHRISTOPHER HANGE   PAGE 2

- Negotiated bridge financing facilities which permitted transactions to be closed according to customers' needs while preserving Universal Capital's ability to manage its debt-equity ratios and maintain its AAA rating.

- Created the financial infrastructure needed to support the business' international expansion, including the establishment of servicing support and routines to manage funding, tax, accounting and foreign exchange risk.

Universal Pump Business   **1994 - 1997**
Trenton, NJ
Manufacturer of residential and industrial pumps and metering devices.

Manager - Business Analysis

- Directed the financial planning and analysis of this $120 million business and coordinated efforts which resulted in a 43% improvement in return on sales and a 12% reduction in real base costs in three years.

- Participated on a task force which overhauled the businesses' hourly wage system, making it simpler, more flexible and more competitive and reducing projected labor costs 30% in four years.

- Reviewed a high-profile new product program and recommended that it be abandoned as too expensive and too difficult to manufacture within established specifications and cost. The program was terminated and the $20 million in program funds was redeployed.

Universal Silicones   **1985 - 1994**
Stamford, CT

Finance Manager   1990 - 1994
Specialist - Business Analysis   1985 - 1990

EDUCATION

Universal's Manager Development Course - 1992

Universal's Financial Management Program - 1989

B.S. in Information Technology and Honors Graduate, MIT, Boston, MA - 1985

Numerous technical and leadership development courses and seminars

JOHN CHISHOLM

89 Lake Hills Road West
Newtown Square, Pennsylvania 19075

Home: (610) 668-3905
Office: (610) 496-2000

CAREER SUMMARY

Senior Financial Manager with 17 years of diverse assignments with Zimmer Incorporated. Experience includes financial planning, forecasting, manufacturing cost control, capital justification, marketing and product line support and acquisition analysis.

PROFESSIONAL EXPERIENCE

ZIMMER INCORPORATED - Malvern, PA   **1990 - Present**

Manager, Systems Integration - *Home Products Division* (2001-Present)
Managed projects and coordination of IS services for high-impact financial applications. Ensured implementation objectives were realized by IS and financial systems users.

- Developed specifications for a $1.4 million automated claims processing system saving $500,000 annually.
- Reengineered customer order fulfillment and claims cycle. Identified 30% cycle time reduction and $11 million cash flow opportunity.
- Justified major enhancements in payable and receivable systems; reduced staffing 15% saving $85,000 annually.
- Participated in vendor analysis and contract negotiations.

Manager, Financial Planning and Analysis - Corporate (2000-2001)
Coordinated planning process for all divisions. Assessed integrity of divisional plans and forecasts. Identified areas of earnings vulnerability and recommended contingency actions. Recommended capital requests to CFO and CEO.

- Developed manufacturing strategy for seasonal products reducing variances $4 million annually and eliminating payments to subcontractors.
- Identified warehousing consolidation opportunity saving $650,000 annually.
- Recommended termination of divisional computer service contracts and full utilization of internal mainframe systems savings $250,000 annually.

Manager, Financial Planning and Analysis - *Home Products Division* (1997-2000)
Directed development of financial projections and budgets for a $900 million consumer products division. Prepared annual profit, competitive action and five year strategic business plans. Managed capital justification and acquisition analysis processes.

- Implemented systems to monitor actual versus planned product costs identifying variances for inflation and productivity.

JOHN CHISHOLM

- Justified capital projects exceeding $50 million annually and over 50 new products.
- Implemented analysis and valuation techniques for seven acquisition targets valued at $500 million.
- Led evaluation and assimilation of $15 million Mexican acquisition.

Manager, Manufacturing Accounting (1995-1997)
Managed inventory and expenses for six manufacturing and distribution locations. Operations included over 200 presses and $150 million in annual overhead expenditures.

- Reduced variances by $2 million per year.
- Established controls monitoring $15 million of inventories consigned to subcontractors.
- Reduced annual physical inventory losses by $500,000.

Senior Manufacturing Accounting (1994-1995)
Approved inventory and cost of sales closing entries. Prepared budgets and reconciled inventories. Reported product line profitability and return on investment.

Financial Analyst (1992-1994)
Prepared operating budgets and annual profit plans. Reported capital spending to corporate management. Completed tax and audit schedules.

Corporate Auditor (1990-1992)
Conducted compliance audits and tests of operational controls. Investigated divisional performance issues related to manufacturing scrap, variances and inventory controls.

ELEXIS CORPORATION - Media, PA   **1989**
Accountant

ESMARK - Richmond, VA   **1987 - 1989**
Manager Policy Services/Business Process Analyst

EDUCATION

M.B.A. - 1997
University of Pennsylvania

B.B.A. - 1987
University of Virginia

Melvin C. Cooke

600 Beach Lane   Home: (714) 546-9837   Fax: (714) 546-9852
San Diego, CA 37497   Office: (714) 646-9083   E-Mail: MELCC@MSN

OBJECTIVE: Senior level business planning position in technology-based organization.

PROFESSIONAL EXPERIENCE:

1996-   Director of Strategic Planning
Present   **Phonecom Communications, Inc. (PCI), San Diego, CA**
                A 100 year-old west coast telecommunications holding company with interests in
                local telephone service, publishing, long distance and network services,
                equipment and telemarketing.

- Architect of PCI's first strategic plan in 1999 which helped transform the company into a market-based, customer-oriented, entrepreneurial organization. Results: Since 1999, revenues have increased by 130%, net income by 172%, and achieved 20% ROI objective two years ahead of Plan.

- Extensive "hands-on" involvement working with PCI's Strategic Business Units in helping develop and implement strategic plans consistent with and flowing into PCI's corporate objectives and strategies. Pursued balance between top-down strategic direction and bottom-up implementation.

- Successfully managed a "turnaround task force" to improve profitability of PCI's business systems unit from 1997's net loss of $950K to current rate of plus $550K.

- Coordinated development of PCI's plans to enter Cable Television, Distance Learning and Internet Access businesses; led to Cable TV acquisition and enhancement of local loop broad band capability.

1991-   Manager of Market Planning
1996   **AeroSafe Corporation, Dallas, TX**
                Manufacturer of air pollution control systems for the automotive industry.

- Developed marketing information and competitive intelligence systems which assisted increase in market share.

- Supervised four major market research projects involving new, high-tech removal systems.

1989-   Senior Planning Analyst
1991   **Howland Corporation, Manchester, NY**

EDUCATION: B.S., Business Admin., 1989, Texas A&M University. Top third of class.
                   Post graduate studies and seminars in: Strategic Planning, Acquisitions and
                   Finance.

REFERENCES: Available on request.

BRANDON HARRISON

78420 Cedar Hollow Drive
Gates Mills, OH 45782
(216) 423-8445 Work
(216) 423-4321 Home

SUMMARY

Extensive experience managing domestic and international manufacturing and logistics operations. Broad range of business responsibilities including purchasing, inventory management, production planning, manufacturing systems and operations analysis.

PROFESSIONAL EXPERIENCE

RC COLA, Cincinnati, OH   **1992-Present**
A $7 billion operating unit of National Can Company and the world's fourth largest soft drink manufacturing and bottling company. Brands marketed include: Tahitian Treat, Orange Wave and Banana Quencher sold in over 150 countries.

Director, Operations Analysis, Cincinnati, OH   1999-Present
Beverages Production Center

Report to the Senior Vice President of Technology. Responsible for developing strategic programs to improve operating costs and organizational efficiency.

- Conducted an analysis of corporate R&D functions and recommended changes that will reduce product development cycle time and technical cost.

- Performed an analysis of U.S. and European manufacturing cost structures. Implementation of recommended changes will reduce product costs by approximately 23%. Also assessed the potential impact of NAFTA on North American manufacturing operations.

Director, Concentrate Manufacturing Operations, Cincinnati, OH   1994-1999
RC Cola, Concentrate Manufacturing

Responsible for soft drink concentrate manufacturing and materials management operations in U.S., Canada, and Mexico. Also accountable for manufacturing quality, technical support, and information systems for facilities in Ireland, Spain, Ecuador, Brazil and Asia. Reported to Vice President of Concentrate Manufacturing. Staff of 75.

- Responsible for managing five major post acquisition manufacturing consolidations resulting in annual savings of $25 million.

- Negotiated raw material supply contracts producing cost reduction of $6.2 million.

- Developed manufacturing sourcing strategies and cost improvement programs for operations in Europe, North America, South America and Asia.

BRANDON HARRISON   Page 2

- Formulated a global manufacturing system strategy for manufacturing facilities in U.S., Ireland, Spain and Canada. Successfully installed Business Planning and Control operating systems utilizing IBM AS400 hardware at each facility.

- Designed and implemented a global manufacturing quality program. Initiative enhanced product quality and reduced product write-offs by 50%.

- Led team responsible for a Philippines manufacturing feasibility study encompassing financial analysis, legal/tax revision, plant design and site selection.

Director, Inventory Planning, Cincinnati, OH   1992-1994
Reported to Director of Materials Management with staff of ten. Directed production planning and inventory management functions for multiple site manufacturing and distribution network for a $600 million business unit whose core business consisted of cocktail mixers and non-alcoholic sparkling wines.

DELMARK FOODS   1984-1992
Pittsburgh, PA

Director, Production Planning & Inventory Control
Major brands include Florida Citrus Marmalade, Sweetwater Onions and Chen's Oriental food products. Managed departments engaged in production planning for four food manufacturing facilities. Responsibilities also included inventory management and warehouse replenishment for a network of 20 distribution centers. Reported to Director of Physical Distribution, with staff of six.

- Member of team that implemented order processing, inventory management, sales forecasting and DRP systems. Inventory savings of $6 million and customer order lead time reduction of 45% were achieved.

- Provided logistics support for numerous new product introductions while maintaining customer service levels at +99%.

PITTSBURGH ELECTRIC   1982-1984
Pittsburgh, PA

- Graduate Student Training and Placement Program.

- Engineering assignments on team responsible for designing a new major appliance manufacturing facility.

- Materials Management responsibility for industrial Battery Charger facility and Mexican sub-assembly operation.

EDUCATION

M.B.A., 1990, Management Information Systems
University of Pittsburgh - Pittsburgh, PA

B.S., 1982, Mechanical Engineering
Case Western Reserve - Cleveland, OH

Henry F. Griggs
143 Sweet Potato Road
Albany, GA 55794

OFF: 402-665-3072   HOME: 402-973-4957   E-MAIL: HFG@AOL.com

Marketing and Sales Executive with extensive experience and a progressive track record within the pulp and paper industry. Strong technical and organizations orientation and an ability to work closely with manufacturing to optimize the fit of mill capabilities to customer needs while maximizing profitability.

PROFESSIONAL EXPERIENCE

RUSHTON PAPER COMPANY, Albany, GA   **1992 - 2002**

Manager, Product Development and Strategic Planning   2000 - 2002
Pulp and Coated Paper Group
Primary responsibilities are to guide pulp and coated paper divisions in developing a new five year strategic plan, coordinate product development activity focusing on recycled paper, and participate in dumping case brought against European producers.

- Developed a full line of recycled coated paper grades to support new de-inking plants in three mills.
- Managed Rushton Paper's efforts and appeared as industry expert in European dumping case. Imports dropped 38% in 2000, 14% more in 2001.
- Directed work of mills and marketing groups for new five-year plan for 375,000 ton, $250MM business. Organized and wrote plan and board presentation.

Manager, Marketing and Sales, Coated Papers Division   1997 - 2000

- Added seven new positions to serve new sales volume and service needs. Increased sales 40% to fill new lightweight coated machine started in Washington in 1999.
- Reversed plan to shut down California mill in 1998 by adding new products that fit the machines better than prior mix. With 53% of sales in 1999, mill had 57% of profits.

Product Manager, New Products   1995 - 1997

- Reorganized product development activities to eliminate poorly researched products and focus on those with market potential. Coordinated expansion at Atlanta mill and development of new in-line calendering process.
- Developed new business proposal for $29MM plant to make non-structural building panels from recycled fiber.
- Led marketing team of joint venture with major petrochemical company in development of synthetic pulp for papermaking. Directed all field studies.

New Product Engineer   1992 - 1995

EDUCATION

B.S. Pulp and Paper Engineering, University of Maine, Orono, ME (1992)

CARLA T. WARRING
127 Clover Terrace
Denver, CO 1394806
(306) 329-1576

OBJECTIVE

Operations Management. . . International Logistics. . . Strategic Planning

EXPERIENCE

ROCKY MOUNTAIN PRODUCTS, INC.   **1996 - Present**

International Planning Manager, Denver, CO (1999-Present)
Responsible for overall logistics direction, analysis and leadership to RMP's worldwide affiliates, licensees and direct customers of household chemicals and cleaning products, representing sales in excess of $4.1 billion in 64 countries.

- Managed all logistics activities for the most ambitious product roll-out in the history of the company, introducing new soup products into 64 countries in six months. Activities included coordinating production on two continents, developing distribution channels and assuring supply of strategic raw materials.

- Saved $3.7 million in transportation costs, by developing more efficient methods of loading and distribution.

- Created a database saving over $1.7 million in raw material costs, by identifying global raw material price differences in local markets.

Mill Planner - RMP Plant, Arlington, VA (1996-1999)
Responsible for inventory management, customer service and production scheduling of RMP's largest facility. Supervised the production planning and customer service staff. Facility shipments were in excess of $800 million.

- Analyzed and implemented 24% downsizing of operation resulting in $18 million savings.

- Improved inventory turns 48% to 37 turns per year.

- Used linear programming techniques to reduce waste, saving an additional $5.1 million.

EDUCATION

M.B.A.,   Wharton Business School, University of Pennsylvania, Philadelphia, PA   1996

B.S.,   Industrial Management, Drexel University, Philadelphia, PA   1994

JAMES PLANT
3414 Washaw Court
Raleigh, North Carolina 27613
Home: (919) 532-7843
Office: (919) 532-2000

SUMMARY

A financial executive with solid domestic and international experience, having performed the full breadth of the CFO function as Controller at a $1 billion corporate headquarters, Treasurer and Controller at a $2.6 billion corporate headquarters, Controller at a $1 billion manufacturing division and as CPA with a "Big Six" firm.

PROFESSIONAL HISTORY

SAMPSON INTERNATIONAL, Raleigh, NC   **1997-2001**

A subsidiary of Fulton Paper Company engaged in the production and sale of pulp and wood products along with the management of timberlands in North America. Over 30% of company's $2 billion in sales are export sales, primarily to Asian and European markets.

Corporate Controller - Sampson International   *12/97-10/2001*

- Directed annual and quarterly SEC reporting for Sampson International, a NYSE listed master limited partnership, as well as reporting related to a $600 million shelf registration, $250 million 7.5% notes and a medium-term note program.

- Coordinated the preparation of operating plans/budgets along with presentations to senior management.

- Evaluated options, performed analysis, prepared presentations, and reviewed contracts related to an acquisition of $500 million of timberlands in Australia.

- Managed accounting, consolidations, external and internal reporting, financial planning and forecasting, risk management and capital planning/expenditure functions.

ALLENTOWN STEEL, Allentown, PA   **1985-1997**

A steel producer with annual sales of $3.4 billion, is engaged in the manufacture and sale of flat-rolled steel products along with the mining and pelletizing of iron ore and the mining of coal.

Vice President - Allentown Steel   *12/96-11/97*
Treasurer   *08/93-12/96*

- Established a treasury function at Allentown Steel when SMP Corporation, a Japanese steel maker, purchased 50% of PSW from Werner Corporation. Established and maintained banking relationships with domestic and foreign banks and obtained credit without guarantees from either parent.

- Negotiated and established approximately $850 million of innovative credit facilities, including $300 million revolving credit agreement and $90 million related letter of credit commitments; $400 million of project financing including construction and permanent financing with vendor and equity sources; $15 million variable rate pollution control issue and various other facilities including lease lines.

- Directed treasury operations, credit, accounts receivable, tax, and risk management.

JAMES PLANT   **PAGE 2**

Controller – Allentown Steel   *09/92-08/93*

- Directed accounting functions, consolidation, internal and SEC reporting, as well as cost analysis and forecasting.

Assistant Controller - Campbell Steel Group (the predecessor of Allentown Steel)   *11/91-09/92*

- Coordinated the development of accounting systems to establish the steel group as a separate company and the development of accounting systems to centralize the management of cash disbursements, accounts receivable, salary payroll and market analysis.

- Represented management in the negotiations and sale of a major division.

- Managed accounting functions, cost analysis and forecasting.

Midwest Steel Division, Cleveland, OH (Allentown Steels's largest division and a fully integrated steel mill with sales of $1.5 billion.)

Vice President and Controller - Midwest Steel Division   *01/90-11/91*
Assistant Controller   *08/89-01/90*

- Defined markets and strategic direction, including the rationalization of facilities to minimize costs and serve markets.

- Directed divisional accounting, budgetary planning, market analysis, cost analysis, methods studies (including industrial engineers), the development and implementation of standards, and management information services.

Manager of Cost and Methods - Midwest Steel Division   *12/86-08/89*

- Utilized standard cost system to improve productivity and costs. Implemented market profitability analysis.

General Supervisor of Accounting - Midwest Steel Division   *11/85-12/86*

- Improved productivity of department and the credibility of data output used in budgeting, planning and market analysis through procedural and system changes.

W.M. Barr & Company, Cincinnati, OH   **1978-1985**

Certified Public Accountant

Managed both tax and audit engagements in a broad variety of enterprises. Experience was obtained in manufacturing, service industries, retailing, banking, investment holding, franchise negotiations, and joint ventures.

EDUCATION & PROFESSIONAL CERTIFICATION

Univeristy of Illinois, B.A. in Accounting, 1978

CPA - State of Ohio. Certificate No. 077145

Member, AICPA

JEFFREY F. CLEMENS

1573 Woodland Road
Chicago, Illinois 66095

Home: 612-631-3485
Office: 612-752-8375
FAX: 612-752-8376

CAREER OBJECTIVE:

Senior management position with a growth oriented, customer focused organization requiring strong leadership, business planning, problem solving and innovative administration skills.

BACKGROUND SUMMARY:

Twenty years of progressive responsibility in the domestic/international environments of the pharmaceutical, consumer products and medical device industries with a strong success record in: cost reduction, reorganization, process redesign, performance management and strategic development.

PROFESSIONAL EXPERIENCE AND ACCOMPLISHMENTS:

BROOKE PHARMACEUTICALS - Chicago, Illinois   **1999 to Present**

Accounting Services Director, Corporate (1998 to Present)
Responsibilities include management of five departments and a support staff of over 30 associates including payroll, accounts payable, accounts receivable, travel/expense administration and benefit accounting. Significant achievements include:

- Reduced voucher payments outstanding over 30% and increased on-time payments by 20% through procurement process redesigns.
- Lowered service expenses by 35% with increased transaction productivity and efficiency through greater utilization of technology and process changes.
- Consolidated benefits accounting with compensation and benefits resulting in reduced service costs, faster claims processing, reporting and communications between trustee, record keeper and corporate.

Prescription Products Division Controller (1992 to 1998)
Responsibilities grew initially from a Sales and Marketing Controllership role to full financial and customer service support for the largest revenue division of the company with $3.4 billion in sales. As key financial representative on the Division President's staff, achieved significant growth and business success in several broad areas:

- Developed performance measurement and incentive plan objectives which successfully launched four new products in six months and grew earnings 25% for three consecutive years.
- Created a strategic intent and long-range business plan as our vision for the balance of the decade.
- Implemented a Customer Information Center which centralized incoming calls, reduced the number of incoming phone lines, reduced the number of dropped calls/busy signals from 60% to 18% and provided call response benchmark statistics.
- Established a managed care/Medicaid rebate claims processing group in response to OBRA legislation

Jeffrey F. Clemens   Page 2

VISION STAR, INC. - Nashville, Tennessee   **1990 to 1992**

International Division Controller
Newly created position provided unique organization, planning and reporting challenges for fast growing $60 mm dollar division. Key accomplishments include:

- Developed and implemented PC-based financial planning and forecasting system.
- Expanded responsibility for customer service and export orders processing. Process and reorganization efforts reduced lost and duplicate shipments, provided improved order confirmations and improved order status reporting.
- Lowered 120 days receivables by 45% through aggressive collection efforts.

PAYLESS SHOES- Newark, Delaware   **1985 to 1990**

International Consumer Products Division
Manager, Financial Planning/Treasury Operations   (1988 - 1990)
Manager, Consolidations and Financial Reporting   (1986 - 1988)
Manager, General Accounting, Dexter, Inc.   (1985 - 1986)
Established financial accounting, reporting and planning functions for the relocated Dexter Corporation and the newly-created International Consumer Products Division. Key accomplishments include:

- Relocated a $100 mm corporate office through planning, organizing and managing the relocation process for accounts payable, cash receipts/disbursements, fixed assets, retail store accounting and inventory management. Hired and trained a staff of 20 in support of five ledgers, 58 retail stores, three manufacturing sites and one distribution center.
- Merged and reorganized five business units under one $300 mm worldwide division. Developed consolidation and operating requirements (internal/external), determined resource needs, hired, trained and developed a six person support staff and established financial reporting credibility.
- Initiated and developed uniform legal entity and proforma planning and financial reporting for 26 foreign subsidiaries utilizing an IBM System 38, M&D ledger software and integrated telecommunications technology. Reduced closing cycle 25% while expanding reporting capabilities to include product, SBU and geographic income, balance sheet and cash flow statements.

WILMINGTON GLASS, BECKER MFG. DIVISION - Wilmington, Delaware   **1983 to 1985**

Senior Financial Analyst
Responsible for capital and financial planning, international reporting and consolidation and capital appropriation preparation and analysis.

JOHNSON & JOHNSON - Rahway, New Jersey   **1981 to 1983**

International Pharmaceutical Division
Consolidations Supervisor
Designed and implemented an automated proforma reporting system that reduced labor time 58%, increased reporting frequency, and expanded reporting capabilities to include product and geographic information. Preparation time was reduced from three weeks to one.

EDUCATION:

Graduate Work:	New York University, Finance and Business Management
Undergraduate:	State University of New York - B.A., Business/Economics, 1981
Continuing:	Sales & Marketing Management Program, Illinois State University

JAMIE CUNNINGHAM
54 Lake Forest Drive
Parsippany, NJ 08742

Residence: (908) 747-3759
Business: (908) 843-3300

DIRECTOR OF CREDIT AND COLLECTIONS, a highly-experienced credit professional possessing strong analytical and communication skills, and comprehensive bankruptcy experience for Fortune 500 companies. Managed all aspects of credit policy, including establishment of terms of sale and accounts receivable management in competitive markets.

ENGELHARD CORPORATION, Iselin, NJ   **1999 - Present**

An $2.4 billion manufacturer of polymer specialties and chemical intermediates for the industrial market.

Director, Credit and Collections
Exercise total management responsibility for corporate credit and collections activities, inclusive of policy making; accounts receivable; consolidation and administration of U.S. and Canadian subsidiaries and divisions. Direct management and support staff of 42.
- Manage monthly accounts receivable portfolio of $55 million.
- Developed and introduced financial analysis program for evaluation and establishment of credit lines, facilitating control and reducing risk exposure.
- Initiated Vendor Credit Review Program as means of protecting long range interests.
- Played major role in integration and consolidation of multiple acquisitions into corporate operation.
- Responsible for all U.S. and Canadian credit/collections activities and resolution of deductions.
- Represent corporate interests in bankruptcy cases.

CORNING MANUFACTURING COMPANY, Parsippany, NJ   **1998 - 1999**

Manufacturer of consumer housewares with annual sales of $500 million.

Consultant
Served as independent consultant at the request of Chase Bank, lender at time of bankruptcy filing.
- Evaluated integrity of accounts receivable.
- Established collections programs and procedures effectively increasing collections over 110% first month and 280% second month.
- Created account reconciliation teams enabling timely identification of problems impacting cash flow.
- Reviewed merchandise return procedures and presented recommendations for improving controls.
- Initiated credit/risk evaluation analysis to identify and approve shipments to credit worthy customers.
- Functioned as finance liaison to sales and customers.

CAPITAL MANUFACTURING, Columbus, OH   **1993 - 1998**

A $185 million manufacturer of sheet metal and lighting fixtures.

Director, Credit and Collections (1996 - 1998)
Responsible for all policy aspects of credit, collections, accounts receivable, cash application, claims functions and co-op administration for U.S. operations. Supervised five managers and 32 clerical employees. Responsible for the subsidiary Canadian Credit Manager.

JAMIE CUNNINGHAM

- Integrated sheet metal products division into the U.S. lighting division resulting in $92,000 annual savings and Dun & Bradstreet contract reduction of $30,000.
- Consolidated co-op administration function in-house with annual savings of $55,000.
- Key member of task force which established a full line distribution center, improving efficiencies and significantly reducing freight cost to customers.
- Consolidated cash application function under the credit department, resulting in quicker application of payments and identification of deductions.
- Applied analytical and negotiations skills in major bankruptcies and/or work-out situations to maximize returns on bad debt receivables and incremental sales.
- Established separate credit operation for Letters of Credit for export business which led to a more expeditious method of credit approval and timely shipments.

Credit Manager, U.S. (1993 - 1996)
Responsible for the extension of credit and collection of receivables for the U.S. division.
- Responsible for staffing and training of division credit personnel in all credit, collections and bankruptcy procedures, producing uniformity in problem-solving.
- Developed a collection program resulting in quicker conversion of accounts receivable for improved cash flow.
- Reorganized the U.S. credit operation resulting in total account responsibility for each Regional Credit Manager and subordinates, facilitating customer and sales relationships.

NCR CORPORATION, Dayton, OH **1986 - 1993**

Manufacturer of office machines and business equipment with revenues of $600 million.

Director, Credit and Collections/Credit Manager
Directed general policy-making and control of corporate credit, collections and accounts receivable departments ensuring profitable growth and sales development. Developed a proactive team approach with marketing and sales functions relating to customer/credit base. Analyzed, advised and projected financial soundness of daily business activity relating to legal, purchasing and marketing departments.
- Developed a progressive and effective collection program which increased cash flow.
- Established independent credit/collection department which facilitated company expansion into video and PC software market.
- Redesigned procedures and systems that efficiently processed orders via "credit by exception".
- Implemented the inclusion of personal computer system which streamlined procedures in credit, claims and collections departments.
- Managed all procedures to ensure timely retirement of investments in accounts receivable.

PRIOR POSITIONS **1982 - 1986**

Credit Administrator, Polychrome Corporation	**(1983 - 1986)**
Marketing Cost Analyst, Werner Enterprises	**(1982 - 1983)**

EDUCATION

B.A., Accounting, Ohio University, 1982

PROFESSIONAL AFFILIATIONS

Regional Board of Directors, National Association of Credit Management

JOHN C. EVANS

237 Demarest Avenue
Little Rock, AR 72230
(501) 372-6539 (H) or (501) 372-5000 (O)
Fax (501) 372-5005

Fifteen plus years as accessible senior-level human resources generalist in diverse large and small corporate cultures... Proven leader, communicator, problem-solver and strategic/tactical planner... Line and staff experience with domestic and international companies... Start-up, continuous improvement, rightsizing, turnaround and union-free achievements... Staffing, training and development, team building and reengineering innovator... Compensation, benefits and personnel practices designer... Due diligence, sale of company, and business shutdown facilitator... Information services and manufacturing background... PC fluent.

SELECTED CAREER ACCOMPLISHMENTS

VICE PRESIDENT - HUMAN RESOURCES   **Hon Industries**   1998 - Present

Selected as Human Resources Executive by Pacific Management, an interim management company for this $75 million manufacturer of pumps and controls. Charged with fostering and leading Human Resource initiatives designed to maintain attractiveness of business during asset sale/due diligence process.

* Delivered high-quality due diligence results for parent, division, and three buyer companies. Restored and enhanced workplace accord and middle management cohesiveness.

* Optimized retention, productivity and motivation in domestic and offshore facilities through effective use of stay-bonuses, employee recognition and severance plans.

* Served as liaison between company, parent and three buyer companies. Orchestrated equipment dispersal and records dispersal and destruction.

* Implemented leadership and project management training to support a reengineering initiative that projected a 50-75% reduction in process time and costs.

* Met ongoing compensation, benefits and employee relations needs. Administered salary continuance, COBRA and outplacement resources for multiple locations.

DIRECTOR OF HUMAN RESOURCES   **Amstar Corporation**   1996 - 1998

Turned around functional operation for an eight site, 1420 employee equipment manufacturer with annual revenues of $650 million. Managed 19 employees.

* Implemented workforce downsizing and realignment of supervision, saving $1.5 million/annum, without disruption in the retained workforce.

* Introduced exempt performance planning and appraisal practices that resulted in significantly higher satisfaction levels among employees.

John C. Evans   Page Two

* Resolved impending $11 million FAS-106 liability problem and saved $575,000 per year with minimal effect on corporate reputation and employees by modifying health coverages and administrative procedures.

* Spearheaded leadership, team building and facilitation training rated as "best ever" by participants and their managers.

VICE PRESIDENT - HUMAN RESOURCES   **American Seating Company**   1990 - 1996

Led department start-up. Teamed with peers to develop and advance a business and people sensitive Human Resource agenda for world class manufacturer of quality leisure furniture. Notably influenced, as officer and executive committee member, the strategic and tactical planning for this $450 million per year business. Key participant in operational decision-making for all functional disciplines.

* Led "start-up" of Human Resource function and designed and instituted "first ever" comprehensive corporate policies, practices and benefits programs. Managed team of eight employees responsible for Human Resources, Community Relations and Employee Services.

* Effectively integrated cultural diversity and forged six years of union-free workplace harmony through supervisor and management development, employee relations and communications programs and rigorous employee involvement.

* Led community relations initiatives which earned an "employer of choice" reputation and positioned the company as a recognized corporate citizen.

* Designed and implemented "first ever" flexible compensation programs, including pay-for-skills, perfect attendance, work-at-home and temporary employment that achieved turnover and absenteeism levels below 1.7% and 1.3% respectively.

* Developed and instituted health care cost control measures that held premiums and increases well below national averages.

* Designed and implemented successful full-featured compensation and benefit plans, exempt/non-exempt performance and salary review programs, wage and salary incentive plans, and executive compensation and retirement plans.

VARIOUS POSITIONS   **Eagle-Picher Industries, Inc.**   1980 - 1990

Performed increasingly responsible functions. Began as hourly technician and ultimately served as Manufacturing Supervisor and Plant Level Human Resources Manager.

EDUCATION

B.A., Business Management, LaSalle University, 1980
(GPA: 3.45)

Robert D. Braxton
14 Daisy Drive
Huron, OH 17490

Home: (206) 665-0982   Office: (206) 658-9238   E-Mail: RBRAX@AOL

Human Resource Executive having 12 years experience with quality *Fortune* 500 companies.

EXPERIENCE:

1999 - Present   **CORBIN STEEL PRODUCTS CORP.,** Sandusky, OH
                  Director of Human Resources
                  Reporting to the VP Administration, responsible for organization, staffing,
                  compensation and benefits, communications, total quality leadership, labor
                  relations, training and development, safety and legal compliance for seven locations
                  with $300 million in sales.

- Managed negotiations of two contracts with the USWA resulting in controlled cost, greater flexibility, and use of teams and "Temporaries".
- Developed new executive and salaried incentive plans including stock options and SERP's with annual savings of more than $1 million.
- Coordinated the organization's first restructuring resulting in $1.5 million annual savings.

1989 - 1999   **DRESSER INDUSTRIES,** Corporate Offices, Dallas, TX
               Director of Human Resources - Industrial Equipment   (1994-1999)
               Division had five locations with over 1,500 employees.

- Led the Division into strategic planning, goal setting, and performance management.
- Planned the consolidation of two facilities resulting in $400,000 savings.
- Negotiated a one-year extension to contract while resolving a termination settlement with United Auto Workers in Detroit.
- Designed and implemented flexible benefit plan.
- Introduced employee involvement at two locations (Cleveland and Philadelphia) changing from strike situations to cost reduction of hundreds of thousands.
- Negotiated a first-time contract with United Auto Workers in Atlanta as the result of an earlier election; employees later decertified the UAW.

Employee Relations Manager - Commercial Products, Chicago, IL   (1991-1994)

Finance and Accounting Intern - Conveyor Equipment, Atlanta, GA   (1989-1991)

EDUCATION: **Michigan State University** - MS in Organizational Development, 1989
               Penn State University - Bachelors in Business Administration with honors, 1987

STACIE BELL
59 Illinois Avenue
Lancaster, PA 15291
Home 717/737-2489
Work 717/737-1000

OBJECTIVE: **Senior Human Resources Management** position requiring a generalist with an MS degree and experience in all human resource management functions emphasizing compensation, management development, recruiting, organization development, employee relations and minority affairs in diverse domestic and international environments.

EXPERIENCE:

Oct, 1999-Present   **HILLMAN COMPANY,** Pittsburgh, PA

Director - Human Resources, Financial Department, Lancaster, PA
Report to Chief Investment Officer. Responsible for all human resources activities for 450 employees in the Investments Group. Promoted from Corporate position as **Director - Staffing & Recruiting** (managed 38 employees involved in local and college recruiting, in-house temporary program, community employment and outplacement center).

- Designed and implemented a non-qualified voluntary investment plan which provided employees with the opportunity to defer bonuses on a pre-tax basis for three to 21 years.

- Designed and obtained management commitment for a banded compensation structure which combined 13 salary grades into five bands.

- Successfully managed numerous employee layoffs, including some sensitive situations, avoiding grievances and potential costly litigation.

- Implemented changes resulting in productivity and/or cost savings. Utilized desk-top publishing to reduce advertising costs, decentralized campus recruiting expenses to reduce corporate overhead, increased use of in-house temporary (clerical & professional) employment organization to 98% of temporaries employed, utilized use of national career fairs and minority organizations to reduce recruiting costs, canceled a costly and inefficient community recruiting/training program.

- Designed a national college recruiting strategy based on needs of business and major field offices incorporating a University Executive concept. Developed strategies for each school and created a national advertising strategy to reduce costs and better target student populations. Developed partnership with I.C.H. Corporation to support funding which corresponded to recruiting needs.

- Developed a concentrated campus minority recruiting strategy which increased minority hires by 22% in the first year and resulted in recognition by *Afro-American* and *Hispanic Collegian Quarterly* of Hillman as a top 100 company employer.

1990 - 1999   **CHASE ENTERPRISES,** Hartford, CT

(1997 - 1999)   **Consultant - Recruiting Issues,** Recruitment Department
Responsible for developing corporate minority and MBA recruiting strategies and recommending actions. Implemented strategies across company's businesses.

STACIE BELL

- Conceived minority strategy and developed partnership with Chase Foundation including scholarship funding of over $1 million. Implemented program by involving Chase University Executive business recruiting teams with historically black schools which resulted in recognition of Chase as a significant player by national minority organizations.

- Re-targeted MBA hiring strategy from corporate business level. New focus coupled with comprehensive communication program increased commitment and hires.

(1996 - 1997)   **Manager - Human Resources**, <u>Chase & Company</u>
Reported to President of this $3 billion international business with over 500 employees worldwide. Promoted from position as **Manager - Organization Development & Staffing**.

- Redesigned organization structure to accommodate changing business requirements including reducing census 50% and consolidating product groups. Actions contributed to one year business reversal from $3 million loss to break-even.

- Analyzed industry pay standards and designed bonus program tied to business goals to place company in more competitive compensation position. Improved new hire acceptance rate 50% and halted loss of key personnel.

- Sourced and hired international and specialty talent in widely diversified commodity and technical fields. Beat all hiring time standards and minimized recruiting costs.

- Led management team in creating and implementing succession plan including employee career development activities which improved retention and speeded staff process.

(1990 - 1996)   **Human Resources Representative**, <u>Chase Consulting</u>
Responsible for managing the full scope of HR activities for 400 employees in this technical consulting organization. Earlier, as **Coordinator/Specialist - Relations Programs** oversaw and executed numerous HR programs.

- Restructured secretarial staff into pooled system. Reduced overtime 80%, turnover 50% and absenteeism 60% while maximizing productivity.

- Developed Affirmative Action Plan conforming to government regulations, met or exceeded hiring/promotion goals and passed federal audit.

EDUCATION: **MS - Human Resources Management**, <u>Drexel University</u> , Philadelphia, PA - 1990
BS - Business Administration, <u>Connecticut College</u>, New London, CT - 1988

HONORS: YWCA Achievement Award for Professional Women - 1995
Chase Enterprises's Key Recognition Award - 1991

PERSONAL: INROADS of Chicago, Board of Directors
Member, National Human Resource Society

Cynthia Edwards
7893 Jenkins Road, #3
Greensboro, NC 27407
(919) 864-3484

OBJECTIVE

Human Resources Director or Vice President responsible for total HR support of a company or division with 20,000 or more employees. Consider smaller start-up or fast growth.

SUMMARY

Strong background in Human Resources management gained through experience in two Fortune 100 corporations, primarily in direct Customer Service businesses. Experience includes overall HR responsibility for a major corporate business including planning, developing and implementing all HR related programs. Supported five different businesses. Responsible for providing HR support to over 24,000 employees in 30 countries. Strategically directed strong build-ups, severe downturns and organizational restructuring. Experienced in domestic and international. Strengths include:

· Ability to integrate HR into the business	· Successful at stabilizing crises and uncertainties
· Providing HR strategic direction	· Innovative problem solving prevention
· Team leader and facilitator	· Understanding of operations (factory & field)
· Effective communicator at all levels	· Reengineering and aligning business to need

EXPERIENCE

HALSTEAD INDUSTRIES, Greensboro, NC   **1999 - Present**

Director of Human Resources
Manage total Human Resources Operations for Halstead Industries including the strategic planning, developing and implementing all HR related programs supporting over 30,000 employees in 35 countries. Responsible for worldwide operations, domestic and international.

- Active member of the management team which restructured three companies into one company unit.
  - Led the restructuring of three HR organizations, in three companies, into one new HR organization.
  - Directed the design, development and implementation of the reduction-in-force package and process.
  - Facilitated reengineering and consolidating of HR processes for speed, quality and consistency.

- Integrated HR with business objectives and aligned HR initiatives to directly impact these objectives.
  - Established HR initiatives, specific projects, project teams and action plans to achieve initiatives.
  - Active on management team to design individual incentives and scorecards focused to achieve business goals.
  - Implemented a management communication plan with all employees focused on achieving specific results.

Cynthia Edwards

BRUNSWICK CORPORATION, Skokie, IL   *1988 - 1999*

Human Resources Director, Marine Division   *1995 - 1999*
Manage total Human Resources for a major corporate business including planning, developing and implementing all HR related programs. Responsible for compensation and benefits, employee relations, employee development, employment health & medical and safety supporting up to 4200 employees. Experienced in domestic and international.

- Integrated Human Resources with the business objectives.
  - Developed and implemented programs which improved the ratio of sales per payroll.
  - Business achieved #1 position in the company for highest employee attitude ever.
  - Established Safety Awareness and Prevention programs reducing lost work days 70% in three years.
  - Instituted Total Quality Management and Communication programs at all levels.

- Pro-actively resolved problems through effective listening, negotiating and preventive measures.
  - Avoided a Union Campaign/Union Attempt by involving employees to set up improvement programs.
  - Resolved all unfair labor charges in company's favor and successfully completed three OFCCP audits.
  - Reengineered processes to reduce cycle time and improve products and service.
  - Restructured HR Corporate Policy to be more competitive while retaining employee sensitivity.
  - Recognized for gaining the trust and confidence of all employees by serving them as customers.

- Provided HR strategic direction to continue profitability through both growth and downsizing cycles.
  - Directed employee involvement, continuous improvement and customer focus.
  - Continually upgraded employee skills and contributions through retraining and restructuring.
  - Instituted Self-Evaluation and Career Reviews to manage people resources and avoid layoffs.
  - Strategically managed development of Self-Directed Work Teams requiring 30% fewer employees.

- Established a reputation for excellent comprehension of operations, both factory and field.
  - Experienced in domestic and international field operations.
  - Strengthened communications between field and factory by establishing annual field meetings.

Human Resources Director, Transportation Equipment Division   *1993 - 1995*
Managed total Human Resources including employment, compensation and benefits, employee relations, development, health & medical, and safety for an operation of 2600 employees.

Group Compensation Manager, SeaRay Boats Division   *1991 - 1993*
Responsible for Compensation and related activities including establishing competitive salary structure for a Division of Corporate with 7500 employees. Coordinated all compensation related activities up through Division President and served on compensation and benefits committees to determine corporate policy.

Employment/Training Manager, SeaRay Boats Division   *1990 - 1991*
Human Resources Representative, SeaRay Boats Division   *1988 - 1990*

EDUCATION

M.B.A., Management, North Carolina State University   1988
B.S., Industrial Management, North Carolina State University   1986

KAREN FLANAGAN

810 Cumberland Road
Wooster, OH 44916

(216) 264-4582 (H)
(216) 358-3400 (O)

SUMMARY

Results-oriented Human Resources Manager with 12 years of progressive experience in high technology and consumer products industries. Primary areas of expertise include **Employee Relations, Staffing, EEO and Compensation & Benefits**. Three years of experience assisting an Application Team in successfully pursuing and winning the *Malcolm Baldrige National Quality Award*.

EXPERIENCE

RUBBERMAID INCORPORATED, Wooster, OH   **1998-Present**
The largest direct sales organization in the consumer products industry. Fortune 500 Company with customers in 20 countries and annual retail sales in excess of $1.7 billion.

Human Resources Manager, Distribution Group
Responsible for establishing, implementing, directing, planning and coordinating all Human Resources activities required to support five Regional Distribution Centers located in Hartford, Cleveland, Seattle, Houston, Delaware and Tampa. Serve as consultant and business partner to management team to facilitate ongoing development of proactive employee relations programs.

- Developed and implemented a decentralization strategy which significantly improved HR services within each of the six regions.

- Negotiated a 24% reduction in the hourly mark-up for temporary personnel provided by contract labor agencies.

- Established cost-effective staffing procedures which resulted in a 62% reduction in the cost-per-hire for exempt professionals.

- Achieved a $120,000 annual reduction in Workers Compensation payments through effective safety programs and aggressive case management.

HONEYWELL, INC., Minneapolis, MN   **1988-1998**
A global, high-technology manufacturing and engineering company with 58,000 employees and annual revenues in excess of $6.2 billion.

Regional Human Resources Manager, Air Transport Systems Division   1996-1998
Responsible for leading, organizing, and developing the Human Resources Team to provide a comprehensive array of support and services for 6000+ employees at multiple sites throughout the United States.

- Implemented a new staffing process that significantly reduced cost and cycle-time while improving the company's overall image on college campuses.

KAREN FLANAGAN   PAGE TWO

- Successfully initiated the policy framework, communication and implementation strategy to establish the company's second smoke-free work site.

- Directed and implemented a new performance development process which resulted in increased employee empowerment and a more effective, team-oriented culture.

- Served as a member of the Malcolm Baldrige National Quality Award application writing and support team for the Human Resources Utilization Section.

Employee Relations Manager, Commercial Flight Systems Division   1992-1996
Responsible for leading and coaching the Employee Relations function to provide value-added support and services for 2500+ management, engineering and manufacturing employees.

- Member of the Human Resources team responsible for developing and implementing a new reduction-in-force policy that guided the company in successfully downsizing several operating units.

- Established a systematic tracking mechanism which provided real-time EEO status reporting capabilities prior to commencing reduction-in-force actions.

- Chaired a Creative Action Team that designed, developed and distributed a *Career Development Guide* to facilitate professional development and career planning for over 2000 employees.

Personnel/Compensation/Staffing Administrator, Space Systems Group   1989-1992
Responsible for providing generalist and specialist support for the Manufacturing, Engineering and Quality Assurance divisions within the Space Systems Group.

- Managed an aggressive College Recruiting Program which hired and relocated over 340 college students annually from the best engineering universities throughout the U.S.

- Established computer systems capabilities which resulted in more effective decision-making with regard to Compensation, EEO and Affirmative Action.

- Designed, developed and delivered a series of training programs to improve employee performance during periods of explosive business growth.

Assembly Supervisor, Space Systems Group   1988-1989
Supervised 35 employees in the assembly of missile components.

EDUCATION

M.S.,	Industrial Relations, Colorado State University, Fort Collins, CO	1988
B.B.A.,	Personnel Administration, North Carolina State University, Raleigh, NC	1983

ALICE P. BROOKE
42 Sutter Place
Drapperville, MI 42736
(735) 974-1476

EXPERIENCE

AGRI TECHNOLOGY, INC.   **1997 to Present**
Publicly held agricultural biotechnology company with four subsidiaries and two major operating joint ventures.

Senior Human Resources Administrator (2000 - Present)
Report to Vice President, Human Resources and Administration of this leading biotechnology company. Responsibilities include managing flexible compensation, the self-insured health plan and other personnel functions.

Major Accomplishments:

- Manage administration of four company 401(k) plans.
- Effectively administered COBRA compliance for former employees affected by the company downsizings.
- Reduced (by 65%) turnaround time from claim to payment of the flexible spending account reimbursement.
- Managed the Summer Intern Program which employed an average of 42 students per year.
- Designed, implemented and managed Human Resources Information System, to track and report employee information for management decision making.

Human Resources Representative (1997 - 2000)
Reported to the Director, Human Resources and Administration. Responsibilities included administration of all company benefits.

Major Accomplishments:

- Established company medical department through subcontracting with private physician which resulted in reduction of workers' compensation lost-time.
- Designed and administered an employee survey, the response to which resulted in changes to the benefits plans to better serve the needs of the employees.
- Designed and implemented new employee orientation procedures which resulted in smoother integration of new hires into the organization.

EDUCATION

Michigan State University (Dean's List)
B.S. Degree, Business Management (1997)

Michigan State University (Fall, 1999)
Certificate in Professional Human Resources

SAMANTHA SHEARA
245 Post Oak Drive
Pittsburgh, Pennsylvania 23589
(203) 799-2456 Home
(203) 942-3500 Office

EXPERIENCE

MELLON BANK CORPORATION, Pittsburgh, PA   **2000 - Present**
Senior Vice President/Director of Worldwide Compensation and Benefits
Principal accountabilities include the strategic design, development and implementation of all direct and indirect compensation programs to include executive compensation, variable pay programs, base pay plans, welfare and qualified and non-qualified retirement plans for all domestic and international locations (20 countries, 70,000 employees and 18,000 retirees). Examples of recent achievements:

- Orchestrated one of the largest compensation and benefit mergers in the financial services industry.
- Designed, developed and implemented one of the first all-employee financial planning programs.
- Managed the company benefit costs at 0% growth over the last three years and down for 2001.
- Introduced a service-based compensation consulting unit to service line business units.
- Developed and implemented flexible benefits program and introduced Managed Care Health Program for all domestic employees.
- Reduced FAS 106 (retiree welfare costs) liability by over $40 million annually, one of few companies to successfully impact past retirees.
- Revised executive compensation program with focus on increased share ownership.
- Decreased growth in fixed personnel expense through increased use of variable pay plans for non-executive population.
- Developed and implemented successful compensation and benefit template for integrating over 18 acquisitions.
- Reengineered HR support areas and initiated outsourcing of all non-value oriented activities; i.e., benefit/pension administration, due diligence, compensation, etc.

FISHER SCIENTIFIC, Pittsburgh, PA   **1998 - 2000**
Director of Worldwide Compensation
Principal accountabilities included the design, implementation and administration of all executive compensation to include long-term restricted stock, phantom stock and stock option programs, short-term management and sales incentive programs, deferred compensation, Board of Director compensation, salary management policies and programs, equity of job evaluations in operating divisions, development of total remuneration strategies for domestic and international locations (95 countries and 110,000 employees) and tactical implementation. Examples of achievements:

- Developed long-term incentive plan with performance based restricted stock.
- Developed extensive compensation communications program to facilitate change and increase executive awareness.
- Converted NQSO/SARs to broker/dealer NQSOs, thus saving $85 million in P&L costs.
- Designed and implemented performance-based long-term deferred cash and phantom stock plans for foreign subsidiaries.
- Developed alternative reward programs to allow management greater flexibility in retaining high performers.
- Introduced new expatriate compensation program to maximize equity and transferability across all operating companies.
- Developed total remuneration measurement strategy to determine overall compensation and benefit competitive posture.

SAMANTHA SHEARA   PAGE TWO

EQUIMARK CORPORATION, Pittsburgh, PA   **1994 - 1998**
Practice Director for the Northeast
Responsibilities included analyzing client business conditions in order to develop effective compensation and benefit strategies, executive compensation programs (i.e., short/long-term cash incentive vehicles, stock based incentive plans, competitive base pay programs, deferred compensation plans); salary management programs, job evaluation systems, compensation audits and surveys. Performed business development activities such as conducting seminars, delivering speeches and designing special topical surveys.

NORWEST CORPORATION, Minneapolis, MN   **1990 - 1994**
Director of Compensation & Benefits
For domestic and international activities (50,000 employees). Responsibilities included designing and implementing management incentive programs, multi-location base pay programs, maintained corporate-wide job evaluation system (Hay), recommended and administered expatriate and foreign national compensation policies and procedures. Recommended, implemented and administered all health and welfare benefit programs including profit sharing, medical, life insurance, etc. Examples of achievements:

- Reduced welfare benefit costs by $3 million by revising benefit funding arrangements.
- Revised expatriate compensation programs to maximize tax effectiveness.
- Recommended termination and recapture of $50 million in excess pension assets.

WHEATON INDUSTRIES, Millville, NJ   **1986 - 1990**
Manager, Compensation and Benefits
For domestic and international activities. Responsibilities included designing and implementing executive and middle management incentive programs, multi-location base pay programs, innovative sales incentive plans, automated salary planning and budget modeling, corporate-wide job evaluation programs, performance management systems and recommended and administered expatriate compensation policies and procedures. Designed, implemented and administered all health and welfare benefit programs including 401(k) plan, self-administered, self-funded medical programs. Examples of achievements:

- Established and implemented sales incentive plans to maximize asset utilization, deployment and margins.
- Revised short-term management incentive plan to better link company and individual performance.
- Developed and implemented corporate-wide computerized job evaluation program.
- Instituted expatriate/TCN compensation program.
- Revised health plans to increase cost effectiveness.
- Designed and implemented 401(k) plan.

TELEDYNE, INC., Los Angeles, CA   **1983 - 1986**
Manager of Administration
Duties involved wage and salary administration, recruitment policy, development, safety, communications, supervision of support services.

EDUCATION

B.S., Management, Pepperdine University, 1983

PROFESSIONAL ACTIVITIES

Frequent speaker at national conferences for ACA, Conference Board, AMA, etc.
Published several articles on mergers and acquisitions, benefits, etc.
Certified Compensation Professional

ALLISON DANIELS

1458 Quarry Road
Dallas, TX 75292

Home: (214) 839-2576
Work: (214) 830-2500

OBJECTIVE: Challenging Benefits and/or Compensation position with a progressive company where broad management skills and knowledge can be fully utilized.

PROFESSIONAL EXPERIENCE:

1977
to
Present

KIMBERLY-CLARK, Corporate Headquarters (Dallas, TX)
World's largest manufacturer and marketer of sanitary tissue products with annual sales of approximately $6.8 billion and 40,000 employees worldwide.

Manager of Qualified Plans (1999 - Present)
Report to Manager of Compensation & Retirement. Primary responsibility for Hourly and Salaried Investment Plans (10,000 participants) and Salaried Retirement Plan (10,500 participants). Design, communicate and, through the use of outside suppliers, direct the administration of these Plans. Manage external relationship for Executive Tax Planning and Preparation Service. Executive contact for compensation and benefits information.

Significant Accomplishments:

- Serve on Project Team to design, implement and communicate new Defined Contribution Retirement Plan for salaried employees (2,500 participants). Project to be completed June, 2001.
- Provided benefits technical support for five divestitures involving 4,800 employees.
- Serve on Project Team to change recordkeeper and voice response system for Hourly and Salaried Investment Plans. Project to be completed June, 2001.

Manager of Job Evaluation & Comparative Analysis (1998 - 1999)
Reported to Manager of Total Pay. Responsibility for managing Corporate Job Evaluation System and completing various compensation surveys used to determine salary line and ranges. Provided compensation and benefits information for input to the annual proxy statement. Managed external relationship for Executive Individual Financial Planning. Executive contact for compensation and benefits information.

Significant Accomplishments:

- Served on Project Team to develop and implement simplified Base Pay Structure ("broadbanding").
- Implemented ten job ladders for non-exempt employees in Dallas.

Manager of Compensation & Benefits Services (1995 - 1998)

Reported to Director of Benefits and supervised two employees. Directed the process of delivering timely and accurate information to Corporate Headquarters, Field Sales, Expatriate and Third Country National active and retiree groups across the spectrum of employee benefits (Group Insurance, Investment Plans and Retirement Plans). Managed Long Term Disability, Total and Permanent Disability and Death claims processing and counseling. Expanded and maintained interactive benefits communication system. On a corporate-wide basis, provided financial planning capability development through seminars and interactive benefits communication system. Responsible for Human Resources Policy formulation, updating and approval.

Significant Accomplishments:

- Developed and implemented Services Group concept.
- Provided benefits technical support for three acquisitions, two divestitures and one plant closure.
- Coordinated financial planning and outplacement assistance for significant work force reduction program.

Manager of Thrift Plans & Financial Planning Assistance (1987 - 1995)

Reported to Director of Benefits and supervised two employees. Managed Hourly and Salaried Investment Plans and Employee Stock Ownership Plan administration and communication. Managed interactive benefits communication system. Managed corporate-wide personal and pre-retirement financial counseling (executive and group) programs.

Significant Accomplishments:

- Implemented hourly and salaried 401(k) programs.
- Implemented company-wide Employee Stock Ownership Plan (ESOP) for all salaried and hourly employees.
- Developed quarterly Investment Plan Newsletter.
- Developed and implemented interactive benefits communication system.
- Developed and implemented Executive Individual and Group Personal and Pre-Retirement Planning Programs.

IR Operations & Administration Project Assistant (1984 - 1986)

Reported to Director of Human Resources - Operations & Administration. Responsible for job evaluation for all plant sites and various administrative projects.

Various Administrative Positions within Human Resources (1977 - 1984)

PC SKILLS: Multi-Mate, Microsoft Office '98, Microsoft Word 6.0, Microsoft Excel 5.0

CARLA JOSEPHS

700 Park Avenue
New York, NY 10034

Office: (212) 779-4305
Home: (212) 843-8844
Fax: (212) 779-4307

OBJECTIVE: Senior level human resources development position responsible for organization development, executive management development, and training.

EXPERIENCE:

1999 – Present

JOHNSON & HIGGINS – New York, NY
A management consulting and training firm whose client organizations are typically in the manufacturing and high tech industries. A leader in attracting New York State Employment Training funding for clients.

As **Senior Consultant**, I am responsible for conducting organization-wide assessments and designing complete training and education curricula for all clients; as well as designing, developing, customizing and conducting training in cultural change, empowerment, leadership and management development, quality communications and other OD implementations. Perform executive assessments, provide coaching, and help develop individualized development strategies and plans. I also operate as a freelance training and development consultant.

- Trained and facilitated over one hundred self-directed work teams resulting in 25% to 75% productivity gains.

- Designed and customized results oriented leadership development programs for top teams.

1995 – 1999

ADVANCED IMAGING, INC. – Rochester, NY
One of the fastest growing medical imaging companies in the world, with $150 million annual sales, 720 employees throughout the U.S.

As **Manager, Management and Organization Development,** I was responsible for internal OD/Management consulting, reengineering studies, corporate-wide executive/management education, training and development, and succession planning. Assisted the CEO and other Executive Team members in determining their development needs, personalized development plans, university executive programs, and coordinated supporting resources.

- Planned and facilitated Business Reengineering studies which trimmed inventory $1.2 million, cut G&A expenses 23%, and restructured Sales and Service from four regions to three.

CARLA JOSEPHS   **Page Two**

- Designed and installed company's first corporate executive and management succession planning system in a six month period; half the time allotted.

- Designed and orchestrated first Leadership and Effective Management Course for high potential middle and senior level managers; 55% below the planned budget.

1990 – 1995   **GENERAL DYNAMICS CORPORATION – Falls Church, VA**
Aerospace company with $8.8 billion annual sales and 80,000 employees.

As **Senior Organization Development Consultant,** my primary responsibilities involved designing executive management programs, coaching senior managers on their succession plans, team building, executive off-site conferences, quality improvement methods, and internal management consulting.

- Redesigned the two-year Executive Development Program to focus primarily on key business strategies and improvement of executive leadership and management practices.

- Improved response to customer's Request for Quotation by 300% and improved delivery time on military spares by 35%.

- Facilitated continuous improvement projects totalling more than $50 million in savings.

- Improved succession planning effectiveness resulting in an 80% selection rate.

EDUCATION: 1990 – MBA   Business Management
                   Villanova University, Villanova, PA
                   1988 – BS   Business Management
                   Cornell University, Ithaca, NY

Organization Effectiveness Consultant Course – Alexandria, VA, 1995
Advanced Organization Effectiveness Program – Alexandria, VA, 1992

Qualified trainer for these international programs:

- "The Right Way to Manage," Conway Quality, Inc.
- "Seven Habits of Highly Effective People," Covey & Associates
- "Situational Leadership," Blanchard Training, Inc.
- "Managing for Productivity," ODI, Inc.

Jill W. Radnor
(908) 792-8133

120 Summit Hill Road
Princeton, New Jersey 80903

CORPORATE RELATIONS

Highly influential team builder with several successful years
in management and governmental affairs.
Effective communicator at all levels.

Selected Career Highlights

Manager, Legislative and Government Affairs
Johnson & Johnson, New Brunswick, NJ   2001 - Present
Protect the interests of one of the nation's leading pharmaceutical, healthcare and consumer products companies, a NYSE listed corporation with over $14 billion in annual sales.

- Represent the corporation at legislative conferences and industry group meetings throughout the U.S.
- Assisted the Investor Relations Department in preparation of innovative presentation shown to 40 securities analysts.
- Coordinated successful nationwide campaign involving more than 100 legislators to pass federal legislation favorable to the industry.
- Led task force of mid-level managers which provided expert knowledge on federal legislation affecting pharmaceutical operations.
- Authored compliance manual and presented training seminars to more than 100 managers and vice presidents.

Product Manager
Johnson & Johnson, McNeil Pharmaceuticals, Springhouse, PA   1997 - 2001
Created and marketed a consulting service designed to assist pharmacists with inventory and pricing.

- Designed and developed marketing brochures, promotional items, various advertisements and training videos.
- Prepared, planned and managed yearly operational budget of $1.6 million and wrote business plan for start-up venture.
- Coordinated and presented continuing education program entitled, *Inventory and Pricing Strategies*, to more than 300 participants.
- Increased gross profits for participating pharmacies by implementing new training programs and consulting services.

Pharmacist
C.V.S., Chester County, PA   1994 - 1997

Education

M.B.A., cum laude, Rutgers University, 1994
B.S. in Pharmacy, magna cum laude, University of Pennsylvania, 1992

David O. Dodds
426 Carver Avenue
Chicago, Illinois 18857
Home: (402) 694-8372   E-Mail: DODS@AOL.com

EXECUTIVE SUMMARY

Public relations executive with proven ability in strategic planning, project management and mass communications.   Strong background in translating corporate messages into appropriate communications media: publications, films, exhibits, entertainment and special events.

PROFESSIONAL EXPERIENCE AND ACCOMPLISHMENTS

BUBBLE-COLA, INC. - Chicago, Illinois   **1999-Present**
Director of Corporate Communications

Directed public relations for nation's fifth largest soft drink company with staff of one communications specialist and two editors. Responsibilities included planning, budgeting, publications, media relations, special events, entertainment production, major exhibit management, and public relations activities to enhance the company's image with its publics.

- Directed development of a strategy to boost the company's support among Hispanics, generating strong national media coverage and on-going ties to Hispanic leaders.

- Recommended, booked and produced local and national entertainment acts including Natalie Cole, Reba McEntire, Kenny Loggins and many others, all of which received standing ovations, creating a favorable impact on customer relations.

- Created and published a 100-page award-winning book, "Bubble-Cola Recipes" which has been reviewed favorably in newspapers across the country and ordered by more than 95,000 consumers.

- Directed the creation and operation of two major image-enhancing Bubble-Cola industry exhibits, effectively managing the million-dollar annual budget.

THE CLEVELAND PLAIN DEALER - Cleveland, Ohio   **1996-1999**
Business Writer

U.S. NAVY   **1992-1996**
Following graduation from Officer Candidate School, served aboard *USS FRIGATE*
as Administrative Assistant to the Executive Officer, and as Public Information Officer.

EDUCATION

B.A., Accounting, Colorado State University (1990)
M.B.A., Communications, University of Chicago (1992)

RYAN PELLINO
7 South 10th Street
Memphis, Tennessee 38952
(901) 753-7143

SUMMARY

Entrepreneurial leader with diversified experience in the development, implementation and operation of projects, services and businesses. Visionary with proven ability to inspire individuals to work toward common goals and accomplish desired results. Demonstrated strength in quickly understanding and handling complex technical and operational issues. Strong customer focus. Easily adapts to foreign cultures and business practices.

PROFESSIONAL EXPERIENCE/ACCOMPLISHMENTS

RICHARDSON-VICKS- Memphis, Tennessee   **1994 - Present**
Division of Richardson-Vicks AB - Hamburg, Germany
Director, Administration   1999 - Present

Directed a 24-person technical team ($2.5 million budget) responsible for telecommunications, multi-platform computers, voice and data networks and administration services.

- Created a central data network and desktop support team providing expanded services while reducing labor requirements by 33%.

- Reengineered the IS work practices, cross-training associates to provide personal and professional growth opportunities while ensuring maximum support capabilities.

- Established key headquarters relationships and gained corporate buy-in to drive technology standards, policies and new system applications.

- Reduced cycle times of business processes by developing concept, marketing benefits and implementing LAN and WAN based information sharing applications.

Director, Customer Affairs and Distribution   1994 - 1999

Directed a 60-85 person work unit at four sites ($5 million budget) responsible for Customer Services, Distribution, Credit Management and Accounts Receivable.

- Negotiated agreement between two adversarial divisions on unified sales policies, terms and conditions necessary for common sales and distribution infrastructure.

- Within nine months, implemented reengineered multi-site national operations supporting more than $100 million in revenue for the consolidated consumer products division.

- Improved customer service levels from 85% to 98%, accounts receivable current from 90% to 95% and transportation cost from 3% to 2% of sales.

Ryan Pellino
Page 2

THOMPSON LABORATORIES - Nashville, Tennessee   **1992 - 1994**
Division of Richardson-Vicks AB - Hamburg, Germany
Manager, Planning   1993 - 1994

Developed new business opportunities. Established business planning concepts and guidelines, directed annual planning process and monitored company performance vs. plan.

- Led a six-person Sales Operations Task Force to identify customer needs, recommend marketplace opportunities and develop restructuring plans for a 125-person organization.

- Evaluated the market rationale, financial implications and business risk of various acquisitions and licensing opportunities ranging in size up to $100 million.

Planning/Financial Analyst   1992- 1993

- Managed the business planning process and provided financial analysis for marketing and sales plans ($70 million revenue) and capital projects ($5-$8 million annually).

RICHARDSON-VICKS S.A.   **1989 - 1992**
Division of Richardson-Vicks AB - Hamburg, Germany
Manager, Pharmaceutical Technology

- Acquired cultural sensitivity and language skills to effectively motivate, negotiate and manage diverse people and operations.

- Accelerated new product introductions by implementing a structural planning process between Marketing, Research and Registration at national and international headquarters.

- In three years, saved the company over $500,000 by improving management practices and departmental work processes for production operations.

EDUCATION

M.B.A., University of Tennessee, Knoxville, TN 1989
B.S. in Pharmacy, Oklahoma State University, Stillwater, OK 1987

CARL D. CROCKETT
102 Clover Hill Road
Nashville, TN 38495
(725) 955-8724   E-mail: Crock@AOL.com

Summary of Experience

Over thirteen years of diversified information systems experience in hi-tech manufacturing and consulting, with 9 years in the management and control of all information systems functions. In-depth knowledge of process re-engineering, large-scale implementation projects, and the economics and use of standardized hardware and software strategies. Extensive financial and manufacturing background.

2001 to Present	**Olympia Corporation, Nashville, TN** $6+ billion worldwide corporation producing automotive and electronic equipment.

Corporate Director Information Systems. Reporting to the Chief Financial Officer. Responsible for applications of computer technologies for the U.S. corporation, including business data processing, CIM/CAD/CAM, product R&D, telecommunications, office automation and advanced computer applications. Staff of 150 with a budget of $39 million.

- Reduced information systems budget to 2% of sales, while supporting a compound sales growth of 14%

- Replaced mainframe computers with cost-effective minicomputers, and eliminated or outsourced remaining legacy systems, saving $2 million annually.

- Implemented common financial systems in three divisions and two joint ventures, saving 1500 accounting staff days per year.

- Received "Quality Systems Achievement" award, 2001.

- Designed and implemented an international communications network that doubled the traffic capacity for all data, image and voice traffic between North America, Europe and Asia while reducing costs by 15%

- Selected and installed standardized manufacturing software/hardware systems and centralized systems support, which eliminated 63 systems positions.

- Implemented customer/supplier EDI, reducing inventories by $25 million.

1997 to 2001	**Darnell, Inc., Kaiser Insurance and Publishing Companies, Atlanta, GA** Specialized publishing/insurance division of a multi-billion dollar conglomerate.

Manager of Information Services. Responsible for financial and publishing systems development, technical support functions, corporate computer center, word processing center and telecommunications.

- Developed a long-range business plan and established computer strategy for a sister insurance division working with its CEO.

- Consolidated five word processing centers into one corporate department, reduced staff, expanded output by 35%, saved $200,000 per year. Project received recognition in national publication.

- Selected and implemented new accounting system which reduced accounting staff by 25% and compressed monthly closing cycles by four working days.

CARL D. CROCKETT   Page 2

1995 to   **Dynamic Electric Corporation**, **Tele Products Division, Arlington, VA**
1997 $75 million division manufacturing computerized telephone switch equipment.

> **Manager of Information Systems.** Responsible for all data processing department activities. Served as member of executive staff. Coordinated MIS functional goals and objectives as they related to the short-term and long-term business plan.
>
> - Directed the conversion of manufacturing system from an IBM mainframe to a Hewlett-Packard minicomputer, which increased services and reduced EDP budget by 15%.
>
> - Implemented an on-line shop floor control system to collect time/attendance, shop order tracking, job cost and payroll information that reduced payroll errors by 98% and increased production information accuracy by 92%.
>
> - Developed inventory analysis program that reduced inventory by 10% and eventually increased inventory turns 250%.

1990 to   **Spacetrac Technology Laboratories**, **Malvern PA**
1993   A high-tech consulting company specializing in government/industrial research.

> **Senior Client Consultant/Analyst.** Responsible for P&L of client projects, system design and analysis contract negotiations, project estimation and management from governmental and industrial projects.
>
> - Programmed computer software to plot maps of the lunar landing sites for the Apollo Lunar Expedition.
>
> - Designed, programmed and managed various large governmental projects for the Department of Defense and Federal Bureau of Investigation.
>
> - Provided technical support for the project to automate the Library of Congress.

SUMMARY OF TECHNICAL EXPERIENCE:

HARDWARE:	IBM (Mainframe & AS 400), NAS and AMDAHL, DEC-IBM minicomputers, Hewlett-Packard and personal computers.
SOFTWARE:	COBOL, FORTRAN, RPG, Assembler and BASIC.
APPLICATIONS:	Manufacturing, Finance/Accounting/Treasury, Distributed Processing, Data Base Systems, Local and Wide Area Networks.

EDUCATION:

M.B.A., Columbia University, 1995
M.S., Mathematics, Drexel University, 1990
B.S., Computer Science, Ohio State University, 1988

KAREN S. SHARPE
2248 Ole Dusty Lane
Cedarville, PA 17473
(645) 447-9847 (Home)   (645) 972-3649 (Office)
E-Mail: KSSHAR@MSN.com

PROFESSIONAL EXPERIENCE

CEDARVILLE TOBACCO COMPANY - Cedarville, OH   **1996 to Present**

<u>Director, Information Resources</u> (1998 to Present)
Executive in charge of company-wide personal computing, office systems, mainframe end-user computing, engineering service, information resource administration, disaster recovery planning, data access security systems availability, business forms design and management and operations facilities planning. Directed the operations of the data centers, telecommunications and software execution. Budgetary responsibility of $10 million and a staff of 15.

- Participated as a member of a steering committee that identified cost savings opportunities and recommended the consolidation of data centers and staff realizing $800,000 in personnel savings and $165,000 in hardware savings.

- Implemented Total Quality Management for the operations staff and supported the creation of self-directed work groups resulting in improved organizational effectiveness and productivity by reducing overtime and absenteeism.

- Directed the development of microcomputer hardware and office systems software standards for an installed base of 650 with annual purchases in excess of $5 million.

- Established an in-house training facility providing technical career development and office systems software training realizing $3.7 million cost avoidance the first year of operation.

<u>Project Manager</u> (1996 to 1998)

- Implemented the consumer products group national sales reporting system.

- Introduced new technologies for program developed and report production.

DREYFUS CORPORATION - New York, NY   **1994-1996**

<u>Programmer/Analyst</u>

EDUCATION

B.B.A., Marketing, Ohio State University, 1994

JASON LARSON
22 St. Vincent Road
Miami, FL 42301
(432) 985-1348
Fax: (432) 985-2593

CAREER SUMMARY

General Counsel for medium and large corporations. Manage legal departments and counsel senior management on mergers and acquisitions, environmental problems and other difficult and controversial issues. Anticipate problems and develop practical solutions with bottom-line sensitivity.

PROFESSIONAL EXPERIENCE

DUTCH SILVER CORPORATION, Miami, FL   **1999 - Present**

$6 billion natural resources company, producing 25% of the U.S. brass supply as well as major quantities of gold and silver.

Vice President, General Counsel, Secretary and Member of Board of Directors

Member of senior management group; responsible for all legal affairs; managed a ten person law department.

- Negotiated and oversaw drafting of engineering and construction contracts for $450 million smelter construction project, saving considerable outside counsel fees.

- Negotiated $800 million acquisition of Fargo, Inc., a mining, oil and gas and heavy metals company.

- Crafted a program for cleanup of ninety years' mining waste while avoiding "Superfund" designation, saving tens of millions of dollars in oversight costs.

APPLEBY WINDOWS, Orlando, FL   **1996 - 1999**

A $275 million manufacturer of building products, including windows, doors, siding and accessories. An LBO company formed in June 1996; previously a wholly-owned subsidiary of Carthage Steel Corporation.

Vice President and General Counsel

- Positioned LBO company for sale by divesting subsidiaries not related to core businesses, thereby maximizing return on LBO investment.

Jason Larson   **Page 2**

- Negotiated the successful sale of company to Lexington, Inc.

- Precluded EPA interference with sale of company by anticipating clean-up requirements, thereby avoiding potential years' delay of sale and several million dollars' oversight expenses.

BETHLEHEM STEEL, Pittsburgh, PA   **1989 - 1996**

Counsel

Responsible for legal affairs of Bethlehem's Diversified Group, including five subsidiaries. Directed internal investigations.

- Supervised antitrust, securities, product liability, toxic tort, real estate and trademark litigation.

- Conducted Carthage Steel Corporation's legal compliance program at 12 major plant locations.

WAPNER & NEWMAN, Philadelphia, PA   **1982 - 1989**

Associate, Litigation/antitrust group.   (1987 - 1989)

Law Clerk, part time, while attending law school. (1982 - 1987)

EDUCATION/MILITARY

Pennsylvania University School of Law, J.D., 1982
Activities: Class President
Honors: Top 1/4; Member, Law Journal

Cornell University, A.B. English Literature, 1977
Honors: Pennington Scholar
             New York State Regents Scholarship

Captain, U.S. Army, Intelligence Corps (1977-82)

BAR ADMISSIONS/PROFESSIONAL ACTIVITIES

- Licensed in Florida, Pennsylvania and Connecticut.
- Member, Ethics Advisory Opinion Committee, Legislative Affairs Committee (Pennsylvania Bar Association).

Barbara A. Stanley

302-A Seventh Avenue
Dayton, Ohio 64136
Office (613) 822-9462 ◆ Home (613) 844-2110

SUMMARY

Senior Manager with division of Fortune 500 corporation. Consistent record of success in increasingly responsible positions. Educated and experienced in materials management, purchasing, production control and integrated business systems.

EXPERIENCE

EAGLE-PICHER INDUSTRIES, INC., Plastics Division, Dayton, OH
A division of a Fortune 500 NYSE corporation with annual sales of $190 million.

Materials Manager, **(2000 - Present)**
Responsible for directing the Division's production and inventory control functions, includes: purchasing, order entry, order engineering, materials planning, production scheduling, warehouse and shipping and receiving. Also responsible for facility and machine maintenance.

- Reduced inventories significantly during a time of expansion.
- Increased service levels while reducing inventory.
- Increased revenue from freight rebates by $80,000 annually.
- Reduced raw materials 45% through stocking program and better scheduling techniques.
- Project leader for the implementation of a new integrated business systems software.
- Implemented preventative maintenance program for production machinery.

Purchasing Manager, **(1996 - 2000)**
Responsible for directing the Division's purchasing function, including the procurement of materials, services and capital equipment for $190 million division, by working directly with managerial and supervisory personnel in four plants including one international plant location.

- Implemented Division purchasing practices and procedures.
- Significantly reduced and maintained highly competitive raw material costs.
- Instrumental in implementing computer software for purchasing.
- Developed method and wrote PC software to aid in inventory usage and vendor analysis.
- Implemented vendor qualifications program.

Production Analyst, **(1992 - 1996)**
Special projects manager reporting to the Vice President and General Manager, working to analyze procedures and develop manufacturing strategies.

EDUCATION

B.A., Business Management, Ohio State University, 1992
Certified by the National Association of Purchasing Management (C.P.M.)

GERALD RAND
589 Portland Avenue
Corning, NY 14813
607/343-2742

SENIOR LEVEL EXECUTIVE with twenty years of line/staff/internal consulting experience in customer service, order fulfillment, logistics and product service. Strong decision-making, team-building, process reengineering, TQM, trouble shooting and cost avoidance skill set. Wharton MBA.

EXPERIENCE:

1998 - Present   **CORNING INCORPORATED,** Corning, NY
General Manager, Supply & Transportation
· Re-engineered purchasing/logistics functions, resulting in 66% reduction in work staff while accommodating 80% growth in work.
· Reduced staff budget from $18.4 million annually to $13.1 million.
· Reduced inventory levels from $17 million to $5.9 million.
· Reduced cycle time from 24 days on uniform/office supplies to two days.
· Re-engineered ordering/fulfillment process from paper to touch-tone electronic entry.
· Set and achieved goal of employee development to benchmark 5% training level.

1994 - 1998   **THE ARBITRAN COMPANY,** Laurel, MD
Staff Director, Logistics and Standards
· Created and directed a team which saved $25 million on $850 million annual purchases.
· Negotiated purchase agreements, saving 48% on switching equipment costs of $285 million and 28% on cable costs of $30 million.
· Served as in-house consultant to senior management on purchasing, distribution, inventory control and incentive compensation in preparation for centralization and corporate restructuring.
· Prepared recommendations and advised on inventory levels, materials standards.
· Provided comparative analysis for eight operating units.

1986 - 1991   **POWER UTILITIES CORPORATION,** Fort Lee, NJ
Northern Region Director, Customer Service
· Provided supervisory and administrative direction, to area encompassing two-thirds of New Jersey's 1.2 million customers, producing 60% of company's New Jersey revenue.
· Directly supervised management staff, reporting to an operation vice president.
· Successfully converted New Jersey from 13 district headquarters to two regional territories reducing operating costs by 50% and increasing operating performance and productivity.
· Represented management at union negotiations and personnel evaluations. Personally evaluated every job in conversion to Hay System.

EDUCATION: 1994 -   **WHARTON BUSINESS SCHOOL,** Philadelphia, PA
Masters of Business Administration
1986 -   **DUKE UNIVERSITY,** Durham, NC
Bachelor of General Studies Degree

CREDENTIALS: · Licensed Pilot
· Member, National Association of Purchasing Managers
· Member, American Management Association
· Certified Purchasing Manager

GREG HARVEY

13 East Hyde Street
Oakland, CA 98234

Home: (516) 735-7829   Office: (516) 834-2000, Ext. 16

OPERATIONS EXECUTIVE

Pro-active executive offering a strong background in production planning, purchasing, warehousing, distribution, inventory management, order processing, systems design, transportation, and customer service. Excellent people management skills, coupled with the ability to communicate effectively, enhancing the management of a large group of professionals.

PAWS & CLAWS., Oakland, CA   1999 - Present
Director of Logistics
Direct all aspects of production planning, purchasing, warehousing/distribution, inventory control, customer service and transportation for Paws & Claws' Grocery Products Division.

- Reduced division-wide inventory carrying costs by 25% or $10MM through implementation of cycle-time compression program. Program encompassed all functional areas within product supply chain.

- Improved overall customer service to wholesale and retail accounts by 10% through institution of CRP/ECR programs. Escalation in O-T-D and product fill-rate performance directly supported domestic and international sales in excess of $600MM.

- Fostered partnerships with suppliers and created formal Vendor Certification Program. Subject program yielded vast improvements in component and raw material quality and cost.

- Reduced base line operating budget by $4.8MM through implementation of accelerated cost reduction program. Program entailed utilization of "ABC" accounting techniques and served as pre-requisite to division's re-engineering of manufacturing/logistics processes.

- Directed all business logistics components of Paws & Claws' $20MM pet food launch into the Asian marketplace.

MAGNUM INTERNATIONAL, Seattle, WA   1991 - 1999
Manager of Logistics

Directly managed multiple site logistics operation for Magnum's Manufacturing Division. Areas of responsibility included material warehousing, distribution, inventory management, order processing, transportation and customer service functions.

- Responsible for operating budget of $9MM, staff of 10 managers and 175 direct/indirect employees. Managed a 300,000 square foot conventional warehouse, a 35,000 unit automated Hi-Rise facility, and all sub-contract distribution centers.

Greg Harvey

- Instrumental in development and implementation of MRP II technologies and strategies. Integrated modules such as MCS, PCS and DRP in support of Sherwood's "Just in Time" production concept. Created and implemented the Inventory Control Department.

- Spearheaded development and implementation of TQM and SPC programs, which eliminated $2MM in cost of non-conformance.

SYSTEM ONE, Portland, OR   1989 - 1991
Distribution Consultant

- Corporate distribution systems consultant serving System One's major subsidiaries and minority-owned affiliates. Direct responsibility for corporate distribution planning and customized application use.

- Project Manager, Corporate-Record Information and Storage Systems Development. Directed all facets of project analysis, functional specifications development and systems implementation for nationwide record/claim data management program.

DELUXE, INC., Sacramento, CA   1986 - 1989
Manufacturing/Distribution Facility
Plant Manager

- Full line responsibility for management of flagship plant servicing Deluxe's largest Forms Management customer base. Managed staff of three departmental managers and operations personnel consisting of 40 non-exempt/exempt employees.

- Directed all facets of facility including plant budgeting, production inventory control and maintenance of multi-plant management information systems program.

- Coordinated all physical plant set-up, in charge of interviewing, hiring and training of selected personnel. Implemented all systems and procedures for the newest operational facility in Deluxe's Business Forms Division.

EDUCATION

B.S., Psychology, Farley College - 1986
Sacramento, CA
Executive Development Program - 1989
Stanford University

HARVEY J. HALLIDAY
460 South Barnes
Cincinnati, OH 43607
Res: 416-832-9795
Bus: 416-832-6500

PROFILE:
International Business, Sales and Marketing Manager with more than 15 years in the Sporting Goods Industry, now seeking a new Senior Management challenge and opportunity. Areas of expertise include:

- Strategic Planning
- Operations Management
- Distribution/Logistics

- International Sales & Marketing
- Licensing/Sourcing
- Product Development

PROFESSIONAL EXPERIENCE:

SPORTS USA, INC., Cincinnati, OH   **1984 to Present**
A division of Athletic Wear Ltd.

Helped manage the International business and marketing growth of this $300 million leader in the Sporting Goods industry to a position where 50% of total revenues came from international sales to 90 countries. Matrix-managed staff of 32 employees, directed purchases of $80 million of goods worldwide, and managed expense budgets up to $500,000.

Director - Global Logistical Systems (1997-Present)

- Developed, implemented and managed the company's global logistical systems and operational procedures.
- Provided effective and efficient control in planning and maintenance of the company's inventory.
- Reduced inventories by 38% ($26 million) in 1998 and consequently reduced credit lines and interest expense.
- Implemented systems and procedures that reduced Asian sourcing lead times by 20%.

Director - International Strategic Planning/Special Projects (1995-1997)

- Managed the company's International Department.
- Worked with the International Field Managers to finalize 1996 business plans inclusive of sales forecasts, budgets, pricing and objectives.
- 1996 Business Plan was achieved and record billings and profit level were reached.
- Participated in the development of strategic plans that addressed future growth, and customer, consumer and corporate needs.
- Identified significant opportunities for improvement within the company then analyzed and developed solutions.
- Decentralized order processing, distribution, forecasting and inventory planning into three business units (U.S., U.K., Asia) to be more responsive to local market needs.
- Fine-tuned and helped link forecasting, inventory requirements planning and sourcing systems between offices in five different countries.

RONALD KNEE
7 Smith Bridge Road
Syracuse, NY 13222

: (315) 437-5400   Home: (315) 547-7524

SUMMARY

...mplished professional with more than fifteen years experience. Areas of concentration include ...chasing, management and production. Specific skills are in negotiation and contract ...hasing, management and production. Specific skills are in negotiation and contract ...nagement, use of databases for sourcing and analysis, budget preparation, materials ...nagement, cost control and facilities management. Recognized by both management and peers ...integrity, dependability and flexibility in meeting objectives.

PROFESSIONAL EXPERIENCE

CONTINENTAL PRODUCTS COMPANY, Syracuse, NY   1999 - Present

Commodities Buyer
Manage staff of five, responsible for purchasing more than $25,000,000 annual volume of catalogs, promotional items, sales aids and collateral materials.

· Developed and implemented strategy to use internal versus external production resources for product catalogs resulting in annual savings of more than $1 million.
· Provided expertise in establishing first formal company-wide purchasing department and developed operating guidelines.
· Utilized Manufacturing Resource Planning (MRP-II) and Just-in-Time (JIT) techniques which reduced complaints, missed deliveries and inventory.
· Analyzed purchasing practices and implemented consolidation and streamlining process resulting in first year savings of $500,000 and continued cost reductions.

PURCHASING PROFESSIONALS ASSOCIATION, New York, NY   1997 - 1999

Administrator
Responsible for day-to-day operations for 325-member organization with annual budget of $1.75 million.

· Re-established operations which included securing office facilities, reorganizing files and renewing membership interest.
· Developed long-term fiscal and strategic plans and managed association operations at the direction of ten-member board.
· Developed monthly meeting programs for membership addressing business, technical and social interests.
· Arranged quarterly business seminar programs made available to members and industry in general.
· Sourced, selected, negotiated and promoted extensive seminar program for bi-annual trade show.

Marketing Manager (1994-1995)

- Negotiated licensing agreement with Warner Brothers and managed the marketing of Sports USA's products.
- Developed *Jock Master* brand, product and collections exposure through television product placement, tie-in promotions and in-store merchandising programs.
- Managed new business development which provided $3.5 million of incremental sales from 1,000 U.S. storefronts and distributors in 20 countries.
- Implemented in-store merchandising program that received "1995 Best of Industry Award" from National Retail Merchandising Association.

International Sales Operations Manager (1990-1994)

- Developed, coordinated and implemented international marketing plans, forecasts, inventory control programs, procedures, policies, budget and administrative programs.
- Developed, managed and expanded international customer relationships. Travelled to 30 countries to work with customers.
- Achieved 392% sales growth in four years.
- International sales grew to account for 50% of total company sales. Grew distribution to more than 90 countries.

Project Manager (1988-1990)

- Directed and managed the product development, sourcing and marketing of racquet strings, sport bags, soft goods, machines and accessories.
- Achieved 113% sales growth in three years.
- *Jock Master* string product line profit margin increased by 20% and the category grew to the #3 position in the U.S.

Technical Manager - Stringer Education & Services (1984-1988)

- Responsible for developing a comprehensive grass roots stripping & technical education program for dealers and distributors.
- Provided *Jock Master* sponsored players with stringing and equipment services at major tennis tournaments.
- *Jock Master* rackets became the #2 choice of tournament professionals during this period providing the company with a major marketing advantage.

TENNIS PROFESSIONAL   1980 to 1984
Taught and developed beginner through world-class players at Lakeland Heights Tennis Club, Lakeland Heights, NJ. Managed club's pro shop.

EDUCATION: Baker University, Columbus, Ohio
                        B.S., Business Administration/Marketing, 1980

YVONNE SEIBERT
(813) 884-3100
43 MERIDIAN STREET
TAMPA, FL 33643

Experienced in all phases of Material Management, Purchasing, Production Planning, Master Scheduling, Production Control, Inventory Management and Distribution.

EXPERIENCE

ANCHOR PRODUCTS COMPANY, TAMPA, FL   1999 to Present
DIRECTOR OF PURCHASING

Responsible for the Purchasing, Inventory and Material Planning for this $150 million industry leader of consumer houseware goods. Report directly to the owners of the company and direct the activities of three professional vendor/schedulers and one inventory manager in the areas of material procurement, inventory levels and on-time performance. Knowledgeable in MRP, SPC and TQM techniques.

- Instituted "state-of-the-art" Partnership Purchasing Programs on key commodities which saved in excess of $2.3 million over a two-year period.

- Developed and expanded off-shore sourcing realizing a net savings of over $750,000.

- Instrumental in the start-up of a new injection molding department. Initiated planning parameters, production scheduling techniques and inventory levels which achieved internal production of over 90% of plastic requirements in less than one year.

- Reduced inventory levels over $500,000 while supporting a 20% increase in sales and the start-up of a new injection molding department through improved ordering techniques and vendor stocking programs.

BROAN MANUFACTURING COMPANY, HARTFORD, WI   1995 to 1999
MANAGER OF CORPORATE PURCHASING AND MATERIALS

Responsible for the Purchasing, Inventory, Shipping/Receiving and Traffic functions of this $85 million world-class electromechanical producer. Directed the activities of five professional buyers and seven vendor schedulers in the areas of material procurement, scheduling and capital expenditures with budgetary responsibility in excess of $32 million. Negotiated all freight carrier contracts for a multi-plant distribution environment with a freight budget responsibility of over $5 million.

- Instituted "Partnership Purchasing Program" and "Vendor Analysis Program" resulting in a 15% average reduction in pricing and a 23% improvement in supplier delivery performance. Bottom line savings over $820,000.

- Reduced inventory levels over 31%, or $3.6 million, through improved vendor delivery performance and implementation of supplier stocking programs.

YVONNE SEIBERT

- Reduced company L-T-L (Less Than Truckload) carrier ba resulting in increased freight discounts and savings in excess o

- Sourced, negotiated, certified and implemented outside fabric for company's major product line resulting in over $1 million in

BORDEN PACKAGING, COLUMBUS, OH
MANAGER OR PURCHASING AND DISTRIBUTION SERVICES

Responsible for the Purchasing, Traffic, Warehousing, Shipping and Wilson-Martin consumer products division with sales of $54 million.

- Through aggressive negotiations, maintained a favorable purchasing p a divisional savings of approximately $500,000.

- Reduced expense spending 22% for a $510,000 savings through order/vendor visibility and control.

- Instituted vendor performance measurements for raw materials suppli delivery performance to 95% on time and successfully meeting MRP (Planning) objectives.

- Implemented a Traffic Program that saved over $325,000 in freight cha freight discounts on combined inbound/outbound poundage.

MANAGER OF PRODUCTION PLANNING AND INVENTORY CONTROL

Responsible for the Production Planning, Production Control, Customer Service Receiving and Inventory (Raw Material, Work-In-Progress, Finish Stock) for the comn division. At the apex of our manufacturing cycle, directed the activities of 24 salaried employees in the areas listed above.

EARLIER EXPERIENCE

Held progressive managerial positions in production planning and inventory control at Bo Corporation (Chicago, IL).

EDUCATION

University of Cincinnati, Cincinnati, OH
Bachelor of Science in Industrial Management, 1981

Member of American Production and Inventory Control Society (APICS)
Member of the National Association of Purchasing Management (NAPM)

RONALD KNEE   PAGE TWO

FARLEY INDUSTRIES, Chicago, IL   1992 - 1997

General Services Director
Supervised and directed 20-person department which included photography, printing, mailroom, warehouse, creative design and facilities management.

- Eliminated wasteful purchasing practices by consolidating purchases which saved $100,000 the first year.
- Restructured warehouse personnel which reduced unemployment expenses and overall salaries while increasing productivity.
- Utilized expertise to modify design and production of printed support materials which provided more efficient and less costly manufacturing.

ROBERT KNEE PUBLISHING COMPANY, Philadelphia, PA   1989 - 1992

Owner
Operated small commercial printing company with full fiscal and production responsibilities. Provided printing for military bases, Commonwealth of Pennsylvania and dozens of small businesses in the Philadelphia area. Gross annual sales averaged $150,000.

U.S. NAVAL PRINTING OFFICE, Atlanta, GA   1988 - 1989

Printing Specialist
Sourced, competitively bid, awarded and administered printing contracts for governmental printing needs in the southeastern United States.

- Sourced and managed a variety of printing requirements valued at more than $1,000,000 annually.
- Developed detail specifications used to solicit bids for printed materials.
- Gained expertise during three-year printing management program which resulted in promotion to GS-11 Printing Specialist.

EDUCATION

A.A.S., Printing Technology, 1988
Drexel University, Philadelphia, PA

Additional Courses:

Frontline Leadership Program
MRP-II Seminar

AFFILIATIONS

Member, Pennsylvania Institute of Technical Printing

JOSEPH P. PARKER
26 High Valley Road
Laguna Beach, CA 80793
(714) 972-1844   E-Mail: JOPAR@MSN

SUMMARY

Manufacturing/operations manager with 12 years experience and accomplishments as a cost reduction manager and innovative leader. Strong P&L track record with functional management experience in all disciplines of manufacturing operations.

EXPERIENCE

TECHTRONICS, INC., Irvine, CA   **1999-Present**
Leading manufacturer and supplier of printed circuit boards with sales of $95 million annually.

Director, Manufacturing Operations
P&L responsibility for a business unit engaged in the manufacture of printed circuit boards. Functional responsibilities include manufacturing, quality, manufacturing engineering, product engineering, materials, and maintenance. In addition to functional responsibilities, position requires strategic planning, leading, and organizing of the operational activities of the unit.

- Increased manufacturing efficiency 20% by implementing a training program which used employee input and involvement.
- Improved yield 28% by restructuring the production operation process.
- Increased unit production 35% through tooling, fixturing, mechanization and automation.
- Implemented team concept by creating functional and cross-functional teams.
- Restructured production environment from high volume/low mix to low volume/high mix.

COMPU-PRO, INC., San Diego, CA   **1992-1999**
Manufacturer and distributor of modems with annual sales of $250 million.

Vice President, Manufacturing
Responsible for all manufacturing activities including production, quality, mechanical engineering, manufacturing engineering and materials management. Key success factors were insuring competitive product cost, meeting exact quality standards, and maintaining optimum inventory levels.

AMP INCORPORATED, Oxnard, CA   **1988-1992**
A world leader in the manufacture and supply of electronics with annual sales of $3 billion.

Production Manager
Site manager of $80 million sales volume facility with 900 employees. Responsible for production, engineering, quality, production control, maintenance and employee relations.

EDUCATION

M.B.A., Finance, University of Southern California, 1988
B.S.,   Industrial Engineering, U.C.L.A., 1986

BARBARA ALBRIGHT

84 Century Road
Chicago, IL 45309

Office (312) 625-1175
Home (312) 438-3479

SUMMARY

Accomplished Operations Manager with extensive experience in Manufacturing, Quality Control, Engineering and Maintenance. Progressive leader with strong team-building skills, focused on quality, productivity and results. Capable of improving profit margin through automation, development of human resources, and continuous process improvement programs. Solid budget development and financial management skills.

Hands on/Take Charge   Strong Communication Skills   Innovative/Progressive

SELECTED HIGHLIGHTS

- Successful, on time start-up of new plant. Hired and trained employees, implemented and directed all major operations. Increased annual production rates by 15% in second and third year of operation.

- Expanded plant bringing in new equipment and automated processes resulting in $1.4M annual cost savings.

- Turned around problem relationship with manufacturing, quality and sales, increased market acceptance of product, cut customer complaints in half in two years.

- Reduced plant downtime and product cost by implementing Continuous Process Improvement programs for plant equipment and processes.

- Implemented "Total Productive Maintenance" program reducing required maintenance personnel by 70% and improving employee ownership and productivity.

EMPLOYMENT HISTORY

NATIONAL MANUFACTURING COMPANY, Sterling, IL   1998 - Present
As **Manufacturing Manager** direct two levels of supervision for a manufacturing and maintenance operation of furniture manufacturing company with sales of $45 million.

- Responsible for the start-up of all plant operations. This was accomplished on schedule and under budget. Turned a projected eighteen month loss into a profit after six months of operations.

- Continuously improved the overall plant productivity. Quality and process losses average typically about 1%. Routinely have groups working together to solve both technical and personnel problems.

- Developed and directed the implementation of production scheduling and reporting procedures. Prepared yearly expense and capital budgets.

Barbara Albright
page two

EMPLOYMENT HISTORY (continued)

- Involved in the implementation of a totally integrated computer network system for handling MRP, inventory, and the general ledger.

- Responsible for corporate safety and environmental compliance responsibility. Directed response to extensive OSHA inspection resulting in no fines or penalties.

- Directed implementation of computerized maintenance work order, spare parts inventory management, and downtime reporting systems, reducing downtime and increasing productivity.

GENERAL CONTAINER COMPANY   1989 - 1998

GENERAL CONTAINER PLANT, Seattle, WA (1995 - 1998)
As **Quality Control Manager** of container manufacturing and distribution facility with annual sales in excess of $43 million, directed department of inspectors responsible for quality assurance and product acceptance.

- Lowest complaint settlement costs of all General Container manufacturing plants.

- Worked directly with customers and sales people to develop comprehensive quality action plan which addressed market weakness and recaptured lost business.

GENERAL CONTAINER TECH CENTER, Detroit, MI (1991 - 1995)
As **Development Engineer**, developed and implemented new manufacturing process for 18 Folding Carton manufacturing plants.

- Assisted in the automation of manufacturing operations through equipment selection and system design.

- Completed over a dozen equipment development projects from design through plant installation. Received two United States Patents.

GENERAL CONTAINER PLANT, Dallas, TX (1989 - 1991)
As **Process Engineer** had sole responsibility for all projects and process engineering functions.

- Construction and start-up of a $5.4 million plant expansion.

- Successfully, handled all dealings with Government Environmental agencies.

EDUCATION

1989   M.S., Chemical Engineering, Pennsylvania State University

1987   B.S., Chemistry, Pennsylvania State University

CHARLES LEWIS

653 Wayside Drive
Seattle, WA 98045
work (206) 543-7850
home (206) 543-3461

SUMMARY

Over sixteen years of broad-based manufacturing experience rising to the position of plant manager with a "world class" Fortune 500 company. Previous assignments included managerial positions in engineering, capital planning, purchasing, finance and systems.

PROFESSIONAL EXPERIENCE

Paccar Inc., Automotive Division, Renton, WA   2000 to Present
Plant Manager

Total operational and financial responsibility for a $63 million, 800-person, non-union, fractional hp, vertically integrated motor plant producing 5100 motors/day.

- Doubled inventory turnover from 12 to 24 by creating cellular manufacturing, focused factories and set-up reduction.
- Orchestrated the ramp-up of production components for an 80% output increase to a highly successful Mexican assembly facility.
- Directed strategic program to transfer production among four plants to improve profitability and create a market focused operation.
- Increased pump motor sales 22% through improvements in cost, quality and customer service.
- Improved productivity 9% through improvements in fabrication and flow.
- Developed plans for ISO 9000 implementation.
- Implemented $2.5 to $3 million in cost improvements annually.
- Guided the creation of empowered hourly/salary teams to improve product quality in a TQM environment.

Walden Pump Corporation, Baltimore, MD   1998 to 2000
Plant Manager

A $60 million annual sales operation with 350 employees involved in machining and assembly associated with the manufacture of pump systems.

- Achieved record quarterly production 17% over previous record.
- Improved production control and MRP systems.
- Installed new production methods cutting cost 22%.
- Reorganized staff improving teamwork and plant performance.
- Reduced inventories 16% in less than eight months.
- Transformed quality mind set from detection to prevention.
- Developed comprehensive strategic plan for new owners.

Tomkins Industries, Inc., Dayton, OH   1985 to 1998
Manager Manufacturing Engineering (1996 - 1998)

Responsible for $9.2 million budget and activities of 220 people for $850 million producer of packaging machinery.

CHARLES LEWIS   page 2

- Developed master plans reorganizing multiple facilities.
- Launched new product introduction, on time and 30% under budget.
- Coordinated activities of seven JIT hourly/salary teams.
- Identified and implemented set-up reductions of 10-80%.
- Installed eight manufacturing cells reducing space by 30%.
- Initiated comprehensive preventative maintenance system.

Information Systems Manager (1994 - 1996)
Headed nine-person department responsible for development, operations and maintenance of information systems in an IBM-4341 DOS/VS environment.

- Implemented a shop order system saving $1.1 million.
- Headed development of long range master systems plan.
- Developed programs to highlight and analyze inventory problems.
- Conducted division-wide information systems training sessions.
- Led systems efforts to consolidate multi-plant purchasing functions.

Manager of Purchasing (1992 - 1994)
Managed 13-person purchasing department responsible for all scheduling and procurement of $175 million of production, sub-contract and support materials for a fabrication/assembly operation.

- Consistently achieved over $1 million in favorable price variances.
- Reduced inventory 23% through JIT purchasing and consignment.
- Negotiated multi-year contracts realizing 5-50% cost reductions.
- Implemented automated purchase order system tied to plant MRP.
- Assumed Materials Manager's responsibilities for nine month period.

Manager of Financial Planning and Analysis (1990 - 1992)
Supervised six individuals in the planning, analysis and forecasting of a $425 million division operating as an independent profit center.

- Developed annual and five year plans with senior management.
- Prepared monthly forecasts for division P&L and cash flow.
- Assumed Controller's responsibility for four month period.

Project Manager   (1988 - 1990)
Manufacturing Engineer   (1985 - 1988)

EDUCATION

B.S. Electrical Engineering (with Honors), 1985
Brown University, Providence, RI
Elected to Tau Beta Pi

ORGANIZATION SERVICE

Member, Institute of Electrical Engineers

ASHLEY HEMPHILL

3 Knolls Road
Buffalo, NY 14552

(716) 623-7837

OBJECTIVE

A challenging position which provides the opportunity for utilization of my manufacturing, financial and managerial skills.

SUMMARY OF QUALIFICATIONS

- Demonstrated ability to effectively manage start-up/turnaround situations
- Consistent record of achieving and surpassing desired results and creating new methods and procedures
- Proven record of people development

CAREER HISTORY AND SELECTED ACCOMPLISHMENTS

CALSPAN, INC., Buffalo, NY (1999-Present)
Operations Manager
Responsible for the management of five manufacturing facilities and a warehouse/distribution center totaling 520,000 square feet and 1,200 employees involved in the manufacturing, packaging and distribution of flexible packaging in a multi-shift environment. Annual sales of $100 million, with direct expense budget responsibility of $15 million and capital budget averaging $1 million.
- Instituted standards and methods resulting in an increase in production efficiency of 20%.
- Installed a safety program that reduced lost work days by 80% with corresponding effect on workers compensation insurance rates.
- Created annual and preventive maintenance programs for both manufacturing equipment and facilities which resulted in greatly reduced downtime saving $200,000 per year.
- Improved inventory controls and reduced physical inventory to book variance by $117,000, or to .003%.
- Revamped quality inspection program resulting in significant reduction in rework expense.
- Started cost improvement program with savings of $125,000.
- Prepared new product costing estimates.

PRIMERICA CORPORATION, Duluth, GA (1995-1999)
Senior Vice President and Chief Financial Officer
President – Primerica Financial (Subsidiary)
President – Commercial Packaging Company (Subsidiary)
Responsibilities included structuring, obtaining and negotiating project financing, corporate finance, coordinating and supervising direct participation program securities sales, cash management, budget preparation, regulatory compliance, asset management, acquisition and divestitures and overall management of flexible packaging company.
- Instituted cash management and investment programs.
- Structured $42 million in project financing in the health care, airport, housing and public/private sectors.
- Restructured $20 million in debt in response to the Tax Reform Act of 1996.
- Broadened relationships with investment bankers, lenders and broker/dealers.
- Reorganized plant management and practices to cause return to profitability.

FIRST EMPIRE STATE CORPORATION, Buffalo, NY (1991-1995)
Vice President and Manager - Financial Institutions Division
Responsible for the overall management of the division which served the Bank's relationship with firms in the financial industries with a loan portfolio of $125 million, deposits of $55 million, and fee income to $5.3 million. Voting member of Regional Loan Committee and member of Strategic Planning Task Force.
- Refocused Division to a corporate finance/investment banking direction.
- Developed and instituted comprehensive marketing plan.

ASHLEY HEMPHILL

- Established both near and long-term goals and objectives and restaffed the Division to provide the requisite base of experience.
- Created syndication/networking capabilities.
- Provided product capability to all bank customers in structured/specialized credits.
- Directed policy creation on off-balance sheet credit products, funds management exposure, and specialized credit products.
- Improved bottom line profitability $900,000.

BINKS MANUFACTURING, Franklin Park, IL (1987-1991)

Director of Operations – Binks Finance Company (1989-1991)

Responsible for the formation of the captive finance subsidiary, all finance programs, documentation, credit and collection procedures.

- Defined the initial scope of business and developed initial organizational structure and inter-company agreements.
- Created new finance and lease programs, implemented marketing support systems and instituted policies and procedures for proper management control.
- Successfully resolved several preexisting accounts saving the company over $1.2 million in bad debt exposures.
- Provided focused financing support of product sales.

Manager - International Credit and Finance (1987-1989)

Responsibilities included making credit decisions on all export shipments from Binks-U.S. locations, arranging export financing for customer purchases from all Jordan worldwide locations, working closely with the Assistant Treasurer in the area of bank relationships, foreign subsidiary financing, capitalization requirements and cash management.

- Created in-house distributor and end user finance programs.
- Developed outside sources of financing.
- Negotiated attractive import financing from the German Government resulting in a $1.5 million savings.
- Effected refinancing of foreign subsidiary debt at significantly lower rates.
- Participated in a major foreign divestiture.
- Traveled to and transacted business throughout Europe, Middle East and Central and South America.

HIBERNIA NATIONAL BANK, New Orleans, LA (1983-1987)

Cash Management Representative (1986-1987)

Responsibilities included designing collection and disbursement systems for major customers of the Bank.

Administrative Assistant - Commercial Division (1985)

Credit Analyst (1984-1985)

Management Training Program (1983)

EDUCATION

GEORGIA STATE UNIVERSITY
   M.B.A., Finance (1983)
   B.S., Accounting (1981)

SECURITIES LICENSES

General Securities Representative (Series 7)
Uniform State Securities Registration (Series 63)
General Securities Principal (Series 24)

WARD L. CHRISTIAN

16 Seashell Drive   (814) 665-2977 (Res.)   Fax: (814)665-8972
Orlando, FL 65233   (814) 996-4126 (Bus.)   E-Mail: WLCH@MSN

OBJECTIVE: Management position in production/operations with a company that will utilize my experience and skills to meet business objectives and support my commitment to customer service, employee development and continuous improvement

EXPERIENCE:

DEVORN PHARMACEUTICAL CO. Orlando, FL
A $9.4 billion pharmaceutical, health care and consumer products company.

Production Manager, Orlando, FL   **1999 - Present**
Reporting to the Director of Operations, directing six Department Managers and 320 employees in all aspects of manufacturing and packaging for divisional sales of approximately $400 million.

- Managed site's profit improvement program which resulted in yearly savings of over $1.8 million for four consecutive years.

- Implemented the establishment of production line teams that resulted in numerous operational improvements including the elimination of line Group Leaders with associated savings of $310,000.

- Successfully coordinated the validation and production start-up of approximately 31 products transferred to Orlando from a sister plant that was closed.

- Worked closely with R&D and Marketing to successfully launch a major new product line with estimated annual sales of $32 million.

Production Manager, Macon, GA   **1996 to 1999**
Reporting to the Plant Manager, directing three Department Managers and approximately 130 employees in all aspects of manufacturing and packaging for divisional sales of approximately $51 million.

- Coordinated the installation of a fully computerized integrated powder manufacturing system resulting in annual savings of approximately $180,000.

- Managed cost reduction program which generated annual savings of approximately $400,000.

- Implemented monthly operation meetings to enhance employee-employer relations, improve communications and provide for employee feedback and ideas.

Supervisor of Aerosol Filling   **1994 to 1996**
Quality Control Manager   **1992 to 1994**
Assistant Supervisor, Aerosol Filling   **1991 to 1992**

EDUCATION:

Florida State University - BA in Biology, Minor in Chemistry, 1991

PETER R. SAILOR　　　　　　　　　　　　　　　(206) 357-9321 Office
106 Radnor Drive　　　　　　　　　　　　　　　　(206) 425-1362 Home
Wheeling, WV 31594　　　　　　　　　　　　　　　E-Mail: PSAIL@MSN

OBJECTIVE

Operations/Manufacturing Management leading to Business Management

PROFESSIONAL EXPERIENCE

WHEELING CHEMICAL COMPANY　　　　　　　　　　**1988 to Present**
Wheeling, WV
<u>Director of Manufacturing, Specialty Chemicals</u> (1999 to Present)
Manage the manufacturing operation of the company's largest business unit. Three primary accountabilities are: optimizing the performance of the production sites, creating an integrated manufacturing strategy that improves the relative competitive position of the business, and coordinating the transfer of technologies and systems among the plant operations in North America and Europe.

Accomplishments and Results

* Developed a cohesive strategy and operational plans for four manufacturing facilities, resulting in a 100% profit gain in two years.

* In a facility operating at a loss, exceeded ROA targets in two years, reduced waste by 40%, increased saleable output by 35%, reduced personnel by 40%, and significantly improved profitability.

* Implemented an innovative management and labor relations strategy in a key facility that initiated a collaborative rather than adversarial relationship and reduced grievances by more than 90%. Production was increased by 25% in one year; value added cost reduced by 30%.

* Co-managed the development of $60 million capital improvement program, with particular emphasis on facility relocation, capacity expansion, and corporate campus planning.

<u>Manager of Site Operations</u> - Seattle Plant　　　　　　　　(1995 - 1999)
<u>Plant Manager</u> - Seattle Plant　　　　　　　　　　　　　　(1994 - 1995)
<u>Plant Manager</u> - Portland Plant　　　　　　　　　　　　　　(1992 - 1994)
<u>Senior Project Engineer</u> - Portland Plant　　　　　　　　　(1990 - 1992)
<u>Project Engineer</u> - Portland Plant　　　　　　　　　　　　(1988 - 1990)

EDUCATION

UNIVERSITY OF CHICAGO – M.B.A., General Management & Finance Major (1988)

OREGON STATE UNIVERSITY – B.S., Mechanical Engineering (1986)

ERIC KILE
15 East 74th Street
New York, NY 10023
(212) 739-3472

PROFILE: Excellent background in Distribution/Transportation Operations and Engineering, with recent experience in the Manufacturing environment.

EXPERIENCE:

1991 - Present   **GIVENCHY, INC.**   NEW YORK, NY

(1999 - Present)   *DIRECTOR, MANUFACTURING OPERATIONS*
Responsible for all operational aspects of this formerly subcontracted $6.3 million thermoforming discipline with documented in-house savings exceeding $620,000 annually. Developed and monitored long and short-term critical path production schedules for over 130 major marketing programs. Responsibilities also included attainment of hourly labor performance against budgeted standards as well as the direct control of all Thermoforming Department financial expenditures.

Major Accomplishments:
- Increased labor productivity by 15%.
- Effected a positive component usage variance in excess of $125M against budget.
- Increased safety performance by 42%.

(1997 - 1999)   *ASSISTANT DIRECTOR, RAW MATERIALS MANAGEMENT*
With an annual budget of nearly $8 million, was responsible for the physical movement of all inbound manufacturing components and raw materials to our Connecticut, New Jersey and Manhattan sites. This included both domestic and international suppliers.

Major Accomplishments:
- Conducted the first ever rate negotiation sessions for Freight In operations, which resulted in a 20% reduction in expenditures as a percent to Cost of Goods.
- Established vendor LTL consolidation programs for each of the three Givenchy sites which resulted in substantial cost savings with no adverse effects upon service.

(1997)   *ASSISTANT DIRECTOR, PARFUME DIVISION*
Was instrumental in the start-up of this uniquely new $240 million operation established in Greenwich, Connecticut.

Major Accomplishments:

- Designed the physical layout of the shipping dock, hired and trained the clerical and hourly staff, and directly supervised the day-to-day shipping and transportation operations during its infancy stages.
- Wrote all procedural manuals related to our functional disciplines.
- Developed tonnage and service statistical reports enabling efficient administrative controls and analysis of operational performance.

(1996)   *ASSISTANT DIRECTOR, DISTRIBUTION*

With yearly expenditures exceeding $9 million, was responsible for all aspects of transportation of finished goods to retail customers and between company facilities, both via common carrier and the Givenchy corporate fleet.

Major Accomplishments:

- Through motor carrier rate negotiations, LTL and small shipment consolidations, as well as improved shipping dock labor methods, effected annual cost reductions of $1.8 million.

(1991 - 1996)   *MANAGER, DISTRIBUTION ENGINEERING*

Prepared, in detail, the annual divisional $7 million plus labor budget. Provided cost versus savings analyses on all operations improvement projects and determined the associated facility capacity and manpower requirements. Planned and developed proposals for capital expenditures related to facilities upgrade and new equipment purchases amounting to approximately $2 million annually.

Major Accomplishments:

- Developed and implemented work performance standards within the Givenchy Distribution Division, which resulted in yearly $750,000 labor cost savings.
- Provided long-term cost savings to justify a $4 million Distribution automation project.

1988 - 1991   ARTHUR D. LITTLE   CAMBRIDGE, MA

ASSOCIATE

Representing one of the largest management consulting firms in the world, duties included extensive travel to client locations performing audits and detailed studies of transportation and distribution operations. Responsible for data gathering, analysis, recommendations development, and final written report preparation.

EDUCATION: **AMHERST COLLEGE,** Amherst, Massachusetts

- M.B.A., 1988
- B.A. Degree, Business Administration, 1986

KIRK LIND
10 Forest Drive
Pasadena, CA 97439
(818) 440-5500

OBJECTIVE: To obtain a challenging senior-level manufacturing position.

EXPERIENCE:

1991 - Present   **THE PARSONS COMPANY**   PASADENA, CA

1999 - Present   *SENIOR PRODUCTION MANAGER, CONTAINER DECORATING DIVISION*
Responsible for total profit/loss, scheduling, purchasing of all production and maintenance supplies, maintenance, acceptable quality of finished components, job completion, safety, GMPS, and utilization of labor.

Major Accomplishments:
- Reversed a divisional loss of $750,000 in 1999 to a profit of $1.2 million in 2001.
- Designed and implemented a scrap program that provided an annual savings of $500,000 and brought job completion to 100%.
- Developed and set up cost savings program which realized annual cost savings of $300,000.

1998 - 1999   *PRODUCTION MANAGER, PROMOTIONAL DIVISION*
Responsible for on-time production of finished work, efficient utilization of labor, acceptable quality of final product, job completion, safety, GMP compliance, and receiving and stores.

Major Accomplishments:
- Designed and implemented $.5 million in cost savings programs.
- Produced all promotions on time, despite being handicapped by late component deliveries and moving our operation twice.
- Had positive labor variance of approximately 20,000 hours.

1995 - 1998   *SENIOR PRODUCTION SUPERVISOR, PROMOTIONAL DIVISION*
Responsible for efficient utilization of labor, setting up and clearing of production lines, acceptability of finished products, safety, GMPS, and receiving and stores.

Major Accomplishments:
- Despite a 50% increase in volume, late component deliveries, and a large, new work force, produced all promotions on time and achieved a positive variance of 10,000 hours.

1991 - 1995   *PRODUCTION SUPERVISOR, PROMOTIONAL DIVISION*
Responsible for running production lines, efficient utilization of labor, acceptability of finished product, and safety.

1985 - 1991   **ACUSON CORPORATION**   MOUNTAIN VIEW, CA

1991   *PRODUCTION AND INVENTORY CONTROL COORDINATOR*

1990 - 1991   *BRANCH MANAGER*

1990   *MANUFACTURING SUPERVISOR*

1988 - 1990   *PRODUCTION FOREMAN*

1985 - 1988   *MACHINE TENDER*

EDUCATION: **SAN DIEGO STATE UNIVERSITY,** BS - Business Management, 1985

AVERY CUMMINGS
19 Broadmoor Street
CANTON, OH 45134

Home: (412) 459-1278   Office: (412) 459-3005

OPERATIONS EXECUTIVE

Proven operations executive with successful results in the management of all functions in manufacturing and plant operations, including P&L responsibility. Particular strengths in cost control, systems, business strategic planning, problem-solving and introduction of new technologies and changes for operational improvement. Resourceful leader with excellent communication and interpersonal skills.

DIEBOLD INCORPORATED - Canton, OH   1999 - present
This company designs and manufactures steam turbines and pumps for the industrial and petrochemical markets. The company required significant upgrades of productivity, equipment and processes to improve its competitive position in the marketplace.

Manager - Manufacturing Operations
Responsible for machining, assembly, test, purchasing, material control, manufacturing engineering, plant engineering and environmental compliance for a $150 million plus sales plant. Managed an organization of 500 individuals, 350 of which were union production and maintenance employees. Responsible for a $50 million expense budget.

- Achieved the highest sales in over ten years and reduced backlogs by 35% through organizational restructuring and attention to details,

- Reduced inventories $3.3 million by setting objectives and measuring against the objectives.

- Improved productivity 10% and reduced costs 12% by implementing multidiscipline task forces to address inefficiencies.

- Put in place a joint procurement program with international divisions, which reduced material costs by $2.7 million annually.

- Implemented state-of-the-art computer numerical control five-axis machining and robotic welding, resulting in product quality improvements.

- Converted an adversarial labor relationship to one of mutual trust through participative management.

AURORA PUMP - North Aurora, IL   1988 - 1999

Manager - Manufacturing Operations - Deerfield, IL (1995 - 1999)
This plant manufactures custom pump systems for the industrial and defense markets. Mature facility that required major upgrades of productivity, systems, equipment and processes to assure survival in a very competitive marketplace. Responsible for machining, assembly, test, materials, production control, quality assurance, manufacturing engineering and maintenance for a $75 million sales plant with a $25 million expense budget Managed an organization of 340 individuals, 285 were union production, maintenance and clerical employees. Promoted from Production Manager to Manager - Manufacturing Operations.

- Reduced cycle times by 25% by implementing eight manufacturing cells.

- Improved costs and reduced budgets 10% through instituting cost control and accountability.

AVERY CUMMINGS

Manager - Manufacturing Operations (Continued)

- Improved productivity 25% by methods improvements, control of direct labor and attention to quality.

- Reduced vendor base 35% and set up eighteen alliances with key suppliers. This resulted in significant lead time reductions and improvements in vendor quality.

- Improved on-time shipment 30% by implementing a disciplined production system.

- Reduced inventories over 45% through attention to control and reduction of cycle times.

- Negotiated three labor contracts that achieved greater flexibility of workforce utilization.

Plant Manager - Oak Brook, IL (1993 - 1995)
This plant manufactured and overhauled specialty pumps for the industrial, petrochemical and utility markets. Profit and loss responsibility for die plant. Responsible for marketing, engineering, manufacturing, finance and human resources functions.

- Strengthened the marketing and engineering functions by recruiting highly qualified personnel.

- Improved productivity 14% by implementing an operator involvement program.

- Improved income 30% by cost reduction and cycle time improvement.

- Reduced inventories 40% through attention to control and reduction of cycle times.

- Improved on-time shipments from 60% to 98% with the implementation of new PC-based production systems.

- Achieved an orderly close down of the facility and transferred products to other plants.

Manager - Technical Services (1988 - 1993)
Implemented an integrated facility and equipment plan involving seven plants, reduced quality costs by 56% on five product lines and transferred product lines between plants.

GENERAL DYNAMICS CORPORATION - Falls Church, VA   1978 - 1988
Selected for the General Dynamics Manufacturing Management Program, which involved rotating six month assignments as Production Control Specialist, Buyer, Q. C. Process Specialist, Value Engineer and Foreman. After program graduation, held a series of increasing responsible positions at various plant locations as Manufacturing Engineer, Manager - Production Control, Manager - Advanced Manufacturing and Process Engineering, Manager - Manufacturing Engineering and Manager - Mechanical Design Engineering.

EDUCATION

B. S., Electrical Engineering - 1978
Boston University
Boston, Massachusetts

OTHER ACTIVITIES

General Dynamics Manufacturing Management Program Graduate

JAMES KOENIG

13 Northwood Avenue
Columbus, OH 66312

Home: 614-655-8048
Office: 614-774-3400

SUMMARY OF EXPERIENCE

Considerable experience in a manufacturing/operational environment, servicing the consumer hardware, industrial and sporting goods industries. Personally responsible for domestic and off-shore manufacturing facilities and processes ranging from $70 million to $200 million. Achieved significant accomplishments within extremely competitive markets via the use of strong leadership skills, creative problem solving methods, new product development and enhanced employee capabilities through self-directed work teams.

PROFESSIONAL EXPERIENCE

DIRECTOR OF CHAIN OPERATIONS 1992 - 2000
Goller Custom Tools, Columbus, OH
Goller is a manufacturer of welded and weldless chain and chain accessories servicing the consumer hardware, industrial, automotive, marine and forestry markets.

- Total responsibility for P&L of this $185,000,000 company which includes four manufacturing facilities, eight distribution centers and 1200 employees.

- Initiated and implemented the following major projects: ISO 9000, OPC/SPC, Bar coded shop floor control system, vendor certification program and the introduction of self-directed work teams.

- Personally responsible for the development of off-shore manufacturing relations offering extreme flexibility in the manufacturing of labor intensive products.

- Established a unique consignment program for the procurement of all major raw materials.

- Relocated a 200,000 sq. ft. southeastern chain facility into the Columbus plant within a nine month time period with no disruption in production of service.

- Realized internal cost reduction programs yielding in excess of $1,000,000 annually for the past six years.

- Responsible for a 40% reduction of inventories and 35% reduction of salaried staff within my employment history at Goller while reducing period costs from 18+% to 9.1%.

- Received two patents for new product.

- Was responsible for new three-tier, two-level wage structure and "management by council" concept to support empowered team philosophy.

VICE PRESIDENT, OPERATIONS 1988 - 1992
Goller Custom Tools/Fisher Chain, Baltimore, MD
Fisher Chain was a manufacturer of fastener hardware for the industrial, consumer hardware and saddlery markets, acquired by Goller Custom Tools.

- Manufacturing and marketing responsibilities for this $7,000,000 per year organization.

- Responsible for the design and manufacture of complete new zinc die cast snap and pulley line.

- Responsible for the establishment of Far East manufacturers for labor intensive processes.

JAMES KOENIG   **Page Two**

- Strongly positioned family-owned company for acquisition by larger corporation via:

  - Leader in marketplace   - Good profitability
  - Low inventories   - Sound manufacturing facility and staff
  - Efficient manufacturing processes

VICE PRESIDENT, MANUFACTURING   1985 - 1988
Process Pumps, Inc., Baltimore, MD

- Responsible for manufacturing facility and new product design for this producer of residential and commercial pumps.

- Responsible for an award-winning submergible pump utilizing a zinc die cast design which eliminated 70% of required machine operations.

- Introduction of in-line manufacturing concept reducing product costs by 20+%.

DIRECTOR OF MANUFACTURING   1981 - 1985
Smith & Wesson Corporation, Alexandria, VA
Manufacturer of Pellet and BB Guns. Hired as a product designer and promoted three times to Director of Manufacturing.

- Directly responsible for the design and development of new products which ultimately grew the company from $1 million to $16 million.

- Received four patents for new product designs all of which were mass produced and sold to the sporting goods industry.

- Wrote and implemented a Total Quality Control procedures manual.

- Implemented a computerized materials planning system for all phases of manufacturing and procurement.

- Was instrumental in the planning and construction phases of new 100,000 sq. ft. manufacturing facility.

- Was responsible for the design and implementation of an in-line process for the fabrication of CO_2 powered products.

- Ultimately responsible for the total manufacturing facilities and processes which included three plants and 230 employees.

  - Decreased inventories by 30%
  - Decreased period costs by 25%
  - Increased EBT to a level of 28%

EDUCATION

VIRGINIA POLYTECHNICAL INSTITUTE, Bachelor of Science, Mechanical Engineering, 1981

SPECIALIZED TRAINING

GOLLER INDUSTRIES, Finance for Non-Financial Managers, 1989
DIMENSIONS INTERNATIONAL, Strategies for Employee Empowerment, 1994

RANDOLPH DILLON
652 MONTAGUE STREET
PHILADELPHIA, PA 19103
(215) 696-3490

OBJECTIVE: Production Supervisor position within a growing organization.

SUMMARY: People-oriented supervisor who believes the ability to change and adapt to new technology is necessary in today's competitive marketplace. I am confident that my knowledge, ability and adaptability will be an asset to any organization.

EXPERIENCE:

1984 - 2001   **AMERICAN METER CORPORATION**   YORK, PA

     1995 - 2001   **PRODUCTION SUPERVISOR**
Supervised 80-100 employees in a high-speed filling, packaging and production process. Responsible for running eight different units, as well as training new supervisors and machinists.
Major Accomplishments:
- Instituted a response team of operators and mechanics who responded to line-stoppages, decreasing downtime between repairs by more than 20%.
- Instituted preventive maintenance program that decreased stoppages by 30% over a two year period.
- Responded to OSHA safety requirements with 92% efficiency for the production floor.

     1993 - 1995   **QUALITY CONTROL SUPERVISOR**
Responsibilities included insuring that the final product at the packaging plant met the assigned specifications. Inspected all aspects of the high-speed packaging process, including line speeds, video jets, coders, cappers, box assemblers, pressure fillers, shrink wrappers and labelers. Promoted to the position of Production Supervisor.
Major Accomplishments:
- Instituted a program using electrical weight checking to insure proper fill height specifications within the aerosol filling units.
- Although this position was offered to me on a temporary basis while I was a union employee, my accomplishments warranted an opportunity to advance to Production Supervisor.

     1984 - 1993   **GRADE A MACHINIST**
Responsible for line changeovers, which included the adjustments and changes of machine parts for valvers, actuators, MRM fillers, Goldberger labelers, crimpers and automatic ferrel coders. Responsibilities also included 85% up-time on all running, filling and packaging machinery on the production floor.
Major Accomplishments:
- Instituted training program for new machinists within the company, using procedure guidelines developed by area directors under the advice of department personnel.
- Directed the use of safety gear on all filling lines within hazardous areas: protective glasses, robes and gloves. This reduced lost time accidents by 35% in one year.
- Trained area personnel on the use of hazardous propane and butane gasses used as a propellant in the filling of colognes and perfumes.

EDUCATION: **ARDMORE SR. HIGH SCHOOL**, Ardmore, Pennsylvania; Graduated 1984

TIMOTHY ALLEN

34 Anaheim Boulevard
Detroit, MI 44187
(813) 774-1805 Home
(813) 774-4500 Office

OBJECTIVE:

Senior operations management position at a major operating facility for a growing pulp and
paper or related company, where broad management skills in operations can be fully utilized.

EXPERIENCE:

2000
to
Present

KIMBERLY-CLARK CORPORATION

Director, Pulping Operations - Detroit Mill

Report to Vice President & Resident Manager of this 1,200 TPD bleached kraft
pulp mill. Direct staff of six department managers, 36 professionals and 157
hourly personnel ($240 million operating budget). Functional responsibility for
pulp manufacturing, utilities and environmental protection.

Key Accomplishments:

- Directed successful start-up of $200 million power and recovery capital
  project with less than 24 hours lost mill production (American's largest capital
  project ever).

- Increased pulp production by 155 TPD in single year through improved
  utilization of existing capacity.

- Reduced pulp manufacturing costs by over $24 per ton (8%) with resultant
  annual savings of $12.7 million.

- Directed start-up of state-of-the-art lime mud dryer and kiln (first of its kind in
  North America).

- Achieved $5 million additional annual cost savings in steam generation
  through optimization of fuel mix.

- Reorganized pulp and utilities department for better focus on multiple
  priorities.

1997
to
2000

LAWRENCE MANUFACTURING

Manager, Pulp Manufacturing - Oklahoma City, OK Mill

Reported to Production Manager, Pulp, Power & Wood of this 550 TPD bleached
kraft pulp mill. Managed staff of eight supervisors and 75 hourly employees ($73
million operating budget). Functional responsibility for all pulp manufacturing.

Key Accomplishments:

- Key member of team responsible for planning, process design and equipment selection for $275 million pulp mill modernization and expansion project.

- Increased existing pulp mill production by 27 TPD, despite planned mill obsolescence.

- Achieved $1.8 million annual cost savings in pulp manufacturing costs.

1985
to
1997

CASCADE PAPER COMPANY

Assistant Technical Director - Little Rock, AK Mill (1995 - 1997)
Reported to Technical Director of this 1,500 TPD brown and bleached kraft pulp and paper mill. Managed staff of eight technical professionals and 20 nonexempt support personnel with functional responsibility for process engineering, pulp and paper quality control, testing laboratory and environmental compliance.

Key Accomplishments:

- Developed mill-wide process database and information system.

- Key member of bleach plant implementation core group ($50 million bleach plant capital project).

Pulping Area Supervisor	(1994 - 1995)
Technical Assistant to Paper Mill Superintendent	(1993 - 1994)
Pulp Mill Tour Supervisor	(1990 - 1993)
Technical Assistant to Pulp Mill Superintendent	(1988 - 1990)
Process Engineering Assistant	(1985 - 1988)

EDUCATION:

M.B.A., Arkanses University, 1997
GPA: 3.4/4.0
B.S., Pulp & Paper Science, Oregon State University, 1985
GPA: 3.2/4.0

MILITARY:

United States Navy, 1976 - 1982
Petty Officer, 2nd Class
Interior Communications Technician
Honorable Discharge - September, 1982

STANLEY JONES
43 Shady Lane
Houston, TX 75003
713-952-1384

CAREER SUMMARY

Experienced general manager with significant P&L operations responsibility. Demonstrated ability in building and managing teams which improve profit performance, generating results in all facets of the operation. Contribute equally well in growth and turnaround environments, domestically and internationally.

BUSINESS EXPERIENCE

EXPERT ENGINEERING, A Sanford Laboratory Subsidiary   **1999 to Present**
Vice President Operations

Responsible for operational profitability, plant management and engineering in eight plants throughout North America for this $52 million contract analytical chemistry subsidiary. Direct environmental efforts, customer service and support and material handling. Manage a $30 million operating budget.

- Co-developed a critical joint venture company with another contract laboratory, generating $5.5 million in sales annually from a key $250 million customer.

- Negotiated the acquisition of a competitor whose combined sales will nearly double the East Coast business and position the organization for greater market penetration.

- Successfully directed the design and construction of a leading-edge, 75,000 square foot, $5 million custom analytical laboratory facility, on time and within budget. Additional profits from incremental sales and elimination of shipping costs will exceed $475,000 annually.

NATIONAL LABORATORIES, INC.   **1994 to 1999**
Vice President/General Manager

Total P&L general management responsibility for two distinct businesses generating sales of $20 million annually. Directed sales and marketing, manufacturing, R&D, finance, procurement, and manufacturing representative organizations.

- Turned around the business and reduced scrap an average of 35% for four major customers by developing and launching a sophisticated scanning device for Amatron, a $10 million division manufacturing printing industry control devices.

- Increased national account revenues $1.5 million annually for Microdyne, a custom sterilization division. Effectively accelerated the construction of a mega sterilization chamber, 25% larger than industry standard.

- Accelerated the availability of $950,000 in revenue generation by successfully bringing a plant (75,000 square feet) on-line early while managing all operations of three other sterilization facilities.

BRAXTON, INC.   **1990 to 1994**
Vice President Operations

Managed the profitability and provided the strategic general management direction to worldwide production, corporate manufacturing engineering, distribution, purchasing, and business planning. Directed five manufacturing plants in the United States and Germany with a worldwide staff of 250. Developed and managed the performance of $80 million operating budget and $20 million capital budget.

- Protected a $53 million product line and saved $1.5 million annually through innovative sourcing, negotiation of vendor contracts, and contingency plans.

- Saved $450,000 in material costs annually by managing the launch of MRP II, including executive education, consultant selection, and company-wide implementation strategy.

- Eliminated $625,000 annually in material spoilage by upgrading operational performance through "best demonstrated manufacturing practices" and comprehensive training.

- Averted increased operating costs of at least $500,000 in key pilot plant with 110 employees by successfully turning aside an aggressive union organizing campaign.

DYNAMIC, INC.   **1980 to 1990**
Vice President Manufacturing   1985 - 1990
Director of Manufacturing   1980 - 1985

Directed production activity, domestically and internationally, in nine plants in the United States, Puerto Rico, Japan and Singapore. Managed manufacturing, materials management, engineering, human resources, finance, and distribution. Developed and managed a budget of $300 million and directed 7,500 employees.

- Contributed $20 million in added profits annually by reducing standard costs 10% for three consecutive years. Gains were achieved through manufacturing efficiencies and off-shore sourcing of materials and production of finished goods.

- Eliminated $4 million in operational costs by strategizing and closing a major Illinois manufacturing facility which improved system-wide plant utilization and product closing.

- Provided the strategic manufacturing and business direction for the successful start-up launch, and ongoing operation of highly profitable production plants in Singapore, Japan, and a key joint venture in Shanghai, China. Shipped 400 million units annually within six years.

PREVIOUS BUSINESS EXPERIENCE

As **Director of Manufacturing Engineering** at Vector, Inc. (1974 - 1980), was responsible for operational planning and analysis, engineering process controls, contract packaging, vendor negotiations and production. Installed inventory investment controls for seven divisions, reducing on-hand inventories $70 million while optimizing manufacturing coverage.

While at Duvall Laboratories, Inc., held increasingly responsible technical management and manufacturing management positions from 1972 - 1974.

EDUCATION

M.B.A.   Industrial Management, 1972
           New York University
           New York, NY

B.A.   Economics, Boston University, 1970
           Boston, MA

CYNTHIA R. BUNTING
304 Rolling Hills Lane
Huron, OH 13948
(206) 543-9774   E-Mail: cbunt@aol

Results-oriented manager with extensive experience in high-pressure, time sensitive businesses and proven record of success in on-time delivery of products/services. Innovator in logistics and scheduling for large, complex, 24-hour a day operation. Decision maker/leader with labor union, reengineering/restructuring, OSHA, and employee development background. Team builder/player able to prioritize and supervise employees. Excellent communication and training skills.

FEDERAL EXPRESS CORPORATION   1993 to Present

REGIONAL MANAGER   **2001**-Present
Manage entire operation (ten centers) with over 600 employees including hiring, inventory, and training for large division of this overnight delivery company.

* Oversee daily operations of ten-center division with **50,000 customers** handling over **200,000 packages per day** and annual budget exceeding $32 million.

* Restructured service operation to reduce management and supervisory personnel, saving company **$250,000 per year.**

* Initiated changes in facility and handling procedures, reducing damage to packages and saving company **$500,000 per year.**

* Developed relationships with staff resulting in contract approval with teamsters union by vote of over 80% and simultaneously cut staff by 20%.

TRAINING MANAGER   1994-2001
A special assignment including intensive three month session as training instructor for newly promoted supervisors.

* Trained supervisory personnel from all 52 states on controlling budget and costs.

* Scheduled other instructors and reported directly to Corporate Training Director.

SORT MANAGER   1993-1994
Coordinated all phases of operational start-up for Scan Sort program in Grand Rapids, MI.

* Planned and implemented **start-up** Scan Sort program which handled over 28,000 packages per day from its inception.

EDUCATION

B.A., Business Administration, University of Toledo, Toledo, OH, 1993

CHRISTOPHER WALLACE
3050 Telegraph Road
Decatur, GA 30330

Home: (404) 382-4389   Office: (404) 371-7000

SENIOR LEVEL OPERATIONS EXECUTIVE SUMMARY

Innovative operations executive with a strong background in logistics and customer service processes. A leader with profit and growth motivation who creates a spirited team and is experienced in distribution network, optimization, information systems design, customer consulting and efficient consumer response initiatives.

PROFESSIONAL EXPERIENCE

ALLIED SYSTEMS, Decatur, Georgia   **2000 - Present**
Leading outsourcing company in logistics and distribution with sales of $250 million.

Director of Distribution
Manage Distribution, Customer Service and Transportation for four major Household and Personal Products Manufacturers. Sales targeted to Grocery, Hardware and Mass Merchandiser accounts. Responsibilities include management of carrier, warehouse and customer service personnel, manufacturing and marketing support, customer process integration, systems design and associate development for personal growth and in support of teamwork. Responsible for $125 million operating budget.

ETHYL CORPORATION, Richmond, Virginia   **1993 - 2000**

Distribution Network Operations Manager;
Transportation Manager; National Planning Manager
Managed National Distribution Network for the Corporation ($8 billion sales). Responsibilities included site selection, carrier selection and measurement, construction, hiring and training, system design, network inventory management, customer consulting and operating budget of $320 million.

- Designed and constructed ten distribution centers including all negotiations of leases and purchases and hiring of entire operations staff.
- Designed distribution computer system resulting in significant savings and customer service improvements.
- Implemented RF terminal/scanner paperless warehouse operating system resulting in savings of $6 million.
- Designed and implemented cycle count and inventory control system resulting in zero inventory loss in six years.

Christopher Wallace   **Page Two**

- Motivated, through total employee involvement, distribution teams to virtual zero defect quality levels in shipping accuracy, inventory accuracy, accident prevention and attendance.
- Introduced customer consulting programs for key accounts.
- Designed and implemented a Supplier Quality Program for the Transportation Network resulting in benchmark performance levels in cost and service.
- Developed operating company measurement and reporting systems resulting in order fill rate improvements of 95%, out-of-service transportation cost reductions of $3 million and inventory turn improvements of 6-9 weeks.

JOSLYN CORPORATION, Chicago, Illinois   **1982 - 1993**

Sales and Distribution Service Manager; Transportation Manager; Manufacturing Supervisor; Distribution Manager
Managed customer service operations servicing one-half of the United States.

- Coordinated the design and implementation of ORACLE order entry system resulting in consolidated customer service, transportation and distribution.
- Implemented customer deduction system reducing claims from 1,250 to 225 in on-hand open files.
- Negotiated Teamster contracts resulting in job combinations from 25 job groups to four.

EDUCATION

B.A., Business Management
University of Chicago, 1982

STANLEY BRICE
3105 Summit Avenue
Boston, MA 02349
(508) 246-7832

SUMMARY:

Shirt sleeves manager with a record of consistent success in meeting profit objectives and in using quality management techniques. Focused experience in operations management, TQM, supply management, ISO 9001 and process improvement. Effective leader who creates a results-oriented team environment.

WORK EXPERIENCE: The Aircoil Company, Mansfield, MA

Director, Quality Systems (1998-Present)
- Reduced, by 28%, nonconformances in the contract review and design control areas through the use of process mapping and benchmarking.
- Led a company of 1800 employees through the ISO 9001 process and received registration. The undertaking was a major project and required proven project management skills.
- Trained personnel in the use of TQM, facilitated team building and benchmarking initiatives.

Director, Supply Management (1995-1998)
- Developed suppliers and negotiated terms for $132M (annual) purchase of material.
- Reduced the number of approved suppliers from 3000 to 800.
- Managed a supplier quality control group and instituted a supplier certification program that resulted in an increase in on-time delivery from 84% to 95% and a decrease in defects by 23%.

Plant Manager - Multiple Plants, Assembly & Distribution (1989-1995)
- Increased gross margin 60% by consolidating operations and cutting overtime from 23% to 8% while directing a $7M, 125-employee plant. Responsible for profit and loss, engineering, machining, purchasing, inventory control, building facilities and union negotiations.
- Boosted turns ratio from 2 to 3.5 on $1.5M inventory by cycle counting.

Project Manager, Air Conditioner Parts Operations (1984-1989)
- Expanded sales from $1.8M to $4.2M by increasing direct customer contact and developing several supplier partnering agreements. Reduced cycle time of proposal and contract administration functions by introducing electronic documentation.

Prior to 1984
- Test engineering, R&D, mechanical and electrical design.

EDUCATION: B.S. - Mechanical Engineering, Boston University

LAURA McKINLEY
902 FORT WASHINGTON DRIVE
ST. LOUIS, MO 45782
(314) 344-7529

An Operations professional with a demonstrated record of achievement in manufacturing management, material control, and quality. Results oriented with experience in planning and implementing production strategies and control projects that contribute to the bottom line. Team player, solid interpersonal skills, strong commitment.

OBJECTIVE: Executive manufacturing position with plant operations responsibility.

PROFESSIONAL EXPERIENCE:

1988 - Present   **ALCAN METAL GOODS**
Fasteners Division, St. Louis, MO

International manufacturer of hardware supplies with sales of $700 million. Certified ISO 9001.

(2000 - Present)   DIVISION MANAGER, TOTAL QUALITY

Responsible for implementation and management of divisional strategy based on a system of prevention and continuous improvement utilizing employee involvement. Crosby concepts form the foundation of the process. Scope includes corporate, sales, R&D, as well as seven International and U.S. based manufacturing facilities. Certified Crosby instructor, trained ISO 9000 internal auditor.

- Planned and completed education of 7500 employees in the concepts of continuous improvement.
- Established requirements in concert with internal and external customers, vendors and supporting business units to eliminate non-conformance and improve business processes.
- Savings of $14MM achieved by identifying and reducing non-conformance.
- Achieved reduction of divisional finished goods reject rate by 60%.
- Implemented cross-functional corrective action and customer/supplier interface teams.
- Provided guidance and support to other divisions and international subsidiaries.

(1998 - 2000)   PLANT MANAGER, FASTENERS

Managed all administrative and manufacturing activities for this multi-functional, multi-facility operation of 820 employees.

Laura McKinley
Page 2

Responsibilities included new product and equipment pilot trials, technology transfer, validation and new product launch interfacing with divisional groups of R&D, Advanced Engineering and Q.A. which reside at plant site. Responsibilities included manufacturing, quality control, materials management, safety and environment, human resources and engineering.

- Achieved annual cost reductions in excess of $2 million.
- Implemented cellular manufacturing reducing lead time by 18% while improving productivity 13% within a four-month period.
- Held indirect operating cost budgets to a 4% increase over a four year time frame offsetting inflation and minimizing cost impact during a period of 20% growth in volume.
- Improved quality, reducing lot rejection by 70%.
- Implemented TQM and chaired the Quality Improvement Team utilizing the Crosby approach.
- Led five successful contract negotiations within an aggressive union environment.
- Managed global and multi-plant task groups to determine global production strategies and plant loading. Task group decisions estimated to save $4 million annually.
- Participated in implementation of MRP and SFC. Trained in SPC. Responsible for compliance to FDA, OSHA, DEP and EPA regulations.
- Recognized as "Global Plant Manager of the Year" in 1999 (the first and only recipient).

(1994 - 1998) PLANT MANAGER, HAND TOOLS

Managed all hand tools production, shop floor scheduling, manufacturing, engineering, and safety for a 750 employee operation.

(1992 - 1994) OPERATIONS MANAGER

Responsible for all hand tools production and related components encompassing 600 employees.

(1990 - 1992) PRODUCTION MANAGER

Responsible for all hand tools assembly and packaging with operations consisting of 260 employees and an $9.2M budget.

(1988 - 1990) PRODUCTION SUPERVISOR

EDUCATION:
- Bachelor of Science-Mechanical Engineering
  Saint Louis University, 1988

- Attended Washington University M.B.A. Program, 1996-1998

PROFESSIONAL AFFILIATIONS:

- Health Industry Manufacturing Association (H.I.M.A.)
- American Society for Quality Control (A.S.Q.C.)

KARLENE S. DAWSON

9 Eagle View Road • Asheville, NC 87163
Office: (912) 874-1739 • Home: (912) 775-2839

SUMMARY:

Technical Director having extensive quality, scientific and operations management experience with a continuous record of increased responsibility and demonstrated excellence in the pharmaceutical/chemical industry. Broad quality perspective, results oriented and technically current.

PROFESSIONAL EXPERIENCE:

BAVER LABORATORIES, INCORPORATED - Wilton, NC   **2001 - Present**
Director of Quality Control
Direct the Quality Control Department and four Lab Groups.
- Led operation into compliance with FDA expectations by restructuring the operations, implementing interlocked tracking logs, upgrading training, taking charge of the methods function, and upgrading the staff.
- Designed, equipped and staffed five new lab buildings, with a budget of $6MM, to meet ISO 9000 standards.
- Directed the development and validation of equipment, tests, methods and procedures in support of meeting CGMPs and GALPs.

TECHNO LABORATORIES, INCORPORATED - Burton, GA   **1995 - 2001**
Manager Laboratory Quality Assurance
Led the Laboratory QA function.
- Developed and implemented systems for lab operations, staffing and auditing including the design of labs (2). Budget $5MM.
- Developed, implemented and managed systems for: sample tracking, raw materials, in process label control, CGMP compliance, stability testing and LIMS ($2MM) as well as methods development and validation.

WAVERLY CHEMICAL CO. - Wrightsville, GA   **1988 - 1995**
Senior Research Chemist (1990-1995)
Supervised a biocides residue/impurities lab and assisted in formulations development.
Research Chemist (1988-1990)

EDUCATION:

UNIVERSITY OF VIRGINIA
  Ph.D., Analytical Chemistry   **1988**

  M.S., Inorganic Chemistry   **1986**

URSINUS COLLEGE - Collegeville, PA   **1984**
  B.A., Chemistry

RICHARD CHAMBERLAIN

2392 South Beach Street   Los Angeles, California 90054   (310) 614-4385
Office: (310) 743-7550

PROFILE

An accomplished professional with fifteen plus years of solid "hands on" background and "practical" experience, encompassing all aspects of package design and development. Well versed in a wide variety of packaging concepts and componentry with superior knowledge relating to primary and secondary manufacturing processes. Equally versed in a variety of project management techniques, with proven ability to effectively define, plan and implement and administrate all project related activity of substance. A pragmatic self-starter who can easily grasp corporate objectives and can respond to same in a most favorable and consistent manner.

PROFESSIONAL EXPERIENCE

MERLE NORMAN COSMETICS – Los Angeles, California (2000 - Present)
A $4.1 billion manufacturer of and direct marketer of cosmetic products.

Manager - Technical Package Development

Focus: Provide technical direction for <u>conceptual</u> development of new packages (Skin Moisturizers). Define, plan, implement and manage all aspects of <u>technical</u> development from concept approval to first production, including initial performance and compatibility testing.

Selected Accomplishments:
·   *Developed 18+ new packages (2001) supporting Skin Moisturizer sales in excess of $190 million.*
·   *Reduced conceptual and final package development time frames 25% via Concurrent Activity Planning and timely follow-up.*
·   *Reduced manufacturing costs $500,000 (2001) via aggressive value analysis, planning and implementation of viable projects.*

GARTNER GROUP, INC. – Stamford, Connecticut (1998 - 2000)
An innovative, multi faceted group, structured to provide technical assessment, direction and administrative support to all major markets.

President of Operations
Focus: Provide technical direction for the conceptual design and development of new packaging, including cost effective redesign of existing. Assist clients in evaluating/improving facilities, planning project objectives, developing time frames and cost structure favorable to marketing strategies. Manage contracted projects from conception to first production.

Selected Accomplishments:
·   *Participated in the evaluation of a Fortune 500 manufacturing facility. Increased production efficiencies 40%.*
·   *Improved condition, integrity and efficiency of first generation production tooling (hair shampoo package) 30%.*
·   *Directed the design, construction and qualification of second generation tooling, improving efficiencies an additional 20%.*

PFIZER, INC. – **CONSUMER PRODUCTS** – New York, New York (1995 - 1998)
A $7.1 billion manufacturer of cosmetics and consumer products.

Senior Tool Engineer
Focus: Provide technical direction for the design and development of general packaging and product delivery systems. Manage approved tooling projects obtaining desired part quality, performance and manufacturing efficiencies. Manage corporate asset base (custom tooling) maintaining condition, integrity and production capability throughout planned life.

RICHARD CHAMBERLAIN

. . . .

Selected Accomplishments:
· *Analyzed tooling capacity of core product line. Developed/incorporated a comprehensive tool maintenance program, extending tooling life 50%.*
· *Developed/implemented a capital project reporting system. Eliminated unauthorized spending. Improved development time frames 20%.*
· *Evaluated supplier resources. Integrated selected activities with internal resource activities, reducing internal labor 15%.*

KENNER PRODUCTS – Cincinnati, Ohio (1990 - 1995)
A $325MM manufacturer of children's toys.

Project Manager - Specialty Tooling
Focus: Provide technical direction in the design and development of cost effective packaging and/or assembled activity products. Define, plan, implement and manage approved tooling projects in support of design objectives. Manage corporate asset base via timely assessment and direction for repair, refurbishment and/or replacement as needed to meet business needs.

Selected Accomplishments:
· *Proposed aggressive Vertical Integration Plans. Utilized $750,000 funding and reduced manufacturing costs $800,000 first year. Coordinated project team focus and efforts second year and collectively reduced manufacturing costs an additional $1,200,000.*
· *Proposed and implemented value added revisions to a failing product line, resulting in product resurrection and $200,000 additional sales (patent awarded). Initiated development of a sister product and increased sales an additional $150,000.*
· *Evaluated competitor product infringement. Developed alternate design recovering lost annual sales in excess of $200,000 (patent awarded).*
· *Developed off-shore tooling support centers in Portugal, England and Switzerland. Reduced annual tooling investment 30%.*
· *Developed and incorporated a Specialty Tooling Data Base for accurate tracking of 300+ custom tools. Data Base instrumental in developing annual budgets and curtailing unnecessary spending on obsolete product lines.*

LAKEVILLE PRECISION MOLDING – Lakeville, Connecticut (1985 - 1990)
A respected leader in the design and construction of custom injection mold tooling used in plastic part fabrication.

Senior Mold Engineer
Focus: Assist client base in the design and development of complex plastic componentry. Recommend revisions where possible for most cost effective molding, decorating and assembly. Design custom tooling, coordinating efforts of engineering and contracted support services. Manage all aspects of construction, qualification testing and revision where needed to meet part design and/or tool performance objectives.

Selected Accomplishments:
· *Participated in the design and development of a proprietary product line, contributing to corporate exposure, growth and profitability. Later, proposed/assisted in development of custom assembly equipment reducing manufacturing costs 23%.*
· *Developed a unique mechanical device to facilitate "in mold" closing of a complex fitment, reducing assembly costs 17%.*
· *Developed various in-house engineering standards, formats and procedures reducing mold development time frames 18%.*

EDUCATION

B.S., Packaging Engineering
Clarkson University, 1985

STANLEY GOODMAN   10 Peachtree Lane, Little Silver, NJ 07648

Office: (201) 934-1705   Home: (201) 934-5667

Senior packaging/purchasing executive with extensive experience in developing and launching new products for the fragrance and cosmetic industry. Broad technical expertise in saleable and promotional packaging, point-of-purchase displays, manufacturing processes and supplier capabilities. Direct complex projects and coordinate effectively with marketing, design, sales, and operations. Develop strategic partnerships with global supplier base. Strong track record in managing staff & budgets.

PROFESSIONAL EXPERIENCE

REVLON COSMETICS CO., Red Bank, New Jersey   **1996-Present**

Senior Director of Package Development
Oversaw and implemented all new brand introductions, seasonal promotional programs, and point-of-purchase displays. Led the development process from the brainstorming stage through final production. Worked closely with marketing/creative departments to determine the feasibility of all projects. Also provided project leadership and tracking for the operations teams.

- Directed the team that launched four of the most successful fragrances in the U.S. (*Ecstacy, Ecstacy for Men, Enrapture, Enrapture for Men*). Opened the Asian market to *Loving and Loving for Men*, which paved the way for the full roll-out of all other brands.

- Technical advisor to Chairman of the Board, his staff, and other recognized designers during the early design stages. This accelerated the process and enhanced the final package quality.

- Converted all saleable SKU's to a universal package design that is environmentally and legally acceptable worldwide. The universal package:
  - reduced corporate inventory by 30%
  - provided major administrative efficiencies in most departments

- Managed, within budget, the $4.0MM capital account for tools, dies, molds, prep and separations for all brands. Controlled the packaging general ledger expenses of $1.5MM.

- Initiated computerization that reduced development time and improved the accuracy of cost estimates and BOM's. Introduced electronically transmitted art work to graphic suppliers.

MAYBELLINE COMPANY, New York, NY   **1994-1996**

Group Director, Group I Cosmetics
Developed, specified and coordinated the production of packages for 250 projects in Maybelline's core cosmetic business. Associated closely with new product marketing to develop patented products such as a nail enamel pen, three-in-one eye shadow palette and nail gel.

- Built and motivated a packaging team of five that controlled multiple new product launches and provided promotional support for those programs.

138

STANLEY GOODMAN   **Page Two**

- Engineered the redesign of the eye and face compact line to an open cell presentation which greatly improved the product merchantability.

BEAUTY, INC., New York, NY   **1989-1994**

Package Development Manager, 1991-1994
Controlled prestige fragrance and cosmetic development for designer brands (Caress, Embraceable, Pour Homme and Béaute). Introduced new product launches, seasonal promotions, point-of-purchase displays, and brand maintenance.

Purchasing Manager, 1990-1991
Managed supplier selection, purchase and delivery of all primary packaging ($14MM) with a team of four.

- Negotiated annual contracts for major commodities (glass, pumps). Monitored performance against contracts on an ongoing basis.

Senior Purchasing Agent, 1989-1990
Responsible for the purchase and delivery of folding cartons and custom injection molding.

MILANO COSMETICS, Princeton, NJ   **1984-1989**

Buyer of Packaging Components and Chemicals

- Purchased primary and secondary components and controlled subcontract filling/assembly for Sophia and Gatsby divisions.

- Bought 12 raw materials that were purchased under a corporate contract for use in all domestic factories.

ARMOUR CHEMICAL CO., Schenectady, NY   **1982-1984**

Sales Representative

- Serviced major existing accounts and cold-called to develop new business for resins.

- Completed 12-month marketing/sales trainee program in nine months.

EDUCATION

B.S., Business Administration, University of Connecticut   1982

DAVID PALMER
205 Round Hill Road
Greenwich, CT 06904
(213) 552-9374

PROFILE:	Results-oriented mechanical engineer with over seven years experience in project management, process engineering and project engineering with a technology leader. Accomplished project manager with ability to clearly define project goals and effectively use resources to achieve them.

PROFESSIONAL EXPERIENCE:

ANALYSIS & TECHNOLOGY, INC., North Stonington, CT (1994 - Present)

Project Manager, Fibers Division (1999 - Present)

- Selected to serve as project manager for Abbot Laboratories. Work with Abbott's Advanced Product Engineers on all aspects of launching a new category of surgical sutures including suture design, material selection, prototype design, failure mode analysis, field trial and production start-up.
- Managed development of new technology to streamline manufacturing process. Directed research efforts of Fiber Products Division to develop a super absorbent polymer structure. Worked with customers to refine the process. Applied for a patent on the streamlined process.

Project Engineer, Fibers Division (1996 - 1999)

- Championed the effort to prevent loss of $3.5 million/year Berlex Laboratories' account due to severe product defects. Directed the efforts of Berlex's material development and manufacturing teams and designers to redesign the materials and manufacturing process. Verified improvements through field tests.
- Collaborated on the development of a patented fluid absorption test.

Process Engineer, Laminated Products Division (1994 - 1996)

- Led a team of 15 manufacturing associates in the start-up of a new fabric lamination production line. Determined process condition for 13 products. Standardized operating procedures to ensure products met specifications. Resulted in $11.5 million annual sales.
- Designed and conducted a statistical experiment to study the effect of four process variables on polymer lamination. Identified key variable which had the most impact. Significantly reduced time and cost to isolate this variable.

EDUCATION:

Bachelor of Science in Materials Science, 1994
Massachusetts Institute of Technology, Cambridge, MA

PROFESSIONAL TRAINING:

Introduction to Designed Experiments and Data Analysis (1994)
Strategy of Experimentation (1994)
Theory of Manufacturing Constraints (1996)
Leadership Effectiveness Training (1996)
Critical Problem Solving (1997)
Critical Problem Solving (1998)
Effective Communicating (1999)

MARVIN C. DRUMOND
1214 Overlook Pass
Costa Mesa, CA 38495
(714) 972-1392   E-Mail: MarDrum@MSN

OBJECTIVE

Engineering management position requiring experience in chemical plant design and start-up in the medical products or aircraft industries.

EXPERIENCE

PHARMA MEDICAL PRODUCTS INC., Los Angeles, CA　　　**1998-PRESENT**
Manager, Process Engineering

Responsible for maintaining existing operations, quality of inventory maintenance and warehousing. As part of the Research and Development function, led the design group in the development of concepts into products and manufacturing processes. Report to Senior Director, Research & Development for this $420MM manufacturer of surgical dressings.

- Improved prototype process for manufacturing of surgical dressings using existing equipment resulting in a five-fold increase in production.
- Improved equipment uptime to 95%.
- As Project Manger for a $60 million absorbent dressing manufacturing operation, developed and installed integrated processes capable of producing 10 million cases per year.
- Managed various aspects of development and construction of $30 million advanced Research & Development Facility.

PRATT & WHITNEY, East Hartford, CT　　　**1992-1998**
Mechanical Design Engineer

Responsible for evaluating aircraft gas turbine engine hardware for fit and function relative to engine performance. Reported to Director of Engineering.

- Coordinated the redesign or modification of parts.
- Evaluated tooling for high volume production of large and small castings to ensure machinability and proper function/fit in products.
- Evaluated and approved all casting layouts provided by vendors, and served as the sole approving authority for all casting tools used at Pratt & Whitney.
- Performed extensive interface with vendors and coordinated corrective action for defective casting and machining operations.
- Audited mechanical design of jet engines.

EDUCATION

B.S., Chemical Engineering, Drexel University, Philadelphia, PA, 1992

DANIEL WALKER, P.E.

4 Hubbard Street	Bus: (312) 762-7000
Chicago, IL 60643	Res: (312) 641-3491

OBJECTIVE: Vice President or Director of Engineering position

EDUCATION: **M.B.A.**
Villanova University, Villanova, PA (1992)

B.S. - Mechanical Engineering
Cornell University, Ithaca, NY (1986)

SUMMARY: Fourteen years diverse engineering experience mostly with customer division of $6 billion multinational consumer products corporation.

- Managed and provided strategic leadership for various Engineering organizations;
- Developed and implemented leading edge Computer Integrated Manufacturing (CM) systems;
- Designed, fabricated and developed proprietary, state-of-the-art high speed automated machinery;
- Developed and implemented strategic vision for engineering;
- Championed implementation of innovative technology;
- Demonstrated superior skills in managing technical people and projects;
- Design to Market champion with extensive project work and coordination.

ATTRIBUTES: Highly professional, organized and demanding management style. Strong leadership and conflict management skills. Proven technical and design competency. Broad-based, accomplished computer knowledge and skills. Outstanding track record for meeting goals and objectives through teamwork. Sound businessman. High energy. Results oriented. Decisive. Committed. Interface with all levels of management. Good listener and communicator. People oriented. Entrepreneurial, takes chances.

PROFESSIONAL EXPERIENCE:

NATIONAL PRODUCTS CORPORATION, Chicago, IL   1986-Present

1999 to Present **DIRECTOR OF ENGINEERING**
Responsible for all technical operations in support of ten manufacturing locations for this $12 billion consumer products manufacturer. Recruited, developed and managed 225 person technical staff. Accountable for $300 million capital and $90 million operational budget. Established organizational objectives and initiatives in line with corporate goals and strategies. Responsible for discovery and assessment of new product and process acquisitions. Evaluate technical capability and processability including level of automation through due diligence process. Managed facilities, energy programs, pollution prevention and environmental compliance efforts. Selected accomplishments include:

- Planned, developed and implemented strategic engineering, re-organization;
- Core team member for major new product launch. Exceeded all program goals;
- Established world-wide communication and team-building programs;
- Attained tenfold increase in knife life utilizing design of experiments, metallurgical and advanced FEA structural analysis;

Daniel Walker, P.E.

- Reduced top consumer complaint quality problem by 40%;
- Reviewed and approved four pending product acquisitions;
- Consolidated three manufacturing operations to one location with no disruption to customer service.

1996-1999 **PROGRAM MANAGER,** *Computer Integrated Manufacturing (CIM)*
Researched, designed and implemented integrated manufacturing software solutions in concert with company's World Class initiatives. Managed team of six direct reports and 30 outside consultants. The $25 million project scope included hardware and software selection, vendor and subcontractor negotiations and project management and coordination. Selected accomplishments:

- Installed leading edge shop floor process control and material tracking system employing 90+ work stations, multiple file servers and LAN's in two manufacturing plants;
- Reduced downtime outages by 25% through accurate data capture and reporting;
- Achieved targeted cost savings via waste containment and obsolete parts reduction;
- Spearheaded academic/industry liaisons with MIT, CMU, Duke, RPI and Bellcore;
- Partnered with Microsoft (beta test site) while establishing advanced working knowledge of leading edge PC LAN technology and networking;
- Installed 20 seat file server-based networked CAD system using AutoCAD.

1992-1996 **PLANT ENGINEERING GROUP MANAGER**
Responsible for plant equipment performance, secondary development and maintenance plant-wide. Managed staff of 12 engineers and 85 craftsmen. Coordinated new product introductions. Implemented major operating cost reduction programs. Selected accomplishments include:

- Aggressively recruited and upgraded personnel to increase department capability. Redesigned job responsibilities and implemented measurable performance objectives;
- Managed $2.5 million department budget. Reduced administrative spending by 12% each year while initiating aggressive operating cost cutting programs saving over $110,000 annually;
- Established intensive PM program and repair part testing program reducing plant downtime;
- Attacked plant fire safety issues (fire rate reduction of 30%). Received National Products Achievement Award recognizing my department's machine safety guarding effort corporate-wide.

1990-1992 **SENIOR DESIGN ENGINEER**
Advanced rapidly from *Associate Engineer* position. Performed conceptual design of new products and processes. Managed and supervised the design, detailing and fabrication of $10 million machine design program. Exceeded overall program requirements. Installed machinery at multiple international locations. Developed and implemented various process and productivity enhancements.

1986-1990 **DESIGN ENGINEER**

OTHER: **Professional Engineer,** IL License 54396, 1992
National Products Achievement Award Winner, 1994, 1996, 1998
Member of the National Society of Professional Engineers

HAROLD HOBBS
23 Parkersville Road
Kennett Square, PA 19384
(610) 388-1284

SUMMARY

Twenty-five years of professional experience as an engineer and manager. Management and technical achievements in process and plant floor engineering; project management; sensors; measurement systems and methods; product and equipment development and engineering; and environmental technology. Significant experience in metals, chemicals, energy, and plastics industries. Results oriented with strengths in leadership, organization, and interpersonal skills; and the ability to drive implementation of manufacturing technology improvements.

PROFESSIONAL EXPERIENCE

BATES & COMPANY, Kennett Square, PA   **1999 to Present**

Section Head, Measurement Technology

- Identified customer needs, managed programs, and provided leadership for the development and implementation of solutions involving: sensors, measurement systems, non-destructive evaluation (NDE) methods and instrumentation—for plants throughout Bates.

- Directed work of a diverse mix of technologists: material, electrical, mechanical, and chemical engineers; physicists; and consultants—to the resolution of historically difficult industry-wide problems and implementation of the technology in Bates' plants (e.g., automated ultrasonic plate inspection, in mill plate temperature measurement, non-contact sheet flatness measurement).

- Commercialized instrument products/technology; some marketed and sold worldwide.

COASTAL STATES OIL & GAS, Oklahoma City, OK   **1990 to 1999**

Senior Engineering Associate, Process Engineering	**1997 - 1999**
Program Director, Process Engineering	**1993 - 1997**
Senior Research Engineer, Process Development	**1990 - 1993**

- Saved over $4.5MM annually with developed natural gas processing technology. Provided engineering and tech support to field sites processing natural gas and refinery fuel gas.

- Conceived and championed through approval, a $21MM program designed to ready Coastal and its venture partner, Texas Oil, for the commercialization of oil shale conversion and to develop the design data for a commercial plant.

- Built and managed a multi-company team for the resulting program, including the logistics and relationships between Texas Oil, Coastal States and representatives of Kuwaiti Oil, the licensee of the technology. The results-oriented team peaked at well over 150 people and successfully executed the above program.

- Served as Project Manager for the design and construction of the $9.2MM grass roots processing facility. It was the first-of-its-kind and was completed on time and within budget.

HAROLD HOBBS....   page two

COASTAL STATES (cont'd)

- Designed and installed an integrated process control and data management system with feedback from many instruments and sensors, monitoring process and stream conditions, quantities, and compositions.

- Developed chemical products and processes; e.g., indene and vinyl toluene.

- Reduced catalyst consumption by developing a process that was implemented in refineries for removing impurities of oxygenated compounds from HF alkylation feedstock.

HERCULES & COMPANY, Oklahoma, City, OK   1987 to 1990
Research Engineer

- Reduced SO_2 sorbent requirement in fluidized bed combustion (FBC) coal boilers by at least 60% with developed high temperature sorbent regeneration process. Received Hercules Recognition Award in 1989.

- Developed several instruments for FBC coal boilers.

MIT, Boston, MA   1985 to 1987
Instructor and Consultant

- Consulted on air pollution control and taught undergraduate engineering mathematics.

CHRYSLER CORPORATION, Detroit, MI   1983 to 1985
Engineer

- Provided engineering design, testing, and technical support for injection molding, extrusion, and other fabrication processes for plastic components. Conceived and developed new application of molded glass-filled polyolefin mechanical body components which was commercialized by Chrysler.

EDUCATION

Ph.D., Chemical Engineering, Cornell University, Ithaca, NY - 1983
B.S., Chemical Engineering, Pennsylvania State University, State College, PA - 1979

HONORS & AWARDS

- Honorary Engineering Member of Tau Omega Pi, 1975.
- Outstanding Employee Contributions Award, Coastal States, 1992 and 1997.
- Honorary Scientific Member of Sigma Pi, 1998.
- Keynote Speaker, 1999 International Engineering Association Conference, Hamburg, Germany.
- 4 Patents, 17 Publications.

JEFFREY McGINTY, P.E.
6 Hemlock Street
Fairfield, CT 06693
(203) 834-2358

OBJECTIVE:

Management position utilizing extensive experience in manufacturing, engineering and project management.

CAREER SUMMARY:

Fourteen years of progressively responsible positions in Engineering and Operations Management with expertise in design, start-up, project management, system optimization, productivity improvement, organizational design/development, manufacturing, inventory control and distribution.

BUSINESS EXPERIENCE:

GENERAL ELECTRIC CORPORATION, Fairfield, CT   1994 to Present

Technical Services Manager (2000 – Present)
- Responsible for Site Engineering, Maintenance, Quality Control and Sanitation.
- Developed and implemented programs to improve QC Department effectiveness and response time.
- Utilized team-based methodology to upgrade site OSHA and GMP compliance.
- Delivered significant cost reductions ($1M) through electric rate savings and packaging line automation.
- Utilized TOM principles to improve utility department efficiencies and emergency preparedness.
- Managed site SARA Title III programs.
- Developed and executed water and sewer contracts with the local municipality.

Group Engineering Manager (1999 – 2000)
- Multiple plant responsibility.
- Reduced natural gas costs by 37%.
- Developed and installed automated material handling system which reduced costs by $420K annually.
- Developed a team-based manufacturing organization.
- Implemented programs which reduced equipment downtime by 32%.
- Developed and installed equipment Vision Systems and automation which reduced costs by $210K annually.
- Automated the plant's finished goods inventory control system (4m cubic foot warehouse).

JEFFREY McGINTY, P.E.

Plant Engineering Manager (1996 – 1999)
- Managed department of 40 professional and 65 hourly employees.
- Developed and implemented manufacturing line improvements which increased output by 40%.
- Converted manufacturing equipment to PLC controls.
- Sourced equipment from Korea and Japan to reduce costs and improve deliveries.
- Responsible for $35M capital budget.

Engineering Supervisor (1994 – 1996)
- Managed department of six professional and 80 hourly employees.
- Responsible for $4.2M annual fixed budget and $8.3M capital budget.
- Implemented automated work order and maintenance management system.

CERTAINTEED CORPORATION, Stamford, CT   1993 to 1994

Operations Manager
- Multiple plant responsibility.
- Managed all aspects of window and door manufacturing, warehousing and distribution operation.
- Developed and implemented a bonus program based on team performance.
- Improved customer service and product quality using TQM principles.
- Reduced manufacturing cost per unit by 10%.

BLACK & DECKER CORPORATION, Shelton, CT   1988 to 1993

Project Manager   (1992 – 1993)

Field Engineer   (1990 – 1992)

Systems Engineer   (1988 – 1990)

PROFESSIONAL CERTIFICATE:

Registered Professional Engineer, State of Connecticut.

EDUCATION:

Master of Business Administration, University of Connecticut   1988

Master of Science, Mechanical Engineering and Metallurgy
Cornell University   1987

Bachelor of Science, Mechanical Engineering, Cornell University   1985

Kimberly Bailey, Ph.D., D.A.B.T., R.A.C.

4 Wheeler Avenue
New Brunswick, NJ 08849
(908) 782-8461 (residence)
(908) 594-3000 (office)
(908) 594-3403 (fax)

QUALIFICATIONS SUMMARY

Extensive experience evaluating the safety of drugs including biologics and a major fat substitute; training/ experience writing INDs, NDAs, PLAs, ELAs and food additive petitions; received regulatory concessions from FDA for approval of new drugs and a fat substitute where test requirements were in a state of flux; obtained funding and managed multi-million dollar safety/toxicity test programs; achieved time/cost savings via competitive bidding and strategic placement of study "packages". Board certified in toxicology and regulatory affairs. Based on this training and experience, a position managing drug safety and/or regulatory affairs at a small- to medium-sized biopharmaceutical/pharmaceutical company would be a good fit.

PROFESSIONAL HISTORY

[1998-present] **Merck & Company, Rahway, NJ**

<u>Director, Preclinical and Clinical EPG Safety Test Program</u>

- Direct the design and conduct of all IND/NDA type preclinical and clinical safety studies to obtain world-wide approval for a low- to no-calorie fat substitute. Responsible for the toxicologic/histopathologic interpretation of data. Manage 15 professionals/five clinical consultants who supported safety studies.

- Successfully influenced FDA and Canada's HPB regulatory approval policy for novel foods/macro additives through private meetings as well as industry activities: publications, FDA/industry sponsored workshops to review/resolve technical issues. Obtained project compliance with GLPs, GCPs, and GMPs.

- Obtained multi-million dollar funding for the safety test program of a new fat substitute working with the executive management of Merck & Company and, most recently, a major chemical company.

- Negotiated and managed a total of over $25 million in contracts at nine outside research facilities. Through competitive bidding and strategic placement of preclinical and clinical safety studies, saved over $3.2 million and 1-3 years off a 4-6 year program.

[1996-98] **Loctite Corporation, Hartford, CT**

<u>Toxicology Consultant/Expert Witness</u>

- Successfully resolved technical issues in Products' Liability, Workmen's Compensation, and DUI cases.

[1994-96] **Abbott Laboratories, Drug Safety Evaluation Department, Abbott Park, IL**

<u>Group Leader - Toxicology</u>

- Served on interdisciplinary project teams for the development and safety evaluation of numerous pharmaceuticals and biologics.

- Set up the in-house GLP-compliant toxicology laboratory for dog, rabbit, mouse and rat studies.

- Managed eight professionals as Group Leader in General Toxicology.

- Directed the planning, scheduling and conduct of in-house and most contract lab drug safety studies.

Kimberly Bailey, Ph.D., D.A.B.T., R.A.C.
Page 2

- Authored numerous preclinical summaries for INDs submitted to FDA in support of new drugs while at Abbott Laboratories.

- Reviewed INDs and NDAs prior to their filing. Negotiated safety test programs for various drug candidates with FDA's CDER.

- Reviewed safety data on new drugs for several potential acquisitions.

- Designed and reviewed protocols and data from clinical studies with particular drug safety issues.

[1988-94] Purdue University, School of Pharmacy, West Lafayette, IN

<u>Assistant Professor of Pharmacology & Toxicology</u> - Tenure granted

- Established and administered this graduate toxicology program which maximally had an enrollment of 30 students. Chairman or co-chairman of doctoral committees for nine graduate students.

- Managed five technicians in a NIDA research program on narcotic drug toxicity related to metabolism.

- While at Purdue, Toxicology Consultant/Expert Witness in FDA Food Adulteration, Products' Liability, and Medical Malpractice cases.

[1986-88] Alcon Laboratories, Inc., Fort Worth, TX

<u>Staff Toxicologist and Study Director</u>

- Managed four technicians in conduct of various toxicity/safety studies.

EDUCATION and TRAINING

[1986-88] **NIH Post Doctoral Trainee in Toxicology** - Schools of Medicine, Public Health and Pharmacy, University of Texas, Austin, Texas

[1986] **Ph.D. in Toxicology** - NIH Predoctoral Trainee, University of Arizona, Department of Pharmacology & Toxicology, School of Medicine, Tempe, AZ

[1980] **B.S. in Biochemistry** - Department of Biochemistry, North Carolina State University, Raleigh, NC

PROFESSIONAL CERTIFICATION

[1999] **Regulatory Affairs Certification [R.A.C.]** - Certified by the Regulatory Affairs Certification Board for biologics, drugs and medical devices.
[1994] **Diplomate, American Board of Toxicology [D.A.B.T.]** - Recertified in 1996 and 1999.
[1989-present] **Expert in Toxicology** - Recognized by various State and Federal Courts.

MEMBERSHIPS in PROFESSIONAL ORGANIZATIONS

- Society of Toxicology
- American College of Toxicology
- International Society of Regulatory Toxicology and Pharmacology
- International Society of Ecotoxicology and Environmental Safety

EDWARD DODGE, Ph.D.

9023 Post Oak Road   (713) 952-1148 Home
Houston, TX 77015   (713) 668-6725 Office

SUMMARY

Manager with over 17 years experience in plant start-up, product development, process development and business development. A troubleshooter with broad range of contributions spanning process technology, new business development, marketing, and strategic planning. B.S., M.S. and Ph.D. degrees in Chemical Engineering from Cornell University.

EXPERIENCE

TEXACO CHEMICAL, Houston, Texas   **2000 - Present**
A $1 billion chemicals and petroleum refining company.

Manager, **Development**

- Responsible for process design, process development, and manufacturing assistance at R&D center.

- Manage 45 professionals. Member of the new business development strategy team.

THIOKOL CORPORATION, Akron, Ohio   **1984 – 2000**
Diversified manufacturer of chemicals and propellent systems for the aerospace and defense industries. Annual sales $2.5 billion.

Manager, **Aerospace & Defense Products**   1998 - 2000

- Assumed P&L responsibility for a $325 million/year business segment with a pre-tax profit of $30 million.

Manager, **Business Development**   1995 - 1998

- Responsible for R&D, manufacturing and marketing new products with a focus on aerospace and defense applications.

- Managed a proposed joint venture to manufacture and market rocket propellent with a minimum of $45 million annually.

- Responsible for a $25 million government contract to develop a liquid gun propellant. Full deployment could result in a new $250 million/year business for Thiokol by end of decade. First orders obtained in 1996 and 1997 exceeded $6.7 million.

- Headed a joint development program for a leading new candidate for advanced bomb fill as part of the Department of Defense's mandate for insensitive munitions. Sales exceeded $2.5 million through 1997; could grow to $200+ million annually by 2010.

EDWARD DODGE, Ph.D.   Page Two

Manager, New Product Development   1991 - 1995

· Transferred to the Technology Center, which was established to focus on new strategic businesses in specialty chemicals. Successfully managed the following programs:
  - Test marketing of residential water treatment systems.
  - Test marketing of revolutionary new electronic coating.
  - Commercialization of an automatic chemical feed system for the electronics industry.

Manager, Process Technology   1989 - 1991

· Organized and staffed a new department and led a development effort in a newly-acquired polymers additive business. Directed a $2.3 million R&D budget. Constructed a multi-million dollar semi-works unit to commercialize new products. Successfully commercialized four new specialty chemicals increasing sales by 27% annually.

· As Technology Representative on a long-range planning task force, identified potential new thrust areas for Thiokol. As a direct result, in 1990, Thiokol acquired National Chemical Corporation, an electronic chemicals company.

Senior Group Leader   1987 - 1989

Project Leader   1984 - 1987

EDUCATION

Cornell University, Ithaca, New York
    Ph.D. in Chemical Engineering   1984
    M.S. in Chemical Engineering   1982
    B.S. in Chemical Engineering   1980

PAULINE C. PARLETT, Ph.D.

1401 Collegiate Way   (908) 655-0987   Princeton, NJ 80932

SUMMARY

Research chemist with international experience in process development and synthetic chemistry. Specific research activities include development and scale-up of crop protection and specialty chemicals from lab to pilot plant. Special expertise in analytical methods such as IR, UV, NMR, GC, and HPLC. Exceptional technical analysis, project management and problem-solving skills.

PROFESSIONAL EXPERIENCE

AGRI-CHEM, INC., Newark, NJ   **2000 - Present**
A chemical company involved with the manufacture of agricultural and specialty chemicals. Annual sales are $128 million.

Senior Research Associate, Process Development
- Synthesized and developed specialty chemicals and processes
- Developed oxidation process for a herbicide intermediate with potential production of several million pounds per year.
- Improved a process in a photo-initiator resulting in potential savings of $44 million per year.
- Generated customer lab samples for evaluation.

ICI AMERICAS, INC., Wilmington, DE   **1995 - 2000**
Agricultural Chemicals Division
A leading specialty chemicals company involved with the development and manufacture of agricultural chemicals and intermediates. Annual sales are $4 billion.

Research Scientist, Process Development
- Coordinated and executed process development of five step process for a herbicide with potential sales of $60M annually.
- Reduced toxic impurities in major chemical to less than 1 ppm during production resulting in a $2.1M savings.
- Developed a co-catalyst system resulting in a potential savings of $2 million per year.
- Developed stripping process for key intermediate resulting in potential reduction of cycle time by 25% at 98% efficiency.
- Implemented toll manufacture of major crop protection chemical with annual sales of $7M.
- Managed Crop Protection Process Development Group supervising 18 scientists, engineers and technicians. Activities involved more than 35 projects having an annual budget of $3.4M.

EDUCATION

University of Delaware, Ph.D., Organic Chemistry, 1995
University of Delaware, M.S., Organic Chemistry, 1993
Penn State University, B.S., Organic Chemistry, 1991

SYLIVA SCHWARTZ, Ph.D.
12 Coast Road
San Diego, CA 92211
(619) 642-8941 (Home)
(619) 453-6000 (Office)

PROFESSIONAL SUMMARY

Results-oriented technical professional with experience solving both research and development problems. Experience organizing, managing and implementing technical projects. Can successfully function in a supervisory capacity, as an individual contributor or in a team environment.

PROFESSIONAL EXPERIENCE

1996 to Present
BIOMAGNETIC TECHNOLOGIES - San Diego, CA
R&D Associate   (1999 to Present)
Senior R&D Chemist   (1996 to 1999)
Consult and collaborate with project scientists on task teams. Collect, analyze and interpret technical data. Develop new analytical methods and supervise laboratory technicians in areas of X-Ray Photoelectron Spectroscopy (XPS), X-Ray Diffraction, Electron Microscopy and Particle Characterization.
- Managed and supervised Slippery Surfaces Evaluation Task Force. Developed polyurethane coating with 30% less surface friction.
- Conceived, designed and developed a data logger to monitor polyurethane coated surfaces on conveyor system slide. Technology enabled business group to increase slide durability and reduce manufacturing costs by 20%.
- Co-conceived and co-developed a new PVC resin that could be spray-painted on to metal surfaces to increase surface slip.
- Co-conceived and co-developed a new coating for pigment filler for PVC resin. The coated filler reduced manufacturing costs of PVC siding 20%.
- Conceived and developed a new quality control procedure for manufacturing polyurethane foam which reduced analysis time and cost by 35%.

1992 to 1996
GE CATALYSTS, INC. - Milwaukee, WI
R&D Chemist
Analyzed and interpreted technical data obtained from test reactors to evaluate performance of developmental and competitor's catalysts. Synthesized and developed experimental catalysts. Technical consultant to plant personnel. Designed and built a fixed bed reactor system for catalyst evaluation.
- Developed test reactions (slurry phase and fixed bed) and analytical methods, GC and LC (gas and liquid chromatography) for catalyst analysis.
- Supervised the work performed by two technicians in areas of GC and LC.
- Identified key variables in production of new proprietary catalysts in bench-top experiments and modified manufacturing process.
- Supervised the technology transfer of modified manufacturing process into the manufacturing plant increasing production by 150%.

Sylvia Schwartz, Ph.D.
Resume - Page 2

1990 to   **UNIVERSITY OF HOUSTON** - Houston, TX
1992   Research Fellow, Center For Advanced Polymer Research
               Collected, analyzed and interpreted technical data obtained on experimental polymers
               using surface science (XPS). Supervised and directed graduate students and had
               research budget responsibility.
               - Synthesized and characterized properties and performance characteristics of
                 experimental polymeric materials using test reactors, chemisorption and XPS.
               - Designed and supervised construction of portions of the Center's Polymer Analysis
                 Laboratory.
               - Consulted for Dow Chemical in polymer testing and evaluation.
               - Consulted for Chevron and Mobil Oil in polymer research, testing and data
                 analysis.

EDUCATION

1990   Baylor University, Waco, Texas
                   Ph.D., Physical Chemistry

1986   Baylor University, Waco, Texas
                   M.S., Physical Chemistry

1985   Tulane University, New Orleans, Louisiana
                   B.S., Chemistry

PROFESSIONAL SOCIETIES

- Member, American Vacuum Society, American Physical Society, American Chemical Society,
  Society for Applied Spectroscopy, Eastern Electron Spectroscopy Society.

PATENTS AND PUBLICATIONS

- Eight U.S. patents.

- Eleven publications in professional journals, books and trade papers.

HENRY A. ANTHONY
6152 Jennifer Street
Blue Bell, PA 19433
(215) 742-8935

Objective: Senior Chemical Engineer or Consultant

Professional Profile

Seasoned senior engineer with record of solving tough technical and environmental problems for Dow Chemical Company. Effective communicator across cultural, organizational and skill-level lines. Diverse and successful research and development background with particular expertise in:

- Lab-to-plant scale-ups
- Flowsheets, simulations, statistics
- Economic evaluations
- Polymerizations, separations, mixing

- Plant start-ups
- Physical and chemical analytical methods
- Experimental (Taguchi) designs
- Electronic searching for information

Professional Experience

Process Associates of America., Blue Bell, PA   **1984 to Present**

Intellectual Properties and Regulatory Affairs, Consultant   (2000-Present)
- Communicated effectively with Koreans to interpret and influence modification of importation laws without exposing proprietary product information
- Solved information-flow problem delaying product shipment by up to three weeks
- Established product composition database and computer program to determine composition of regulated substances
- Prepared Material Safety Data Sheets (MSDS) for over 3,500 polymer products, using electronic searching to find latest toxicological and regulatory information
- Searched electronically for patent and research prior-art for use by Legal and Research
- Compiled five years of import data on over 1500 products for Canadian and Philippine inventories

Polymer, Engineering Research, through Research Associate   (1994-2000)
- Led team in completing two lab-to-plant transfers of major product lines more than ten percent ahead of schedule and twenty percent under budget; included planning and scheduling, assembling design basic data, interfacing with design and construction, training operators and leading both start-ups
- Initiated independent research in mixing, waste incineration, polymer stability, films and foams; each study met the goal of significantly improving product and process performance or lowering operating cost
- Designed and conducted experiments and computer simulations to identify crucial chemical principles or four process development teams—two fluorelastomers, one polyester and one polyether-ketone product line, make all supporting economic evaluations and serve as interface for analytical and process instrumentation

Plant Technical, Manufacturing and Planning, through Senior Engineer   (1984-1994)
- Developed a sophisticated purification procedure to recover and sell a by-product from acrylonitrile plant that launched a very profitable new Dow product within two years of my arrival at the site
- Solved start-up problem in two weeks that had delayed new line of TiO_2 flame reactor for months by applying self-authored computer program and statistical process control analyses
- Rotational assignments at four sites with monomers, TiO_2, polymers, textile fibers and elastomers
- Supervised operators of semiworks and commercial continuous and batch processes in day-to-day operations, plant tests and cost control

Education
MS, Chemical Engineering, LaSalle University, 1984
BS, Chemical Engineering, Pennsylvania State University, 1980

ORVILLE T. HAVISTOCK

826 Pine Cone Lane   Residence: (208) 772-3662   Fax: (208) 785-4312
Seattle, WA 23918   Messages: (208) 433-7950   E-Mail: OHAV@AOL

CAREER OBJECTIVE

Innovative research/customer-oriented problem solving targeting composite/materials concepts and solutions involving project conception, time-line development, personnel and equipment allocation.

CAREER HISTORY

COMPOSITE MATERIALS CORPORATION, Seattle, WA   1994-Present

Project Leader - Special Projects   2001-Present

- Served as international technology liaison transferring $32MM of intellectual property to foreign companies. Specified equipment, suppliers, tolling sources, markets and cost analysis.

- Conceptualized and commercialized high density foam composite. First year sales of $1MM with an ROI of greater than 40%

- Played an instrumental role in the development process of thin film, spirial wound membranes for specific gas/liquid phase reactions with a potential market of 4000MM pounds.

Senior Research Engineer   1998-2001

- Served as technical expert in non-woven wet process development/troubleshooting and scale-up of composite materials for specific customer applications.

- Interacted with numerous aerospace companies for commercialization of structurally reinforcing composite foams for radar absorbing applications having a potential market value of $12MM/year.

- Designed, set up and specified equipment for a Resin Transfer Molding (RTM) laboratory. Supervised and trained five people on theory, principles and operation of equipment. Studied inmold flow characteristics of resin/pre-form geometry.

Research Engineer   1994-1998

- Optimized fiber reinforced composite materials for fast compression molding. Studied blank size distribution and placement, in-mold flow studies, thermal stability and optimization of physical properties in relation to geometric shape.

- Designed, set up and specified equipment for a Reaction Injection Molding (RIM) laboratory. Supervised and trained eight people on theory, principles and operation of equipment.

EDUCATION

MS   Polymer Chemistry and Materials Science   Washington State University, 1994
BS   Chemical Engineering   University of Washington, 1992

JASON ROBERTS, Ph.D.
82 Franklin Street
Chicago, IL 43029
216-941-0328 (H)
216-436-5090 (O)

OBJECTIVE: A senior management position in the Research and Development area of a pharmaceutical, related health care or chemical company.

SUMMARY: A pharmaceutical executive with extensive experience in the identification and management of Research and Development Programs. Management and scientific experience includes:

- Developed and implemented new and ongoing discovery research programs.
- Transferred technology of candidate drugs to kilolab and pilot plant scale.
- Reviewed and submitted CMC documents to INDs and NDAs.
- Developed regulatory strategy for Candidate Drugs.
- Effectively managed $3.7 million chemistry department budget to support $5 million research and development effort.
- Lectured extensively on original research and topics in medicinal chemistry.
- Served as Adjunct Professor of Bio-Chemical Engineering at the University of Chicago, College of Pharmacy.

PROFESSIONAL: FLO MED CORPORATION, PHARMACEUTICAL PRODUCTS DIVISION
EXPERIENCE: Chicago, IL (1993 - Present)

Director of Chemistry
Report to Vice President, Research and Preclinical Development with responsibility for discovery chemistry and chemical development projects, including four direct reports and a staff of 32, 17 of whom are Ph.D.'s. Approximately one-third of the staff was recruited during the last four years. Together with the Director of Pharmacology, organized and managed discovery teams, reviewed progress with senior management and consultants and recommended initiating of clinical trials on discovery compounds.

- Established programs to maintain and increase professionalism: dual ladder career path, seminar programs, scientific meeting presentations.
- Served as permanent member of Preclinical Research and Development Management Team, Patent Strategy Committee and Research Council.
- Led the Inhalation Anesthetic Discovery Team that synthesized novel structure classes of new chemical entities that are in advanced preclinical testing.
- Organized a receptor-based approach to antiemetics that led to a recommendation for clinical testing of a promising compound.
- Managed an intravenous Anesthetic Program that led to clinical trials of five Candidate Drugs.
- Worked with Licensing and Acquisition group to evaluate potential in-license drug candidates.

- Discovered a novel neuromuscular blocking agent that began clinical trials.
- Hired ten Ph.D. and M.S./B.S. chemists for discovery and development.
- Developed synthesis for new chemical entities that were scaled up to kilolab and pilot plant.

HEBELER CORPORATION, Evanston, IL (1983 - 1993)

Assistant Director of Regulatory Affairs (1991 - 1993)
Reported to Senior Director of Regulatory Affairs, with responsibility for developing regulatory strategy for development projects. Reviewed and submitted documents to INDs an NDAs. Attended FDA Advisory Committee meetings.

Section Head, Central Nervous System Research (1983 - 1991)
Started as a laboratory scientist synthesizing new chemical entities in the gastrointestinal, cardiovascular and central nervous system disease areas. Led a section of 12 chemists (mostly Ph.D.'s) in discovering analgesic and anti-ischemic compounds. With biology section head, developed and implemented research plans.

- Personally conceived and synthesized three Candidate Drugs that entered clinical trials.
- Organized and chaired a symposium on New Initiatives in Central Nervous System Research

EDUCATION:
Ph.D. - Biochemistry, Michigan State University (1982)
M.S. - Medicinal Chemistry, Michigan State University (1980)
B.S. - Pharmacy, University of Illinois (1978)

Postdoctorals
Drexel University - Peale Sabbatical Program (1986)
Georgetown University, NIH Fellow (1982 - 1983)

Ongoing professional development courses

PATENTS: Awarded 24 US Patents

PUBLICATIONS: Published 12 articles in refereed journals

MEMBERSHIPS: American Society of Chemical Engineering
American Association for the Advancement of Science
New York Academy of Sciences
American Pharmaceutical Association

CERTIFICATIONS: Registered Pharmacist

Foster T. Johnson

33 Phillips Drive
Glens Falls, NY 13648   Phone: (513) 775-0983   E-Mail:FTJOHN@MSN.com

Objective   Engineering or R&D Manager in product or advanced technology development.

Experience

1998-Pres.   *Manager Materials Development*, Farthing Glass, Inc.
Held a variety of increasingly responsible technical, staff and management positions. Developed a broad base of skills leading engineering and R&D work on novel glasses, ceramics, and processes for state-of-the-art applications in electronics. Applications have spanned a diverse array of technologies including flat panel computer data displays, magnetic data storage, microelectronics packaging, fiber optics and precision specialty materials. Accomplishments include:

- Pioneered an innovative materials system that led to the commercialization of a new flat panel data display product which generated $85 million per year new business revenue.

- Established and staffed a state-of-the-art laboratory facility for the development of sophisticated glasses, glass-ceramics, metals, composites and thin/thick film materials.

- Developed materials and processes meeting performance, reliability, and cost objectives which were key to attainment of business strategies.

- Transferred and commercialized technology from R&D to manufacturing which enhanced competitiveness and productivity.

- Established and administered industrial and university R&D contracts.

- Fostered collaboration, teamwork and innovation that led to numerous inventions and technical breakthroughs.

1994-1998   *Project Engineer*, Tileen Glass Co., Memphis, TN
Member of the engineering staff at a corporate RD&E center. Initiated and conducted projects in glass science and manufacturing technology for cathode-ray tubes, scientific apparatus and electronic devices.

Education   B.S., Chemical Engineering, N.C. State University, 1994

Patents   • Holder of four U.S. patents

Marilyn Feeney
34 Holly Brook Lane
Secaucus, NJ 08937
Home: 201 836-1458

SUMMARY:

Senior executive/general manager with extensive experience in marketing/sales and profit and loss responsibility and graduate of The Wharton School, University of Pennsylvania.

EXPERIENCE:

Curtis-Wright Corporation (1999 - Present)

<u>Vice President</u> - Direct the sales and marketing of three divisions which total $118 million with 18 direct sales people and four manufacturing representative organizations. Assist the President with strategic planning. Product lines include automated manufacturing equipment, precision machining, precision stamping and contract manufacturing. Markets served are mainframe computers, telecommunications, semiconductors, medical instrumentation automotive and disk drives.

- Grew sales to OEM market $5 million in one year and quoted over $60 million in potential new business over five years.
- Member Corporate Quality Council - implemented "Sigma Program" throughout the company to improve quality three orders of magnitude in three years.
- With $750,000 in capital, justified a rapid prototyping facility that delivers over 70% ROI per year.
- Justified capital investments with ROCE of 25% or greater, e.g. CAD/CAM, Wire EDM, Machining Centers, etc. Over $2 million invested in 24 month period.
- Chairman Corporate Rewards and Recognition Committee.

Harvard Industries (1995 - 1999)

<u>Business Manager</u> - Supervised direct staff of eight with total organization of 35 including product managers, application engineering, pricing and program management functions. Product responsibility included broad-band network products, high-speed cable assemblies, RF connectors, "Thin-Net" LAN tap.

- Charged with responsibility for $150+ million of bookings; a 50% increase over the previous year at 20% gross margin.
- Improved sales from $100 million to $145 million for a 45% increase. Chairman of the acquisition committee which developed a strategy for RF connectors. Implemented forecasting by part number which improved lead times from 12 weeks to three weeks on high volume components.
- Served on several committees including premise network, electronic distribution, competitive analysis.

<u>Director of Business Planning</u> - Supervised staff of four product managers and an application engineer.

·   Implemented cable assembly strategic plan which focused on high-speed assemblies in the computer, instrumentation, medical and automatic test equipment markets.

<u>Morse Operations, Inc. (1992 - 1995)</u>

<u>Director of Marketing</u> - Supervised staff of five with a total marketing organization of 40 people including product managers, industry marketing, customer service and order entry. Products included commercial connectors, ribbon connectors, cable assemblies and cable. Markets served were telecommunications, industrial, computer and peripherals and commercial and military.

·   Charged with sales of $50 million; a 20% increase over previous year, at a 28% gross margin.
·   Introduced nine new products in 1993 that produced $4 million sales first year with a $12 million potential in five years.
·   Implemented distributor policies to improve part number turnover and increase gross margin.
·   Increased exports and imports 80% ($6MM) and 40% ($6MM) respectively.
·   Negotiated private label agreements with Asian suppliers to address $500 million market not served.
·   Developed strategies for commercial products for investment of $2 million which would generate sales of $15 million at 40% gross margin.
·   Coordinated marketing for commercial products worldwide; including Europe, South America, Far East, Japan and United States.

<u>Douglas & Lomason Company (1988 - 1992)</u>

<u>Product Manager</u>   (1990 - 1992)
<u>Marketing Manager</u>   (1988 - 1990)

Responsible for the computer and electronic interconnect products for board-to-board, wire-to-board and wire-to-wire applications which included investment justification, managing the programs through engineering, pricing, manufacturing and sales organizations.

·   With a capital investment of $1.9 million, developed seven new products that generated sales at a rate of $12 million annually with ROI of more than 50%.
·   Directed the development of 16 new products that have $30 million potential in sales producing a divisional growth rate of 25% annually with ROI of 80% - 100%.
·   Developed 18 additional products, incorporating robotic insertion, surface mounting and automated discrete wire cable assembly systems.

EDUCATION:

M.B.A.   The Wharton School, University of Pennsylvania, 1988
B.S.   Electrical Engineering, Massachusetts Institute of Technology, 1986

MARIA WAGNER

7 Belmont Circle
Richmond, VA 23291

(804) 886-3486

PROFESSIONAL SUMMARY

Innovative marketing and product development/management professional with strong communication, negotiation, and decision making capabilities. Extensive technical background provides the ability to perform successfully in a variety of technical disciplines.

EXPERIENCE

Product/Marketing Manager, Media General, Inc. *(1999 - Present)*

- Established product development process to streamline development cycle, reduce costs, and effectively use resources.
  - Reduced development cycle from one year to three months.
- Successfully penetrated new markets through development and launch of two service offerings.
  - Consulting Services resulted in $500,000 in revenue bookings in first six months.
  - Speech Writing Services resulted in over $250,000 in revenue bookings during first year.
- Cultivated partnerships with industry vendors to increase services sales and perform joint product development.
- Coordinated R&D Budgeting process for new product development.
  - Analyzed budget to assure proper allocation of funds.
  - Tracked development process versus expenditure of funds.
- Created effective marketing programs which resulted in a 50% increase in commercial services business.
- Conducted market research to determine feasibility of offerings using internal and external resources.
- Designed and developed marketing materials for service business offerings including:
  - Trade show exhibits, Video and audio tapes, Product brochures and data sheets.
- Developed and conducted sales training courses for services sales consultants.

Account Representative, NEC Technologies *(1996 - 1999)*

- Identified strategic marketing opportunities through relationship management of senior executive staff of Keystone Financial Services.
- Maintained direct responsibility for developing and implementing NEC workstation marketing strategy for Keystone nationwide. Efforts resulted in 10% increase in market share over two years.
- Directed five month consulting study to analyze the feasibility of imaging technology use within Keystone's Financial Services business unit.

EXPERIENCE (cont'd)

- Effectively coordinated resources and activities with nationwide IBM marketing teams to provide solutions across all Keystone business units.
- Negotiated special contracts for volume bids with internal NEC headquarters management.
- Consistently achieved 100% of quota.
- Received *Branch Managers Award for Excellence in Line of Business* for contributions to marketing effort.

Senior Technical Buyer, NEC Research Center   *(1993 - 1996)*

- Responsible for evaluation and purchase of optical and laser systems for research community, including specification, analysis, negotiation, and installation planning.
- Negotiated and reviewed purchase contracts, service contracts, and software license agreements.
- Functioned as liaison between research community and external vendors and organizations.
- Successfully developed pc-based database of vendor information to streamline buying process.
- Scheduled and hosted technical talks and seminars for research community members.
- Represented Compaq at various technical shows and exhibits.

Technical Buyer, NEC Research Center   *(1990 - 1993)*

EDUCATION

Bachelor of Science - Physics, 1990
Brown University

ADDITIONAL SKILLS

PC Environments: DOS, MacIntosh
Applications: Excel, Word, Lotus 1-2-3, Persuasion, Harvard Graphics, Paradox, DBase IV

FRANKLIN SILVER

20 Billings Road
Minneapolis, MN 55443

Res: 612 458-3483
Bus: 612 648-8700

OBJECTIVE: Managerial position in Marketing Consumer Products or Services.

SUMMARY: Broad consumer marketing experience with major corporations, the last four years with General Mills, Inc. Demonstrated ability to develop and implement advertising and promotional strategies, increasing share and ROI (return on investment). Strong written and verbal communication skills, with ability to interface effectively at all levels. Computer literate and aggressive user of spreadsheet, word processing and graphic software packages, including Lotus/Excel, Harvard Graphics, Power Point, Word for Windows and ProWrite.

WORK EXPERIENCE:

2000-Present   **GENERAL MILLS, INC., Minneapolis, MN**

<u>Marketing Manager – Cereal Division</u>
Recruited to assume line marketing responsibility for developing and implementing plans and programs for worldwide sales of $40 million annually of General Mills consumer products. Frequent interface with sales and marketing management in three divisions in development of sales/expense forecasts as well as implementation of strategic and tactical marketing and promotional plans.

- Reduced marketing expenses 25% and maintained sales volume in the face of a 20% contraction in the cereal market.

- Developed and implemented an integrated marketing approach that built established brand to a record 52% share.

- Streamlined development and delivery of sales and marketing communications and support materials on accelerated schedules at reduced costs.

- Introduced special pack promotions to highly resistant cereal market generating incremental volume through increased display support.

- Designed and initiated "government required" forms utilizing shared computer technology, allowing sales to customize presentations for headquarter accounts.

- Increased productivity of critical manager's meetings by restructuring the format into logical, easily digested segments.

1988-2000   **HAGGAR APPAREL COMPANY, Dallas, TX**

Retail Brand Director (1998-2000)
Established marketing objectives and strategies, integrating all advertising, point-of-sale, and promotional plans and programs for 200+ retail outlets accounting for $150 million in annual sales. Frequent interface with advertising agencies, vendors and field sales force. Supervised three-person brand team.

- Initiated and implemented consumer targeted radio station in-store, enhancing the audio environment, allowing for promotional messages, and generating revenue by selling air time to vendors.

- Developed retail color coding system that simplified shopping, visually reinforced store positioning and energized the environment through effective use of point-of-sale strategy.

Advertising Manager (1995-1998)
Developed creative and media placement strategies in support of grand openings, promotions, image advertising and ongoing campaigns. Acted as communication liaison among management, agencies and sales. Supervised TV and print media production.

- Initiated first co-op advertising effort that generated $500,000+ in media exposure at a cost of $100,000.

- Increased advertising effectiveness by adapting TV advertising to point-of-sale through creation of video programs nationwide.

Merchandise Distribution Manager (1992-1995)
Frequent interface with Sales, Buying, and Manufacturing with responsibility for establishing sales forecasts and assignment of inventory to 200 retail outlets. Also trained associate merchandise managers, and provided in depth sales analysis for buyers.

Associate Merchandise Manager   (1990-1992)
Management Training Program/Store Manager   (1988-1990)

COMPANY SPONSORED TRAINING:

- Kellogg Graduate School of Management: "Consumer Marketing Strategies"
- American Management Associates: "Management in a Team Environment"
- David Bootnick Associates: "Improving Communication Effectiveness"
- Karras Associates: "Effective Negotiating"

EDUCATION:

DePAUL UNIVERSITY, Chicago, IL
B.S., Business Management, 1988

CONNIE FORREST

400 Sycamore Street
Philadelphia, Pennsylvania 19101

Business: (215) 344-1895
Residence: (215) 579-3749

CAREER SUMMARY

Senior executive with over 18 years of progressively responsible experience in new Products Marketing and Marketing Research at leading U.S. food companies including, Campbell Soup Company, Vlasic Foods Incorporated and Godiva Chocolatier, Inc. Outstanding record of developing award-winning new products as well as building and leading effective organizations. Results-oriented, strong team player and creative problem solver.

BUSINESS EXPERIENCE

MRS. PAUL'S KITCHEN, Philadelphia, Pennsylvania   **1995 to Present**
A $2.5 billion manufacturer of frozen and convenience foods and a subsidiary of Campbell Soup Company. Mrs. Paul's Kitchen is a $1.3 billion international food business with operations in 40 countries.

Vice President Marketing, Convenience Foods   **(1999-Present)**
Responsible for directing a major corporate initiative to enter the convenience foods market through internal development. Direct all aspects of new product development and marketing, including concept generation, product formulation, naming, packaging, positioning, advertising, marketing research, marketing plan development and capital planning.

- Generated new product revenues of over $45 million in 1999 with the successful national launch of Cranberry Chocolate Chippers and Pastry Favorites lines.
- Named one of the Top 100 Marketers in the country by *Advertising Age* magazine (June, 1999).
- Introduced ten major new products and drove revenues of Mrs. Paul's Kitchen from $825,000 in 1999 to over $1.5 million by 2002. Brands launched over this period included:

  - <u>Oven Toasters</u> - Generated annual sales approaching $125 million, became the #1 selling brand for Mrs. Paul's and was named an AMA Edison Award winner as one of the Top 10 New Products of 2000. Also won award for outstanding package graphics.
  - <u>Pastry Favorites</u> - Generated first year sales of $95 million, won the AMA's Edison Gold Award as one of the Best New Products of 2001, and received a Silver Level Award for excellence in advertising.
  - <u>Microwave Treats</u> - Was developed in less than one year and achieved sales of $50 million, exceeding plan by 10% in first year.

- Mrs. Paul's Kitchen named New Products Marketer of the Year by both the American Marketing Association and *Food Business* magazine in 2001.

Director, Marketing Research   **(1995-1999)**
Responsible for the leadership and overall direction of the Marketing Research Department. Thoroughly knowledgeable in a full range of research techniques including all types of custom research, syndicated data sources, decision-support systems and forecasting and volumetric modeling.

- Successfully "turned around" the Marketing Research function by upgrading and training the staff, introducing improved research methods and techniques and re-established credibility with brand marketing and senior management.

- Directed the development of an internal new products forecasting model which was significantly more accurate than simulated test market services.
- Served as strategic advisor to the President's Staff on such issues as changing consumer lifestyles and overall market trends.

VLASIC FOODS INCORPORATED, Farmington Hills, Michigan　　　　　**1991 to 1995**

Manager of Marketing Research Department
Responsible for marketing research support on all retail and food service product line including new and established brands.

- Significantly enhanced brand management analysis and planning capabilities by developing a state-of-the-art computer-based marketing decision support system.
- Significantly improved forecast accuracy through development of a model-based forecasting system.
- Reviewed and helped develop long range plans and annual operating plans.

GODIVA CHOCOLATIER, INC., Reading, Pennsylvania　　　　　**1987 to 1991**

Research Manager　　　　　**(1989-1991)**
Research Supervisor　　　　　**(1987-1989)**
Performed a broad range of marketing research studies on assigned brands including concept and product testing, advertising, packaging and name testing, A&U's and test marketing. Recipient of Chairman's Award for business analyses and econometric modeling on Raspberry Crunch chocolate bar which led to development of marketing plan resulting in record sales and profits.

CULLUM COMPANIES, INC., Philadelphia, Pennsylvania　　　　　**1983 to 1987**

Senior Analyst
Progressed from Analyst to Senior Analyst with responsibility for three of the company's largest clients: RJR Nabisco, Nestle Food Company, and Very Fine Products. Responsible for the design, analysis and presentation of consumer research findings to client management

EDUCATION

M.B.A. Cornell University, 1983
Graduated third in class of 105. Full tuition scholastic scholarship

B.A. Georgetown University, Psychology Major, 1981
Graduated tenth in class of 1200

PROFESSIONAL ASSOCIATIONS

American Marketing Association
Association of National Advertisers

ALEXANDER J. NEWCOMBE
343 Oak Ridge Road
Parsippany, NJ 08803
Voice/Fax (908) 854-8934

Summary: General Management/Marketing executive with 13 years domestic and international chemical industry experience.

Specific expertise: Sales, Marketing and Marketing Research, Strategic Planning, Acquisitions, Joint Ventures, and Business Strategy development and implementation.

Professional Experience:

BASF CORPORATION – Parsippany, NJ   **(1999 to Present)**
($5 BILLION CHEMICALS MANUFACTURER)

Vice President Marketing & Sales-Paper Chemicals Division, Parsippany, NJ

Worldwide P&L responsibility for marketing and sales of paper chemical lines manufactured in five countries with sales in 62 foreign countries, sold through direct sales forces in major markets and distributors/agents in other countries. Promoting sale of starch-based chemical system (SBCS) manufactured at new plant is top priority project. (Sales: $17 million, Operating Budget: $1.75 million; Staff: 25)

- Initiating empowerment culture in stifled environment.
- In first year achieved 27% Sales and Volume growth in SBCS 10% overall products.
- Evaluating strategic product line additions, with possibility of significantly changing entire character of division through growth and acquisitions.

ETHYL CORPORATION, Richmond, VA   **(1997 to 1999)**
($2.6 MILLION, INTERNATIONAL SPECIALTY POLYMER COATING MANUFACTURER)

Vice President, International Specialty Group
President, South America
Member, Board of Directors, Europe

Established new business unit to support manufacturing, marketing and sales of specialty finishes in South America. (Operating Budget: $2.5 million; Staff: 38)

- Achieved $2.1 million in annual sales and cumulative profit of $1 million in three years.
- Established two wholly-owned operations in France and Germany.
- Converted JV in Spain to 100% owned subsidiary.
- Formed JV in Netherlands, adding $3 million in sales revenues in second year.

HUNTSMAN CHEMICAL, Salt Lake City, UT   **(1985 to 1997)**
($900 MILLION WORLDWIDE MANUFACTURER OF COMMODITY AND SPECIALTY CHEMICALS)

Director of Marketing & Sales, *Coatings Division*   (1995 – 1997)

Profit and Loss responsibility for worldwide marketing and sales of paper coating product lines. (Sales: $32 million; Operating Budget: $2.75 million; Staff: 65)

- Improved sales efficiency and customer coverage by 32%.
- Resolved three complex claims saving $550,000.
- Negotiated new two-year contract, increasing sales 17%.
- Rewrote agent/distributor contracts reducing company's liability exposure by $1.3 million.

Manager, Strategic Planning, *Pulping Chemicals Division*   (1993 – 1995)

Determined internal consistency of strategic plans for two pulping chemicals divisions and submitted recommendation to senior corporate management; reviewed joint venture projects and made further recommendations for international acquisitions. (Staff: four)

- Analyzed over 150 companies and recommended ten international acquisition candidates.
- Developed and presented additional value criteria to acquisition specifications for European investment bankers, resulting in identification of three candidates.

Region Sales Manager, Southeast Region   (1991 – 1993)

Turned around sales and profits for 30 industrial chemical products (Sales: $15 million; Operating Budget: $2.0 million; Profit: $1.7 million; Staff: three)

- Achieved 20% growth in sales and profits.
- Concluded sales of $3 million to three new business areas.

Product Sales Manager, *Paper Chemicals Division*   (1988 – 1991)

Responsible for marketing, sales and overall business operations for this $60 million product line as it moved from order control to active selling mode. (Budget: $500,000; Staff: three)

- Developed and implemented strategic marketing plan for Europe and contributed to global strategic plan.

Sales Representative, Southwest Region   (1985 – 1988)

Accountable for $5 million sales for 30 industrial chemical products serving eight industries in New Mexico, Utah, Colorado and Texas.

- Increased sales and profits 15% per year in recessionary period.
- Negotiated exclusive contract resulting in annual sales of $400,000.
- Launched three new products resulting in $750,000 additional revenue.

Education: B.S., Chemistry, Drexel University, 1985

BEATRICE A. LESSER

560 Hummingbird Lane
Princeton, NJ 08893

Residence: (908) 874-3481
Office: (201) 540-9000

OBJECTIVE

A senior level sales and marketing position requiring demonstrative skills in leadership, planning, and communication which result in increased profitability.

Qualified by 16 years of experience of positions of increasing responsibility for the profitable marketing of products within the consumer products industry. Background includes consistent record of achievement in the following areas:

- Sales & Marketing Management
- National Account Management
- Advertising
- P&L Management
- Sales Promotion
- Product Development
- Market Research
- Strategic Planning

PROFESSIONAL EXPERIENCE

WARNER-LAMBERT COMPANY   **2000-Present**

Direct all marketing functions including consumer advertising and promotion, marketing services, account marketing programs, and special product development for Warner's top 75 accounts (sales volume - $940MM). Manage budget of 6.3MM and staff of 36.

Vice President Sales and Marketing

Accomplishments:
- Directed effort to expand and recognize Account Marketing department. Increased staff from 18 to 36 members. Reassigned accounts by dollar volume and geographically.
- Produced an additional $25MM in sales from account specific product development. Expanded this service to cover Warner's top ten accounts.
- Developed national promotional strategy to complete with competing shaving products companies. Promotions produced $4.8MM in increased profit.

BIC CORPORATION   **1991-2000**

Fourteen years of results-oriented experience within this $1.9 billion manufacturer of consumer shaving products. Experience includes directing all sales and marketing functions for assigned accounts (or region) covering all consumer trade classes (mass merchant, food, drug, deep discount, catalogue, specialty, etc.)

Senior Sales Manager, National Accounts   *1999-2000*
Created and executed marketing and sales programs for Wal-Mart Corporation. Coordinated activities and provided direction for 150 sales representatives with regards to Wal-Mart sales volume - $300MM.

Accomplishments:
- Produced 20% increase at Wal-Mart versus previous year.
- Introduced first promotional pack featuring free audio cassette with purchase.
- Directed and managed the inventory of all Wal-Mart products at their 105 distribution centers.
- Secured distribution for triple track razor at Wal-Mart.

District Sales Manager   *1997-1999*

Managed, motivated, and directed 14 sales representatives in the Hartford, Connecticut district. Was held accountable for quota achievement, P&L management, promotion, advertising activity, and forecasting as well as career development of team members.

Accomplishments:
- Number one ranked district (nationally).
- Number two ranked district (nationally).
- Three marketing representatives were promoted to managerial positions.

Major Account Manager   *1996-1997*

Created and executed marketing and sales programs for the following national accounts: Rite Aid, CVS, Acme and Super Fresh.

Accomplishments:
- Received Performance Excellence Award signifying Number One Sales Manager in nation.
- Achieved 30% increase in sales at assigned accounts.

Special Markets Manager   *1996*

Managed and directed eight (8) food brokers accountable for all Supermarket business located in the Northeast region.

Accomplishments:
- 100% quota achievement in all product categories.
- Secured new distribution for the Flex Trac razor at Shop Rite (only supermarket chain to carry this product).

Marketing Representative   *1991-1996*

Met and exceeded sales quotas at assigned accounts through the planning and execution of account specific marketing programs and promotions.

Accomplishments:
- 1996 - Excellence Award winner signifying the nation's number one marketing representative.
- 1995 - 100% quota achievement in all product categories.
- 1994 - 100% quota achievement in all product categories.
- 1993 - Ranked number two marketing representative nationally.

FULLER BRUSH COMPANY   **1986-1991**
Account Manager   *1988-1991*
Account Supervisor   *1987-1988*
Account Representative   *1986-1987*

EDUCATION

PRINCETON UNIVERSITY, Princeton, NJ
  B.S., Marketing

Continued professional development includes participation in programs in the areas of leadership, coaching, presentation, interviewing, and writing skills.

BRADLEY DUNLEVY

500 South Central Avenue, Chicago, IL 60063   Office 312/578-9500 · Home 312/685-2323

CAREER SUMMARY

Seasoned sales and marketing professional with extensive experience in the areas of:

- Pricing
- Product line P&L
- Competitive analysis
- Forecasting
- Sales force management
- Market research

- Strategic planning
- Distribution channel design
- Contract negotiation
- New product commercialization
- Competitive acquisition
- Customer service

Results-oriented, self-motivated team contributor with a proven ability to lead efforts in the areas of account acquisition, competitive strategies, market segmentation and profitability improvement.

BUSINESS EXPERIENCE AND ACCOMPLISHMENTS

FARLEY INDUSTRIES, Chicago, IL   **1989 to Present**
A $100 million global business, providing specialty engineered laminates to the electronics industry.

Marketing Manager (2000 – Present)
Report to the Director of Sales and Marketing with key responsibilities in national and international coverage of end use OEM accounts, applications development and new product launch.   Directly supervised a staff of six marketing and technical professionals.

- Led a successful customer-linked commercialization effort from which a new product category was launched, capturing more than $2 million in sales in the first year.
- Established product application teams within the industry supply chain, achieving cost containment and cycle time reduction at all levels.
- Facilitated an alliance with a major OEM, resulting in exclusivity for product qualification testing in a computer application. Successful testing will lead to more than $10 million in new product sales annually.
- Formulated programs, working with sales teams and regional managers, to initiate and introduce new products and productivity options to customers and distributors.

Sales Manager (1997 – 2000)
Responsible on a national basis for all sales activities, pricing policies, sales contracts, competitive analysis, forecasting, customer and technical service associated with a $40 million network of 11 distributors at 22 locations. Reported to the Director of Sales and Marketing.

- Analyzed markets and prepared accurate sales forecasts with distributors' senior management.
- Implemented a mix-driven, volume-based incentive rebate plan increasing sales by 30% in 1995.
- Prospected, recruited and secured long-term arrangements with new distributors resulting in revenue increases exceeding $9 million.
- Planned and initiated distributor training programs.
- Established requirements for distributor certification to comply with MIL-SPEC and other institutional approval ratings.
- Promoted and applied Total Quality Leadership techniques to streamline distributor policies and reduce overall bureaucracy, with regard to claims, special pricing requests and transportation.

BRADLEY DUNLEVY

District Sales Manager (1995 – 1997)
Reported to the National Sales Manager, responsible for $25 million in sales throughout the Northeastern U.S. and Mexico via an organization of three directly reporting salespersons, four distributors and two manufacturer's representatives.

- Exceeded regional sales quotas by 10% in 1991 and 15% in 1992 while maintaining a 5% price premium over competition.
- Re-established Mexican sales base, growing sales from $2 to $6 million.
- Mobilized cross-functional teams to capture new accounts.

Market Research Manager (1993 – 1995)
Responsible for establishing and maintaining product line pricing to meet corporate profitability goals on a national basis. Also responsible for conducting research for competitive and strategic purposes. Reported to the Director of Marketing. Directly supervised four employees.

- Implemented pricing mix strategies enabling price increases exceeding 3%, resulting in profit gains of $4.2 million.
- Managed and negotiated all pricing and contracts for $60 million SBU on a national basis.
- Successfully prepared and justified appropriations requests for capital expenditures in excess of $4 million.
- Led competitive analysis efforts in all segments of market in order to develop and implement appropriate business response.

Product Manager (1992 – 1993)
Reported to the Marketing Manager, responsible for management of three basic product lines. Primary focus included: P&L, market share, forecasting and product line rationalization.

- Organized product rationalization effort in the aftermath of a business acquisition.
- Assisted in the commercialization of new products.
- Focused efforts on the assimilation of the acquired business into the existing one.

Contracts Manager (1991 – 1992)
Sales Associate (1989 – 1991)

EDUCATION AND PROFESSIONAL TRAINING

B.S. Business Administration – LaSalle University, 1989
Graduated Magna Cum Laude – Major: Marketing

- Company-Sponsored Professional Training -

Management Development Conference · Total Quality Leadership Training
Strategic Pricing Seminar · Value Selling Workshop
Total Quality · Middle Management Training · Leadership Training Workshop

HAROLD M. BUNDY
7643 Forest Drive
Columbus, OH 43414

Work: (614) 225-3500
Home: (614) 343-4589

SUMMARY: Senior Marketing executive with strong leadership skills and a proven track record of profitably growing both large national brands and smaller niche products. Strengths include strategy development, consumer marketing and team building. Successful career includes marketing, business development, strategy and finance assignments.

PROFESSIONAL EXPERIENCE:

THE MURPHY-PHOENIX COMPANY, Solon, OH   **2000 – Present**

Category Director – Cleaning Products Unit
Report to Vice President of Marketing with overall responsibility for three major brands: WONDER CLEAN, AMAZE and GLORY SHINE. Received additional responsibility in 2001 for WIZZARD Glass Cleaner, the company's largest brand. Manage existing base business, new product development and Marketing organization's total quality roll-out. Supervise staff of nine.

- Led Floor Wax business turnaround through aggressive in-store promotion focus and product improvement. Additionally developed and launched one new product into test market. Grew volume and increased profits 30%.
- Initiated AMAZE new products program and launched AMAZE PLUS premium product to regain category leadership. Increased share and profits 20% and 12%, respectively.
- Developed and implemented GLORY SHINE EDLP sales strategy which has significantly exceeded payback requirements.
- Revised WIZZARD Strategic Plan to address emerging competitive issues and new product opportunities. Managed advertising development process which delivered superior copy.

BORDEN, INC., Columbus, OH   **1987 – 2000**

Brand Manager – Spread Fast Peanut Butter (1998 – 2000)
P&L responsibility for Borden's largest brand representing $500MM in sales. Duties included managing a $60MM advertising and promotion budget and staff of four.

- Established successful long-term category/brand volume growth strategy.
- Developed record testing advertising designed to reposition the brand and extend product usage.
- Implemented aggressive short-term sales and consumer programs to stabilize share.
- Led development of innovative market level event sponsorships designed to address local consumer and trade opportunities.
- Led development of several value-added spreadable products for test market.

Brand Manager – Red Hot Barbecue Sauce (1996 – 1998)
Managed P&L for this $30MM brand, including a $6MM advertising and promotion budget and one Associate Brand Manager.

- Successfully defended brand against a major new competitive entry and achieved best volume growth (25%) of any Borden brand.
- Developed three new television ads designed for use in regional/seasonal copy strategy.
- Designed and implemented a local marketing program to enhance national consumer events, including USTA and professional horse show sponsorships.
- Developed several new Meat Sauce products for test market and successfully introduced Bull's-Eye Hot-N-Spicy nationally.

Brand Manager (1994 – 1996)
Managed P&L for this $80MM business (ice cream) and supervised one Assistant Brand Manager.

- Repositioned Borden Ice Cream as "fantasy" dessert and increased sales 10%.
- Increased distribution during key periods through special packaging and targeted trade/sales incentives.
- Aggressively managed and increased Toppings profits through developing low cost copacking relationships and short-term sales incentives.
- Recommended and implemented Borden's Pineapple Ice Cream market withdrawal.

Manager of Business Development – Grocery Products Group (1992 –1994)
Reported to the Vice President of Marketing & Strategy with responsibility for developing a growth plan, including acquisition, for the Frozen Foods Group.

- Developed five category-specific growth strategies and prioritized internal and external development activities.
- Established Frozen Foods Group Acquisition Plan and coordinated the strategic planning process.
- Purchased Porter Foods retail brands for $100MM in 1989.
- Led several acquisition studies and coordinated both internal analysis and outside consulting/investment banking teams.

Senior Analyst – Marketing Strategy (1991 – 1992)

- Assessed financial and strategic implications relating to the uncoupling of Wilson Company and Borden Foods.
- Provided Chairman and Chief Executive Officer with operating group performance analysis.

PREVIOUS POSITIONS (1987 – 1991)

Held a series of increasingly responsible assignments in Finance and Strategy which included an 18-month field assignment working on cost and capital planning at a major manufacturing facility; a traditional financial planning and reporting assignment in an operating division; and financial/strategic planning for a divested business unit.

EDUCATION:

- MBA, **Harvard Business School,** 1987
- BBA, Finance, **Harvard University,** 1985

ACHIEVEMENTS:

- Received President's Award (1999)
- Received Borden Frozen Foods Leadership Award (1997)
- Received Borden's Creativity Award (1995)

BERNARD HUTTNER

17 Baybridge Road
Weston, Massachusetts 02139

Home: (781) 457-1987
Office: (781) 457-9196

BACKGROUND SUMMARY

Fifteen years proven experience in international marketing and business development. Experience in country, regional and global business units. Demonstrated ability to improve sales and profits. Assertive, motivated results oriented. Innovative problem solver with ability to implement. Trilingual -Spanish and German.

WORK EXPERIENCE

CUSTOM MANUFACTURING - Boston, MA   **1998 to Present**
A worldwide, $7 billion+ manufacturer and marketer of consumer products.

Manager, International Marketing - Primarily responsible to develop and market the soap and shampoo product lines in all international markets. Manage a staff of six professionals to ensure that appropriate strategies and product launch goals are developed and implemented. Hire, train and conduct performance evaluations.

Accomplishments:

·   Provided necessary management that has increased current divisional sales to more than $300 million annually.
·   Personally developed the soap line and broadened the scope of soap and shampoo business.
·   Introduced new shampoo line into Japan that generated an increase of over $20 million in business.
·   Successfully introduced new scented soap line into Europe.

BABY SOFT - Boston, MA   **1993 to 1998**
A $50 million+ manufacturer and distributor of infant goods.

International Marketing and Sales Manager - Hired with specific objective to establish an international presence for Baby Soft infant goods business.

Accomplishments:

·   Established markets in Canada, U.K., Germany and Spain, resulting in a four-fold increase in sales.
·   Negotiated and developed distributor contracts and established international pricing policies.
·   Initiated trade/consumer advertising campaign in the U.K., resulting in 1500 new sales outlets and establishing a foothold with major retailers such as Beal's and J.C. Penney's.
·   Initiated and implemented bilingual packaging program for Canada which allowed the company's entry in that market.

LENSMAKERS - Miami, FL   **1986 to 1993**
A worldwide manufacturer and distributor of consumer/industrial photographic and imaging products.

Marketing Manager - Worldwide Export Operations (1992-1993) - Promoted to direct worldwide export sales and marketing programs for all consumer photographic and video products. Developed marketing plans, strategies, budgets, pricing strategies, sales promotion campaigns and advertising program for export markets.

Accomplishments:

- Directed marketing programs for worldwide offices in Hong Kong, Paris, London and Florida.
- Redesigned Wide Lens camera system to reduce cost per unit picture.
- Successfully entered export market with profitable new video products.
- Shifted advertising strategy from national media to more localized advertising and sales promotions. Increased sales while reducing advertising budget by $500,000.

Regional Marketing Manager (1988-1992) - Originated and implemented sales and marketing strategies in Colombia, Ecuador, Panama and Venezuela to increase market share. Responsible for developing sales programs, distributor relations/contracts and advertising campaigns.

Accomplishments:

- Conceived, planned and implemented new street photography program in Latin America, increasing market share by 35%.
- Redirected industrial marketing programs which doubled hardware and film sales.
- Negotiated, administered and monitored distribution contracts to ensure exclusivity of product sales.
- Significantly increased amateur camera sales through creative sales promotions and advertising campaigns.

Resident Marketing Director - Germany (1986-1988) - Hired, trained and directed a staff of seven professionals, all German nationals. Increased sales by $1.2 million.

ASHLAND CLEANING PRODUCTS - New York, New York   **1983 to 1986**
Ashland is a worldwide $2.0 billion diverse manufacturer of ethical, OTC and household products.

Various Assignments in New York, Mexico and Colombia - Joined the company in the Marketing/Product Management area and was assigned to various marketing functions (i.e., marketing research, product management for new products) and overall orientation to subsidiary operations in Mexico and Colombia. In 1978, reorganized regional sales territory in Colombia, which was completed without a reduction in sales. Promoted to National Sales Manager for Colombia.

FLO-MED CORPORATION - New Brunswick, New Jersey   **1981 to 1983**
Worldwide manufacturer of ethical pharmaceutical products.

Medical Sales Representative - Awarded Regional Salesman of the Year in 1975, ranking second in the nation in overall sales.

EDUCATION

LaSalle University, Philadelphia, Pennsylvania
Master in International Management, 1981

Lehigh University, Bethlehem, PA, B.A., Economics, 1979

ERNEST T. STRICKLAND

22 Briar Patch Lane   Home: (302) 625-9762
Dover, DE 19898   Office: (302) 687-4215

SUMMARY

International sales, marketing and business development executive serving Fortune 250 chemical companies. Specific responsibilities in large account management, staff recruitment and motivation, new product introduction, pricing and profitability. Demonstrated successes in European and Asian cultures in joint venture companies.

PROFESSIONAL EXPERIENCE

ICI AMERICAS   **1998 – Present**

Director, New Business Development (Commercial Development)

- During initial four years, generated project opportunities providing $400 million in revenue. Provided three year return on $95 million of investment.

- Managed total project including sales and marketing, contract negotiations and investment proposal preparation for a new specialty intermediate product ($8.5 million revenue, high margin).

- Delivered market opportunity for new herbicide intermediate family of products ($200-300 million annually, $55 million investment). Single source position for 10 million pounds with newly developed account.

- Directed the plan preparation for market entry into remediation chemistry ($60 million revenue, $29 million investment).

DOW CHEMICAL COMPANY

Manager, Marketing Development   **1992 - 1998**

- Established a group of new pesticide intermediate products from zero base to $30 million sales in two years.

- Developed applications for existing products for specialty uses resulting in $50 million of additional sales.

- Negotiated contracts for this joint venture company to include: JV agreement, plant services contract, land lease agreement, technology licensing contract, utilities agreements.

International Marketing Manager   **1989 - 1992**

R&D, Technical Service Purchasing   **1986 - 1989**

EDUCATION

B.S., Chemistry, University of Delaware, 1986

CATHERINE A. BROWN

76 Hawbrook Street
Kirkwood, Missouri 63112

413/597-8599 (Residence)   413/597-8500 (Business)

SUMMARY

Fourteen years' experience in consumer packaged goods marketing and sales, with an emphasis on business strategy and new product initiatives. Functional experience includes business planning and profit delivery, television, print and radio advertising development; promotion concepts and execution; brand repositioning; new products exploration/launches and personnel recruiting and development.

EMPLOYMENT HISTORY

1992 to Pres., GREAT LAKES FOODS, INC., Kirkwood, Missouri

2000 - Pres.   *General Manager - New Business Ventures*

Responsible for new product strategy and execution; trade marketing start-up and personnel development of eight marketing professionals and three support staff. Responsibility for $40MM in sales and $8MM in marketing spending; $400MM G&A. Report to Vice President - Retail Marketing Division.

- Restarted new products function for retail marketing, led venture teams on new products/acquisition efforts (including Mexican food category); launched Gravy Master line.
- Repositioned Far East brand noodles with business and product strategy improvements.
- Successfully developed the trade marketing function.

1998 - 2000   *General Manager - Vinegar, Sauces and Gravies*

Responsible for Vinegar, Steak Sauce, Barbecue Sauce, Specialty Sauces, and Gravy business planning; strategy and execution and personnel development of six marketing professionals and four support staff. Responsibility for $300MM in sales and $80MM in marketing spending; $2MM G&A. Reported to Vice President - Consumer Products Division.

- Improved departmental profitability by +16%; formed a "sauces" business unit.
- Initiated new media usage with co-op radio on Gravy during peak season; drive leadership share.
- Repositioned Barlow Vinegar as "the good food vinegar"; initiated Great Lakes Cleaning Vinegar Spray as a new product idea.

1997 - 1998   *General Manager - Ketchup and Sauces*

Responsible for Ketchup, Steak Sauce and Specialty Sauces business planning, strategy and execution and personnel development of seven marketing professionals and three support staff. Responsibility for $250MM in sales and $75MM in marketing spending; $500MM G&A. Reported to Vice President - Consumer Products Division.

- Initiated and developed proposal to launch new recyclable, unbreakable, clear Ketchup bottle.

- Initiated and coordinated NFL event sponsorship representing Great Lakes in a "60 Minutes" interview with Harry Reasoner and an "NBC Nightly News" segment on the NFL.
- Repositioned steak sauce as an "adult ketchup" to build new usage; improved household penetration by +3.5%; increased volume +10%.

1996 - 1997   *Group Product Manager - Ketchup*

Responsible for Ketchup business planning, strategy and execution; administration of $65MM in marketing spending and personnel development of three marketing professionals and one secretary. Reported to Vice President - Consumer Products Division.

- Developed, tested and nationally expanded a new award-winning advertising campaign targeted to teens. Helped reverse category consumption and share declines.
- Coordinated the addition of a consumer-friendly handle to the 32 oz. plastic container.

1994 - 1996   *Product Manager - Baby Food Products*

Responsible for assessing the potential, planning and executing the national launch of Great Lakes' baby food product line. Reported to General manager - Marketing.

- Planned and participated in the national sales meeting; took the show "on the road" for broker visits; helped sell-in on various account calls; introduced shelf management to Sales.
- Developed the consumer 800 line and coordinated the first medical marketing program at Great Lakes.
- Achieved 99% ACV nationally (only one holdout account) and sold 2.9MM cases year one.

1992 - 1994   *Associate Product Manager - New Products, Baby Food*

1988 to 1992, **NABISCO BRANDS, INC.**, Cleveland, Ohio

1989 - 1992   *Brand Assistant - Cake Mixes*
1988 - 1989   *Sales Representative - Case Food Division*

EDUCATION

M.B.A., Marketing Concentration, University of Ohio, (1988)
B.S., Marketing, Ohio State University (1986)

RELATED INFORMATION

- Total Quality Management Training, Crosby and Juran.
- Recognized in various publications (e.g., *Fortune, Business Week, Executive Report, USA Today, Savvy Woman, Executive Female*) as a "person to watch."

FRANK A. MANHEIM
2014 Blue Spruce Trail
Everett, Washington 50739
(216) 694-3782

PROFESSIONAL SUMMARY

Management Professional with significant experience building and leading high-volume, high-profit sales, marketing and product management teams. Combines sales, marketing and technical expertise with an excellent knowledge of industrial markets and products to gain a competitive advantage and win major market share.

PROFESSIONAL EXPERIENCE

WEYERHAEUSER COMPANY   **1991-Present**
A worldwide leader in the forest products industry ($9 billion sales).

Product Manager-Plywood & Lumber   **1999-Present**
Broad-ranging authority for developing strategic business plans, innovative product offerings, training field sales teams, developing product pricing and distribution channels, launching nationwide advertising/marketing campaigns, investigating acquisition alternatives, generating a TQM program and implementing all phases of the business plan. Led the entire new business product development cycle from initial concept and management approval through full-scale roll-out.

- Increased sales 45% and profits 20% within two years.
- Spearheaded the development of a nation-wide network of over 30 distributors during a two-year period which accounted for over 50% of product sales.
- Developed and introduced eight new products and systems in 2000. Five-year sales are projected to exceed $95 million with a solid 18% gross profit margin.
- Initiated a new job title, job description and incentive program for specialty products sales representatives which helped fuel aggressive growth.

Regional Sales Manager   **1995-1999**
Directed all sales and business development activities for Southeast Region (12 sales representative, $20 million sales volume).

- Received the 1998 Sales Management Award for outstanding performance.
- Successfully penetrated Home Depot during account's entry into market.
- Achieved significant 15% sales improvement during a period with flat market opportunity by capitalizing upon specific markets with demonstrated growth potential.
- Trained and sponsored a sales representative who received the 1997 President's Club Award.

Sales Representative   **1991-1995**

EDUCATION

Bachelor of Science - Civil Engineering, Oregon State University, 1991

CARL BILLINGS
879 Ocean View Drive
Pasadena, CA 92781

Residence: 714/963-7678   Office: 714/785-3485

QUALIFICATION SUMMARY

Client-oriented executive with over 18 years of senior management responsibilities in product management, client and technical training, and technical support for two computer companies. Consistently recognized for exceptional organizational and planning abilities, balanced with excellent interpersonal and people-development skills, with staffs of up to 150 people and annual budgets to $5.5 million. A strong record of proactive problem-solving, program innovation and high achievement of financial performance goals.

EXPERIENCE PROFILE

FHP INTERNATIONAL CORPORATION (Fountain Valley, CA)   **1992 - Present**
A $1.3 billion company which develops, markets, and services automated systems for the health care industry in the United States and Canada.

Director, Product Management (2000 - Present)
Responsible for planning and implementing product strategies to complement national marketing strategies for the health care industry. Researched, defined and managed the development process for computer-based products and services marketed to the U.S. health care channel.

- Developed executive relationships within health care companies, leading to joint product planning agreements and shared investments in software development; resulting products had shorter development cycle and were produced at lower cost.

- Planned and implemented expansion of primary product initial line from MacIntosh to IBM-based systems, thus realizing significantly wider market penetration.

- Defined and acquired "super processor" product to penetrate health care conglomerate account not previously serviced by FHP. First year sales netted in excess of $5.1 million.

- Chaired divisional time-to-market improvement team which exceeded first-year objectives in product introduction processes by 20 percentage points.

- Raised staff morale and accountability through new communication programs, training assignments and formalized position descriptions; also converted department managers to MBO-based evaluation program. Earned rating in top 5% of Division for personal managerial effectiveness.

Director, Client Training Services (1998 - 2000)
Responsible for developing and delivering full-line product training for clients and technical support personnel through classroom programs and on-site seminars. Provided telephone "help desk" support across all product lines for U.S. clients and FHP field staff.

- Significantly improved group profitability and productivity by consolidating staffs and facilities while raising department rating to "exceeds expectations" level on annual client satisfaction survey.

- Consistently exceeded services revenue and student activity objectives while lowering costs; final year accomplishments included 130% of training revenue objective, 112% of service billing objective and 10% under budget.

- Defined and initiated a client training service for HMO's as an incremental revenue source to FHP. First year revenues were 128% of plan.

Director, Educational and Consulting Services (1995 - 1998)
Responsible for developing and delivering all product training and documentation services for clients and FHP technical support personnel. Planned and managed product certification and field-release processes for the FHP Service organization.

- Defined, staffed and implemented a systems consulting group to provide product optimization services to clients, and a new revenue stream for FHP; this has since become a major internal profit center with multimillion dollar annual sales.

- Initiated contractual training services for health care companies to absorb excess staff capacity and generate incremental revenue; independently acquired and fulfilled contracts worth more than $500,000 in first year.

- Organized and staffed the first centralized documentation services function within the company; established standards, formats and processes which significantly improved quality and product image, reduced costs and earned national awards for the materials.

Director, Product Training & Support (1992 - 1995)
Responsible for providing all product training for clients and for FHP technical support personnel, plus all sales training for systems sales representatives. Defined and established all educational policies and procedures for internal and external representation.

- Proposed, planned and successfully managed transition of client training services from a cost-center to a profit center operation; annual revenue level exceeded $500,000 within three years.

- Designed and implemented centralized inquiry and enrollment system to streamline administrative processes; saw immediate payback in reduced costs and increased class attendance.

- Restructured Sales Training organization to streamline programs, reduce costs and focus industry-specific sales knowledge; resulted in improved sales-call success ratio and employee retention.

- Initiated standardized sales techniques training and first interviewing skills training for field sales organization.

DATAPRODUCTS CORPORATION (Woodland Hills, CA)   1984 - 1992
An international organization which develops, manufactures, and markets computers, peripherals and communications systems and services to worldwide markets.

Manager, Client Educational Services (1988 - 1992)
Responsible for managing a staff of computer education specialists providing technical instruction for client and corporate personnel involved in the programming, operations, and installation activities of USI products and systems; responsibilities evolved from local line manager to functional direction for eight geographic centers.

Instructor, Marketing Educational Services (1984 - 1988)
Responsible for conducting computer systems classes for client and USI personnel; course content ranged from logic fundamentals to file design to languages and executive seminars.

EDUCATION

California Institute of Technology, Bachelor of Science, Computer Science, 1984

RONALD T. GRANGER

1200 Broadway, NY, NY 18236   Phone: (212) 534-9827   E-Mail: RTG@AOL

OBJECTIVE: Senior level Corporate Advertising position in a consumer products corporation or a major division, depending upon size of company and job content.

EXPERIENCE:

1995 - Pres.   **RANCOR, INC.**   NEW YORK, NY

1999 - Pres.   VICE PRESIDENT, ADVERTISING SERVICES
1995 - 1999   DIRECTOR, ADVERTISING SERVICES
Responsible for development, management and control of 38 brand advertising budgets totalling more than $88 million. Supervision of outside agencies and in-house agency planning and executing of print and broadcast media. Managed Rancor's in-house advertising agency. Responsible for the administration of the entire Advertising Department.

Major Accomplishments:

- Achieved significant prime positioning of company's advertising in major magazines and on network television.
- Produced all the *Sinbare* fragrance and hair care commercials from the brands' introduction in 1997 until 2001. *Sinbare* was world's #1 selling fragrance and country's #2 selling hair care product during that period.
- Conceived and implemented the first and only tie-in promotions with the Miss America Pageant beginning in 1999.
- Successfully negotiated more than 30 major super models/actresses/actors exclusive contracts. Worked with them and supervised the production of the advertising in which they appeared.
- Supervised a 22-person in-house advertising agency handling over half of company's annual media and production expenditures.
- Negotiated a significant reduction in agency compensation, saving $3 million a year.
- Managed and controlled all expenditures without ever exceeding a budget/forecast.

1991 - 1995   **GRANGER ADVERTISING**   NEW YORK, NY

ASSISTANT TELEVISION PRODUCER
Arranged studio facilities and assisted in casting talent for television and radio commercials.

EDUCATION: **COLUMBIA UNIVERSITY**
Bachelor of Business Administration, 1991

HILDA B. KROUSE

1201 Sunset Circle
Berkeley Heights, CA 89731
(810) 694-3020   E-Mail: HILK@MSN

SUMMARY

Results-oriented sales professional with experience in medical equipment product sales. Performance areas include sales and marketing, relationship management and staff training and development. Proven ability to select, develop and promote motivated employees within an organization. Consistent outstanding record of exceeding personal and corporate sales objectives. Awarded company's top sales award six times.

PROFESSIONAL EXPERIENCE

SMITHKLINE BEECHAM, Philadelphia, PA   **1992 - Present**
(A multi-division international pharmaceutical and chemicals company with sales of $5 billion.)

Regional Accounts Manager - West Coast   (1998-Present)
Responsibilities include all major accounts in Arizona, California, Washington and Oregon. Directed sales efforts for four different product areas - imaging systems, nuclear medicine, anesthesiology and catheterization - for selected institutions.

- Managed a business area and 12 regional sales specialists. Area had combined sales of $55 MM.
- Liaison with national accounts buying groups, regional purchasing networks and hospital affiliated networks.
- Achieved top volume sales nationally out of 12 regions.

Regional Sales Manager - Imaging Systems   (1994-1998)
Responsible for imaging systems operations in the mid-west region, which had sales in excess of $25M. Geographic area included Wisconsin, Illinois, Michigan, Indiana and Ohio.

- Managed 14-person sales force whose responsibilities included both direct sales and sales through distributors.
- Grew the region assigned by approximately 150% over a four-year period. Sales grew from $10MM to $25MM.

Sales Representative - Imaging Systems   (1992-1994)
- Sold imaging systems to hospitals and clinics.

EDUCATION

B.S., Biology, Clemson University, 1992

TRACY SCOTT

1715 Oliver Street • *Dallas, TX 75439* • *Telephone (713) 433-8743*

PROFILE: Results-oriented General Manager with strong sales and marketing background. Demonstrated ability to build winning organization, establish trade relations with key customers and grow brands into market leaders. Recognized innovator with strong analytical and strategic planning skills.

PROFESSIONAL EXPERIENCE: THE CROWELL COMPANY, Dallas, TX (1999-Present)

Vice President, Sales & Marketing

Revived flagging $325MM franchise. Within six months, built strong sales and marketing ream, developed and implemented new advertising campaign, revitalized brand sales, and reorganized for market driven focus.

- Launched new product line, increasing retail sales 40% over test market.
- Directed and motivated 220-man, DSD sales force and distributor network.
- Improved media efficiencies 35% over previous year.
- Achieved $500MM annual savings on market research suppliers.
- Reduced days of supply and set program to eliminate short-dated inventory.

Direct Reports: VP Sales, Marketing Directors, Marketing Services, Public Relations, Shops and General Manager Canada/Mexico/Latin America.

ELI LILLY AND COMPANY, Indianapolis, IN (1983-1999)
Consumer Products Division

Vice President, General Manager (1996-1999)

Responsible for long-range strategic plan and short term operating results of $150MM consumer health products division.

- Increased division sales 17% over prior year.
- Increased division operating profit 21% over prior year.
- Successfully defended against competitive threat.

Direct Reports: VP Marketing, VP Sales, Market Research, Business Development, Training, Medical, Regulatory and Clinical Development.

Vice President, Marketing (1994-1996)

Responsible for strategic direction of all brands and new product development.

- Continued sales and market share growth on all key brands.
- Implemented new products program, including an Rx to OTC switch.

Direct Reports: Products Group Directors and Media Director.

Product Group Director (1992-1994)

Responsible for all nutritional and OTC products.

· Launched Slim-Cal, achieving the second leading brand position in category.

Direct Reports: Product Managers and Assistant Product Managers.

Senior Product Manger (1991-1992)

Responsible for Slim-Cal, Vitatabs and Fibertabs.

· Turned around declining Vitatabs franchise into second leading brand in category.

Product Manager (1989-1991)

Responsible for Slim-Cal.

· Turned around declining Slim-Cal franchise into #1 brand in category.

National Sales Merchandising Manager (1988-1989)

Responsible for trade class specific programs.

District Sales Manager (1987-1988)
Coordinator, Sales Training (1985-1987)
Territory Sales Manager, Pharmaceutical Division (1983-1985)

EDUCATION: **INDIANA STATE UNIVERSITY**
B.S., Biology, 1983

EXECUTIVE
EDUCATION: **AMERICAN UNIVERSITY**
General Management (1983)
Marketing Management (1990)

CORNELL UNIVERSITY
General Management (1997)

DREXEL UNIVERSITY
Marketing Management (1988)

SANDRA B. WILSON

209 A Baskins Blvd.   Home: (416) 694-3080   Fax: (416) 694-4327
Ocean Park, CA 08135   Office: (416) 722-5143   E-Mail: SBW2@AOL

Results-oriented sales professional with proven record of success in route sales and account management. High-energy, innovative, and self-directed marketer/salesperson with experience in large and small corporate environments. Seeking position in which I can fully apply my marketing, sales, and management skills to help a company grow.

SELECTED ACCOMPLISHMENTS

SALESPERSON/CUSTOMER LIAISON   **1999-Present**
Frito-Lay, Inc.
A $4 billion snack food corporation, largest such corporation in the world, employing approximately 50,000.

* Generated **over $350,000 per year** in sales by managing customer relationships and increasing shelf space and promotional efforts.

* Consistently **exceeded prior year sales** by 10% and sales projections by 3-4%.

* Received several **awards** for maintaining highest percentage above prior year in specialized promotions and overall sales performance.

* Served as troubleshooter for accounts where problems developed, **saving division $175,000** in two years.

SALES/MARKETING REPRESENTATIVE   **1996-1999**
San Francisco Bottling Company
Soft drink bottling/distribution company employing approximately 200 in San Francisco area and serving large and small store customer base.

* Opened 24 new accounts within **first six months** increasing revenues by over $31,000 per year.

* Re-established/strengthened customer relationships and improved customer service increasing sales **in excess of 10%** over prior year for an average sized account.

* **Attained or exceeded goals** in each period, significantly increasing overall sales over prior year.

EDUCATION

San Diego State University, 1996
B.A., Marketing

NATHANIEL BLOOM

8745 Stone Mountain Road
Raleigh, NC 27906

Home: (919) 656-3498
Office: (919) 874-3420

BACKGROUND SUMMARY

A creative, goal oriented Sales Manager with broad experience in the consumer products packaged goods industry. Successful in the analysis and planning needs for strategically developed business building programs. A history of progressively increasing responsibility for effectively managing personnel, operations and sales performance.

PROFESSIONAL EXPERIENCE

GOODMARK FOODS, INC., Raleigh, NC   **1997 - Present**
A $500 million frozen foods processor and marketing company.

<u>Managing Director – Southern Region</u> (1999 - Present)

·   Manage $250 million sales, marketing and customer support operation extending from Florida through Georgia and Washington, DC. Responsible for all business activities including P&L, systems support, financial reporting, logistics and personnel development.

·   Developed regional strategies involving product mix, promotional spending and merchandising activities that exceeded profit objective by 4.5%. Region is the most profitable in the company ($145 million).

·   Redesigned regional workforce into multi-functional core and dedicated customer teams in order to efficiently meet customer systems, research and product supply needs while designing and implementing profitable volume building promotional opportunities.

·   Directed category management planning processes with our customers. Typical result was the implementation of a revolutionary "Store within a Store" program, strategically designed to attract retailer's targeted consumers of frozen meals. Increased weekly sales by 23%.

·   Developed and delivered in-house software application training program in order to improve the effectiveness of a division wide roll-out of computers.

·   Implemented cost containment measures to achieve savings of $1 million from a fiscal 2000 operating budget of $7.7 million. Identified further cost savings opportunities to produce a 2001 operating budget 11% lower than the 2001 actual spending (-$720,000).

NATHANIEL BLOOM
Page Two

Manager - Sales Development Group (1997 - 1999)

· Developed product variations targeted at wholesale membership club business. Involved in packaging design, pricing and business forecasting.

· Devised alternate promotional program on items to generate merchandising support through convenience store channels of distribution.

CONSOLIDATED PAPERS, INC., Wisconsin Rapids, WI   1992 - 1997
A $1.5 billion manufacturer of consumer paper products.

Divisional Sales Manager

· Managed sales operation in seven-state area including personal accounts and a three-person sales team. Exceeded assigned sales quota every year.

· Secured new customers through cold calling, business analysis and demonstration of products and support benefits. New customer examples include Schnuek's Markets, St. Louis; Venture Stores, St. Louis; Dillons Supermarkets, Springfield, MO; Malone & Hyde, all divisions; and Wetterau, all divisions.

· Grew business base of existing customers through the development of strategically targeted line extensions.

GARDEN STATE PAPER COMPANY, Garfield, NJ   1990 - 1992
District Sales Manager

FIRST BRANDS CORPORATION, Danbury, CT   1988 - 1990
Unit Manager - Coffee Division

EDUCATION

B.S., Economics, Connecticut College, 1988

INTERESTS

Athletics, Flying, Computers
Habitat for Humanity
Little League Coach
Sunday School Teacher

THORNTON T. WILLIS

15 Oak Drive • Detroit, MI 72530
(912) 754-1837

SUMMARY:

Fast-track achiever in sales/sales management with 11 years' experience in medical testing services and equipment. Extensive, in-depth expertise in medical technology and research including degree credentials and registration as Medical Technologist (ASCP).

PROFESSIONAL EXPERIENCE:

CULVER HEALTH CARE CORPORATION - Detroit, MI   **2000 to Present**
National Accounts Manager, Testing
Responsible for the consultative sale of clinical laboratory and substance abuse testing. Prepare proposals and presentations, bids and contracts. Present laboratory services to corporate medical personnel and other groups and individuals using various video materials.
Results:
- Focused on Fortune 1000 corporations as well as small and medium-size private and public companies requiring NIDA and Forensic Drug Testing as well as clinical testing.
- Developed Michigan/Illinois area into a $2.4 million territory in two years for Industrial/Corporate Testing.

FERNWELL INSTRUMENTS - Fort Smith, AK   **1996 to 2000**
Territory Manager
Responsible for training of distributor representatives, as well as for direct sales of blood analyzer product line. Participated in distributor sales meetings, conventions and functions involving end-user relationships.
Results:
- Developed 8-state territory achieving 136% of quota in first eight months.
- Established close working relationship with sales and management personnel of Medical Scientific, Inc.
- Successful in identifying key independent laboratory distributors in 8-state territory and negotiated contracts to sell new analyzer system to end-users.

KARTEEN LABORATORIES - Jacksonville, FL   **1991 to 1996**
Medical Lab Technologist

EDUCATION:

GEORGIA INSTITUTE OF TECHNOLOGY - Atlanta, GA
B.S., Medical Technology (Honors), 1991

PROFESSIONAL MEMBERSHIP:

American Society of Clinical Pathologists

GARY HAYNER

1314 Old Navy Road
Cincinnati, OH 45349
(413) 879-4237 (H) or (413) 542-8905 (O)

Problem solving, top-performing, results oriented sales/marketing leader with ten plus years of comprehensive sales management, sales/marketing and operations experience...Spearheaded significant sales and profit growth, built strong teams, motivated employees, and initiated cost effectiveness programs...Hands-on manager with proven operations, P&L, start-up, business development and customer service achievements.

SELECTED CAREER ACCOMPLISHMENTS

SENIOR SALES MANAGER   **Kaman Corporation**   **1997 - Present**

* Exercised complete sales, operational and P&L responsibility for a start-up service company.

* Increased sales from $0 to $1.5 million/annum, trained sales teams and cultivated partnerships.

* Opened key national accounts, led entry into new markets, built sales/marketing team, instituted strong customer service program and organized operational team.

* Instituted productivity improvement and cost reduction programs, subcontracted services and built working relationships with financial institutions, fleet leasing and insurance companies.

* Developed/implemented strategic and tactical business and sales/marketing plans.

REGIONAL SALES MANAGER   **Waldorf Corporation**   **1988 - 1997**

* Built sales tenfold from $150,000 to $1.5 million/annum.

* Developed customer service/sales support teams and marketing infrastructure to support a $20 million business.

* Instituted business plans, established functional responsibility, directed supervisory team and managed three department heads with 40-50 employees and a sales team of seven.

* Developed/implemented flexible rate/pricing schedule and fostered cost effectiveness programs that saved more than 25%.

* Regional sales team ranked #1 or #2 based on highest percent of sales growth from 1992 to 1996.

SALES MANAGER   **John Alden Life Insurance Company**   **1986 - 1988**

* Built Life/Health Insurance sales force that increased sales revenues 40% in first year.

Other employment: Department Manager (Home Depot), District Manager (Ball Corporation)

EDUCATION

B.A., Business, University of North Carolina, 1985

CHARLES WADE
705 Kensington Road
Los Angeles, CA 90225
(213) 795-3487 Home
(213) 547-8320 Office

SUMMARY

A results-oriented professional sales and account manager with a proven track record managing national accounts in the plastic resin and plastic film industries for a major Fortune 500 chemical company and a regional plastic converting company. Key successes in penetration, issues/service management and developing new business and increasing market share.

PROFESSIONAL EXPERIENCE

ATLANTIC RICHFIELD CHEMICAL COMPANY – Los Angeles, CA   **2000-Present**

General Sales Manager - Films Division
Responsible for the marketing plan, sales implementation and consumer base for the films division of a newly-organized polyethylene plastics operation.

- Directed all management efforts to establish the creation of a new polyethylene film division including resin selection, quality control parameters and equipment utilization.

- Grew the film customer base from 0-31 customers, taking them from development status to commercial status in the first year of operation ($6 million sales).

- Generated new business opportunities in the second year which increased business by 150%.

DOW CHEMICAL COMPANY – Midland, MI   **1983-2000**

Account Manager – Detroit, MI   1995-2000
Responsible for $40 million polystyrene and polyethylene film territory managing the business issues and relationship with the largest distributor ($12 million) of polystyrene film sold into the envelope window market and increased direct sales of specialty polymer film products in the Northeast region.

- Exceeded sales plan in 1996, 1997 and 1998 by 8-10% per year.

- Initiated and managed a Quality Task Force utilizing the Continuous Improvement Process to improve product quality - reducing returns from 2.8% to .3% with annual savings of $250,000.

- Instituted and chaired an innovative "make and hold" program to overcome lengthy lead time problems generating 100% supply positions at three major olefin film customers and an additional $400,000 in sales revenue per year.

- Reduced collection time of past due receivables saving over $500,000 annually.

Charles Wade   **Page 2**

<u>Account Manager – St. Louis, MO</u>   1991-1995

Responsible for $35 million sales territory, managing the largest Dow Chemical polyethylene account in the disposable film market and increasing sales volumes of resins at major extrusion and molding accounts.

- Negotiated and signed a three-year, $40 million contract at the largest disposable film account under extreme competitive pressures producing 20% additional sales volume and limiting competitor participation.

- Initiated relationship; focused on technology fit; and closed sale to a new injection molding customer leading to $25 million sales in four years.

- Sold a specialty food packaging account generating $3 million of new business in the first year.

- Exceeded sales plan in 1991, 1992, 1993 and 1994, earning sales achievement and cash awards.

<u>Senior Sales Specialist – Harrisburg, PA</u>   1984-1991

Responsible for polyolefin, polystyrene, and engineered resin sales to new and developmental accounts in the Delaware, Pennsylvania and New York areas and New England states.

- Generated $1 million per year in new business from a new specialty blow molding account.

- Managed a new product introduction at a specialty roto molding account yielding $3.2 million of new business over three years.

- Grew territory sales volume 120% in six years.

<u>Sales Representative – Harrisburg, PA</u>   1983-1984

EDUCATION

Villanova University (1983)
Bachelor of Business Administration

PROFESSIONAL AFFILIATIONS

Member S.P.I. (Society of Plastic Industries)
Member S.P.E. (Society of Plastics Engineers)
Committee Member EMAA (Envelope Manufacturers Association of America)

CHRISTOPHER SHAY
3 Oakbourne Drive
Minneapolis, MN 55440
(612) 540-4512

SUMMARY

Accomplished sales executive with 12 years of experience in managing, selling and marketing with food service companies in a high profile role directing the sales success of an organization. Previous background includes both operational and sales management in the Food Service Industry.

PROFESSIONAL EXPERIENCE

1999 to Present   GENERAL MILLS, INC., Minneapolis, MN
   A $7 billion international manufacturer of specialty foods and food ingredients.

Vice President - Chains
Developed and led the first national account sales effort for the company. Report to the Senior Vice President, Marketing & Sales. Responsible for $2.1 million sales budget which contributed 20% gross profit for the company, selling specialty foods and seasonings.

· Instituted sales and marketing program directed towards national account business which successfully sold 15 major national restaurant chain accounts within the first two years.
· Grew the department's sales from start-up to $1.4 million in four years, contributing $350,000 in company profits.
· Trained and directed the chain account efforts of the 53 Regional Sales Managers. In the first two years, company added 12 new regional chains, increasing annual sales by $750,000.
· Developed national account marketing and promotional programs which stimulated the addition of seven national account purchasing contracts. These contracts added $500,000 in sales annually at a gross profit of $125,000.

1997 to 1999   H.J. HEINZ COMPANY, Pittsburgh, Pennsylvania
   $6.6 billion manufacturer and distributor of gravies, sauces and food seasonings.

Vice President, Sales & Marketing
Responsible for sales budget of $90 million dollars, $14 million in profits; managed staff of six Regional Sales Managers and three R&D scientists. Reported to the President.

· Directed team which developed 20 new products to be sold to food companies. These new items achieved $2 million in sales within first two years.

CHRISTOPHER SHAY   <u>Page 2</u>

- Increased sales volume by 20% the <u>first</u> year through a revamped outside sales force. This $18 million increase exceeded the first year sales budget and returned $2.7 million in profit.
- Successfully led the first focused national account sales effort, selling $4 million to six national accounts. This generated $600,000 gross profit.

1989 to 1997   NABISCO FOODS GROUP, East Hanover, New Jersey
A $200 million subsidiary of $15 billion RJR Nabisco, Inc. which manufacturers and sells ready-to-eat convenience foods to the food service industry.

<u>Director of Chain Sales</u>   **1993-1997**
Managed eight Regional Account Executives; three Marketing Professionals; four Research and Development Scientists. Reported to Vice President of Sales & Marketing. Sold wide range of ready-to-eat cereals and convenience foods (i.e., waffles, sauces, gravies, food bases, etc.) to large national restaurant and food chains.

- Reorganized and restructured the national account department to be "account targeted". Increased sales from $30 million to $65 million in three years.
- Developed first multi-functional business team (Sales, Marketing and Research & Development) devoted exclusively to the growth of National Account sales. This change allowed National Account sales to grow by $25 million in three years.

<u>Regional Sales Manager - West</u>   **1992-1993**

<u>District Sales Manager</u>   **1990-1992**

<u>Sales Representative</u>   **1989-1990**

EDUCATION & AFFILIATIONS

B.A. - Business Management, Rutgers University, 1989

Completed numerous IFMA workshops and seminars on management, selling (Development & Managing Brokers; Developing a National Account Department); segment sales courses. How to sell different sales segments such as: mid-size chains; growth chains; contract feeders; specialty chains; Cash N' Carry.

SALES AWARDS

- Regional Sales Manager of the Year, 1992, 1993
- District Sales Manager of the Year, 1991
- Sales Rookie of the Year, 1989

BRADLEY FOX
63 Enfield Drive
Lancaster, PA 17934
(717) 833-7842

OBJECTIVE

Senior management position requiring international sales and marketing expertise.

SUMMARY

Fifteen plus years of increasing responsibility in sales, marketing and general management.

- Extensive multi-national experience
- Strong leader and team builder
- Strong technical background
- Expertise in licensing joint ventures and start-up operations

EXPERIENCE

ARMSTRONG WORLD ENTERPRISES, Lancaster, PA   1999 – Present
$65M U.S. manufacturer of industrial pumps for the rubber, petrochemical and plastics industries with manufacturing operations in the U.S. and Germany and sales offices worldwide.

Director, International Sales
Report to Vice President – Sales & Marketing. Responsible for managing and growing business for the Corporation in the Pacific Rim (Latin and South America, the Far East/Asia-Pacific).

- Established and managed international sales management and coordination department at corporate headquarters.
- Restructured international field sales organization for Far East and Latin America. Reorganized and relocated Armstrong Asia from Hong Kong to Singapore. Staffed and managed Armstrong Asia, a sales/marketing company for the Far East and Asia.
- Increased new equipment sales from $5M in 1999 to $20M in 2002.
- Restructured/managed sales representative network for the Americas and Asia Pacific. Personally led breakthrough in Far East by winning contracts in petrochemical, plastics and rubber sectors. Negotiated major contracts in China, Taiwan, Korea, Thailand and Mexico.
- Concluded license arrangement with Westinghouse joint venture for pump repair and overhaul in Singapore.

INDEPENDENT CONSULTANT   1997 – 1999
Awarded contracts in defense, aerospace and industrial markets sectors in U.S. and Europe.

BRADLEY FOX   Page Two

COOPER SYSTEMS, INC., Houston, TX & Frankfurt, Germany   1994 – 1997

Division of Cooper Industries, a $500M U.S. manufacturer of computer control systems for the industrial, defense and aerospace markets with manufacturing operations in the U.S., U.K., Germany, France and Japan.

Director, International Sales, Cooper Systems, Inc. and General Manager, Cooper AB
Reported to President. Responsible for managing and growing business worldwide.

- Restructured international organization. Created, staffed and managed Cooper Systems, a sales/marketing company for Europe, Africa and Middle East. Achieved 78% sales growth to $32M between 1994-1997. P&L responsibility for Cooper Systems, Inc.
- Personally led breakthrough of in-tech product line by winning contracts with aircraft OEMs in Italy, India and France. Negotiated five major aerospace contracts.
- Established/managed sales network for Pacific, the Americas and the Far East.
- Restructured European organization in 1996 to be consistent with new management's philosophy.

A-C COMPRESSOR, Appleton, WI   1989 – 1994

U.S. manufacturer of industrial gas turbine power and compression systems for the oil/gas, petrochemical and industrial markets.

Director of Engineering Services

- Recruited to develop and manage all technical functions in major expansion of company activities in Europe. Reported to Vice President and Managing Director.
- Established/staffed technical group engineering, project management and procurement.
- Won/completed two major turnkey projects ($40M) in Sweden, Germany and the U.K.

EVANS SYSTEMS, INC., Bay City, TX   1986 – 1989

Project Manager

EDUCATION

BSME, Texas A & M, 1986

LANGUAGES

Fluent French and German; knowledge of others.

SANDRA KAUFMAN
12 Duckling Road
San Francisco, CA 98103

Home: (415) 592-4592   Office: (415) 435-9000

SUMMARY

Experienced sales professional with 16+ years of proven performance selling to industrial distributors.

- Hiring & Training
- End-user Penetration
- Evaluating, Local Markets

- New Product Introduction
- Local/National Marketing Programs & Promotions
- Competitive Analysis & Sales Strategies

PROFESSIONAL EXPERIENCE

KELLY-MOORE PAINT COMPANY   **1985 – Present**
Industrial chemical and paint manufacturer with annual sales of $135 million.

Director of Industrial Sales (1999-Present)
Sell complete line of industrial paints (both aerosol and bulk), electronic coatings and specialty products with sales of $85 million. Manage national sales manager, three national account managers, three regional managers and 25 manufacturer's reps. Products sold through 900 industrial, contractor and specialty distributors.

- Increased sales 17% in 2001 and exceeded all budgeted goals on top and bottom line, as well as reducing selling expense. Increased sales 12% in 2000.
- Combined the selling of Easy Way and Spread Right from two rep forces to one allowing greater opportunity for distributor to consolidate product lines.
- Negotiated exclusive membership with large independent contractor marketing group, increasing sales from $500,000 to $1.6 million.
- Negotiated exclusive agreement with West Coast Distributors overcoming competition from RustOleum. Projected 20% sales increase with members and growth of business from $750,000 to $5+ million over a two-year period.
- Developed special incentive structure for manufacturer's reps by combining financial and sales recognition award, which increased enthusiasm, motivation and fostered a 20% sales growth for 75% of reps.

Manager of Sales & Marketing (1995-1999)
Managed sales and marketing functions worldwide.

- Introduced first international sales meeting with classroom breakout sessions for training and developed forum for the exchange of information between sales force and top management.
- Introduced new line of mold inhibitive paint called Clear Flow. Sales grew to $2 million in three years.

SANDRA KAUFMAN *Page Two*

- Introduced new rust inhibitive chemical intermediate, achieving sales of $4 million in first year.
- Launched new line of environmentally safe mold release intermediates that grew business to $3.2 million over a three-year period.
- Marketed and negotiated exclusive rights for sale of a paint mixing system. Sales grew to $2 million at 30% gross profit in first year.

National Sales Manager (1991-1995)
Grew sales through industrial distributors using three regional managers working closely with manufacturer's reps. Worked closely with marketing to assist in relabeling, cross reference charts, fine-tuning sales/policies and timely promotions on key products.

- Increased sales 34% in 1994 and all regional managers and national sales manager won the President's Circle Excellence award.

Regional Sales Manager (1990-1991)
Managed $3 million in sales and $3.1 million in regional manufacturing sales.

- Established network of 12 master distributors resulting in increased sales of 35% annually since 1990.

Regional Sales Manager (1988-1990)
Managed $1.2 million, one direct sales rep, and ten manufacturing reps covering three territories.

- Received award for largest dollar gain in 1989.

Inside Sales (1985-1988)
Worked closely with manufacturing, technical and outside sales as well as assisting industrial distributors.

EDUCATION & TRAINING

B.A., Marketing, UCLA, 1985

WILLIAM A. WATSON

23 Magnolia Lane
Mobile, AL 97263
(205) 745-9827

OBJECTIVE: A position in Product/Brand Management or Marketing

SUMMARY: Six years Marketing and Sales experience in the consumer product industry. Expertise in marketing research, competitive and trend analysis, merchandising strategies, category management and new product launches. A track record of growing market share and sales volumes with focus on the most profitable items.

EMPLOYMENT HISTORY:

Southland Foods, Inc.
Sales Accountant Representative, Tastemaster Coffee Division   1999 to Present
Manage accounts generating $27 million in annual sales. Responsible for increasing distribution points, sales volume and profit margins. Manage $195,000 merchandising budget. Supervise three field assistants.

- Grew market share 42% in the first three quarters of new product roll-out. Directed a market research program that resulted in the highest district rate of growth.

- Tripled annual growth rate of Tastemaster flavored coffees by introducing special packaging and shipper programs. Improved product loyalty and recognition.

- Increased category sales 24% and product turns 20% for a major retail chain.

- Focused merchandising dollars and marketing campaigns on the most profitable brands. Resulted in 28% sales increase of products with a 35% or higher profit margin.

Field Merchandiser   1995 to 1999
Developed and sold account programs and designed shelf layouts for 82 stores in the Alabama territory. $2 million annual sales.

- Ranked #1 in the district due to superior display sales and in-store merchandising. Led to job promotion.

EDUCATION:

M.S. - Organizational Management (GPA 3.79), 1995
Auburn University
Masters Thesis - Total Quality Management

B.S. - Business Administration/Marketing, 1993
University of Southern Alabama

STEPHANIE WILSON
81 Rock Ridge Road
Seattle, WA 98376
(941) 452-7839 Residence
(941) 584-3205 Business

PROFESSIONAL SUMMARY

Sales and Marketing Executive with strong leadership skills and track record of proven results. Twelve years of broad, in-depth experience in management, P&L, restructuring, team building, employee development and succession planning. Consistently exceed profitability, productivity and sales objectives.

PROFESSIONAL HISTORY

BIOTECH INSTRUMENT CORPORATION, Seattle, WA   **1995 to Present**
A leader in the field of services and instrumentation for the biotechnology and medical markets.

Regional Director   **2001 to Present**
Responsible for all aspects of sales, service, local marketing, administration, office management and employee development. Accountable for $37 million in revenue and 90 employees. Full P&L responsibility.

- Highest sales growth in 1999/2000.

- Overall profitability/employee highest in corporation.

- Reorganized entire division into multi-functional work-teams, dramatically improving customer service quality and response time, and empowering employees to "take risks".

- Developed and implemented key programs in marketing and sales management resulting in increased business at targeted accounts. Key account business increased by 25%.

- Implemented targeted selection interviewing process.

National Sales Manager   **1998 to 2001**
GPSC Laboratory Systems Division of Biotech Instrument Corporation. Accountable for sales force, tactical marketing programs, promotional and advertising programs.

- Profit increase of 68%.

- Improved market share 15%.

- Headed task force responsible for 29% reduction in product development time.

- Promoted to Regional Director in 2001.

PROFESSIONAL HISTORY

BIOTECH INSTRUMENT CORPORATION (Continued)

District Sales Manager   **1997 to 1998**
Accountable for staff of 18 sales and support personnel and $7.3 million in revenue.   Promoted to National Sales Manager of Biotech Instrument subsidiary in 1998.

Sales Representative   **1995 to 1997**
Responsible for key accounts in Seattle area. Doubled territory revenue in 15 months.   Promoted to District Sales Manager in 1997.

MET-Rx, INC.   **1992 to 1995**
Medical supplies division of Orth Pharmaceuticals

Sales Representative
Consistently recognized in "Top Ten" of company. National "Sales Representative of the Month" three times.

EDUCATION

UNIVERSITY OF WISCONSIN
Bachelor of Science - Biology, Chemistry - 1992

WASHINGTON STATE UNIVERSITY
M.B.A. in process - 2000 to Present

REFERENCES

Furnished Upon Request

WAYNE ALEXANDER
14 Sunset Lane
New Milford, CT 06777
(206) 437-9185 (H)
(206) 437-2020 (O)

SUMMARY

Sales professional with the ability to communicate well with clients who are primarily sophisticated, well-educated and wealthy entrepreneurs, CEOs, doctors, lawyers and other executives, as well as those from other professions who are purchasing "big ticket" items.

WORK EXPERIENCE

Regional Sales Manager, Team Builders, Stamford, CT   **1993 - Present**
Responsible for sales of pre-engineered, single family contemporary homes to a wide variety of affluent customers throughout Pennsylvania, New Jersey, and Connecticut.

- Sold over 300 individually designed pre-manufactured homes for years on a 100% commission basis.

- Established trust, confidence and rapport with individuals and couples who were about to spend an average of $500,000 on a new single-family home -- their dream house.

- Marketing and sales strategies I developed in New Jersey were so successful over a five-year period that my territory was split. I trained the new sales staff.

- First to market and advertise Team Builders in major home shows throughout Pennsylvania and New Jersey which increased regional business by 25% annually. Emphasis on home shown was then duplicated in all other regions of the country at the insistence of the corporate marketing department.

- Designed custom contemporary single family homes as a modification of the standard architecture. This "Masters in Architecture through Experience" was achieved on my own (no corporate training) by hard work and self-study.

Owner - Alexander's Painting & Contracting Business, Greenwich, CT   **1990 - 1993**

Director - Stamford Youth Program, Stamford, CT   **1988 - 1990**
Responsible for creation, organization and implementation of all youth commission programs. Responsible also for writing funding proposals to state and federal government agencies. Interviewing, employment of staff, community relations and solicitation of funding was part of the job.

EDUCATION

B.A.   Sociology, 1986, Plymouth University, Laconia, New Hampshire
M.Ed. Psychological Services, 1988, Westminster College, Westminster, Massachusetts

OTHER ACTIVITIES

State of Connecticut, Racquetball Champion, Singles, 1998
New Milford Township Recreation Commission, Planning Committee

KAREN M. LANGFORD
1400 Sutton Place. Apt. 3C
New York, NY
(212) 457-3403 (Res.)
(212) 582-3400 (Bus.)

PROFILE:

Customer Service and Sales Manager with 14 years of varied experience with a major financial institution. Particular expertise in:

- Centralized customer service/staffing/phone volume management
- Training employees and monitoring results
- Quality control development and implementation
- Complaint management tracking and follow-up implementation
- Strategic business planning, budgeting and expense control
- Inbound Telemarketing/Sales

PROFESSIONAL EXPERIENCE:

BANK OF NEW YORK, New York, NY (2000-Present)

Assistant Vice President, Loan/Telemarketing Services
Manage staff of 18, personnel budget of $425,000. Direct phone volume tracking, full and part-time hiring, product and office equipment training, sales goal tracking, evaluation and incentive planning, and multiple telemarketing project implementation.

Selected Accomplishments:

- Successfully managed Loan/Telemarketing Unit that produced $65 million in booked credit outstandings through 2000. This produced $1.5 million in margin income to the bank.

- Created and trained a team of senior sales consultants to test telemarketing of a high-end specialized bank product to existing clientele. As a result of this test, the bank's multi-product customer base increased 20% when overall telemarketing was completed by branch personnel.

- Designed and implemented a monthly evaluation for all sales consultants which produced individual improvement prior to annual review and increased unit productivity.

FIRST NEW YORK BANK, New York, NY (1988-2000)
Assistant Vice President, Centralized Customer Service (1994-2000)

Managed staff of 17, personnel budget of $374,000. Directed personnel hiring, customer service and sales skills training, bank product training, complaint management, development of quality control standards, and staffing in conjunction with phone/time management.

Karen M. Langford
Page Two

<u>Selected Accomplishments:</u>

- Utilized innovative hiring practices to create a quality team of customer service consultants to respond to the needs of both internal and external customers. As a result, this team consistently out-performed competitors in areas of customer service and sales, as measured by an independent Customer Service Shopper's Study.

- Expedited new employee training by creating a "mentoring" program and developing a self-taught training manual. These techniques increased trainee confidence and enabled them to assume customer service responsibilities faster.

- Successfully developed and implemented career pathing within unit. This innovation coupled with creative staffing led to a turnover percentage of under 2%, well below the customer service industry average. Overtime expense was also eliminated.

- Created quality control standards to enhance service provided to internal and external customers. This reduced errors in work forwarded to other units.

- Created a management process to follow up on customer complaints. The utilization of this process enhanced the customer's image of First New York Bank.

- Successfully controlled expenses within planned budget allocations throughout the history of the unit.

Assistant Vice President, Banking Officer, Teller (1988-1994)
Various staff sizes and asset, liability and personnel budgets. Directed teller operations, training of tellers and platform personnel, audit controls, customer servicing, budget control, new business planning, staffing, and marketing and sales objectives throughout the retail branch system.

EDUCATION: New York University, New York, NY
B.A., Accounting, 1988

American Institute of Banking
Principles of Banking, Commercial Law, Marketing and other courses

PROFESSIONAL DEVELOPMENT COURSES:		
	Power and Influence	Performance Appraisal Development
	Effective Business Writing	Coaching and Counseling
	Interviewing Skills	Interpersonal Relationships
	Sales Management	Customer Service Management

BARBARA A. BABSON

816 Crimson Way
Baltimore, MD 19736

Home: (312) 933-4487   Office: (312) 774-9827   E-Mail: BAB@MSN.com

OBJECTIVE

A position in healthcare field sales that allows me to take advantage of a successful career in Customer Service.

PROFESSIONAL EXPERIENCE

MADISON HEALTHCARE, Baltimore, MD   **1997 - Present**
Scientific Products Division

Customer Support Supervisor   1999 - Present
Report to Area Customer Service Manager with responsibility for coordinating activities of nine Customer Support Representatives handling $6.7 million in capital equipment purchases, $9 million in sales contracts, $8 million of Madison's Quality Assurance Program (QAP), and $10 million in vendor rebates.

- Responsible for selection and training of all department members.
- Developed a protocol that increased customer phone service levels by 45% within thirteen months.
- Ongoing program implemented to reduce QAP inventory write-offs.
- Decreased department operational overhead by 19% within eight months.
- Direct multi-functional interface with Sales, Sales Management, Area Vice President, Marketing, Finance, customers and Manufacturing.
- Instrumental in assisting with the consolidation of the New Jersey, Pennsylvania and Delaware regions.

Customer Service Representative   1997 - 1999
Coordinated activities for key accounts in greater Baltimore area involving 65,000 products.

- Directly handled orders and special pricing for accounts generating annual revenue of $14 million dollars.
- Direct responsibility for Abbott Laboratories, the largest reference lab in the northeast.
- Voted Employee of the Quarter for Eastern Regional Office.

EDUCATION

Bachelor of Business Administration - 1997
University of Delaware

ANTHONY JACKSON
30 Churchill Street
Teaneck, NJ 07665
(201) 837-6749

SUMMARY

Professional with 20 years of management experience in bringing state-of-the-art high-tech products to national and international markets. Broad experience in program/project management, marketing, merchandising, development engineering, manufacturing, financial analysis and operations management. Exceptional communication, interpersonal and leadership skills. Excellent background in staffing professional teams, OEM, trade shows, foreign negotiations, semi-conductor process/manufacturing, equipment and tool design.

PROFESSIONAL EXPERIENCE

ADVANCED COMPUTER CORPORATION, Teaneck, NJ   1983-Present

OEM PROGRAM MANAGER/SENIOR PLANNER   2000-Present
Developed OEM executive accounts; negotiated comprehensive technical requirements and developed non-ACC logo solutions. Negotiated OEM contracts; provided lines of delivery to meet supply/demand, manufacturing and delivery. Developed a working team to assure customer quality and satisfaction.

- Planned and implemented the infrastructure for new OEM business opportunity within PC company which generated sales revenue of over $150M/per year.
- Established generic OEM contract that became corporate standard.
- Provided turnkey implementation for customer quality satisfaction while maintaining profit margins.
- Planned and implemented team building training sessions that formed a cohesive unit from teams located at four different geographic locations.
- Bid Manager for large airline account that resulted in millions of dollars of revenue.

PROGRAM MANAGER   1997-2000
Developed and implemented strategic direction that provided technical, marketing and merchandising assistance to all vendors developing Anstar hardware for PC systems. Managed over 25 trade shows worldwide and special events activities, planning, staffing, show venues, demonstrations, logistics and PR after show activities (Asia, Pacific Rim, South Pacific, Europe and Russia).

- Demonstrated to the industry that Anstar Architecture was a viable PC platform which generated a 10% increase in sales.
- Received Excellence Award.
- Planned, developed and implemented the infrastructure to technically support over 500 hardware developers of personal computer adapters/cards.

SENIOR ENGINEERING MANAGER   1995-1997
Managed project office team of professional engineers who provided design criteria to Advanced-related products utilizing the PC as a development base. Also designed customized solutions to meet special bid requests for quotations from different industries.

- Developed and implemented requirements and specifications for innovative PC hardware technology.
- Negotiated multiple industry solutions and generated sales revenues in the multiple of millions of dollars.

- Implemented controls and processes which resulted in reducing turnaround time and increasing productivity.
- Managed R/3 development engineering project office for Model 3A; 3B; 3C; and 3D. Released from development engineering to manufacturing all systems within schedule and cost objectives.

LASER PRINTER DIVISION (LPD)
PRINTER MANAGER   1992-1995
Managed a $150M Personal Computer Printer Program with a team of 15. Responsible for worldwide profits, tactical/strategic planning, development engineering, quality and customer satisfaction.

- Directed technology development and financial requirements for PC printers; negotiated with vendors worldwide to establish the first vendor printer for PC usage within Advanced Computer Corporation.
- Succeeded in establishing LPD into a profitable PC printer business.
- Received Division Excellence Award.

HARDWARE TECHNOLOGY   1989-1992
Directed worldwide off-shore development and procurement activities of products for early PC hardware development which included power supplies, motherboards, keyboards, displays and printers.

- Negotiated and contracted various products that established a savings of both dollars and resources in developing early PC hardware.
- Implemented the first vendor-purchased products for internal PC hardware.

POWER-MISER DEVELOPMENT   1988-1989
Development Engineer responsible for mechanical design and implementation of power supplies.

SEMI-CONDUCTOR PROCESSING
EQUIPMENT DEVELOPMENT   1983-1988
Development/Manufacturing/Process/Equipment Engineer for semi-conductor devices.

- Co-founder of Advanced Computer Corporation's Contamination Control Committee which established clean room standards.
- Received Contamination Control Award.

Prior to 1983
Design Engineer/Quality Engineer

- Mechanical design engineer for upper atmosphere sounding devices (Government Contract).
- Mechanical design engineer for oceanographic calibration facilities and installation (U.S. Navy contracts).

EDUCATION

Rutgers University, New Brunswick, NJ
Graduate Studies in Business and Finance

Columbia University, New York, NY
B.S., Mechanical Design

MICHAEL HULSE

5 Sunrise Boulevard
Roanoke, VA 23620
(804) 261-4580

EXPERIENCE

1999-Present

VICE PRESIDENT OF DEVELOPMENT – A.H. Ross Company   Roanoke, VA
Responsible for: Management of 30-person Residential Development Department; work out of company's residential portfolio; entire development process through design, construction, marketing, sales and property management.

- Resurrected a $65 million, 700-unit golf course community.
- Settled a failed $8 million defaulted bond issue in Federal Court.

1995-1999

DEVELOPMENT MANAGER – Telstar Properties, Inc.   Alexandria, VA
Responsible for: All multi-family development, marketing, leasing, property management and asset management; all financial and feasibility analyses; selection of development team. Design sequence and liaison with construction management.

- Developed one of the finest institutional grade, 20-story apartment buildings in the Virginia area.
- Consistently leased above market rents for the residential and office component.

1993-1995

DIRECTOR OF DESIGN & CONSTRUCTION – R&J Contractors   Columbia, MD
Responsible for: Implementation of new project, site selection and master plan, pricing; contract control in selection of design team and general contractor; managing product design; project construction; leasing and property management support.

- Saved $18 per square foot during development of company's typical office product.
- Reduced the development schedule on each project by six months.

1989-1993

VICE PRESIDENT OF DEVELOPMENT - Toll Brothers Developers   Baltimore, MD
Responsible for: Entire development process for $33 million of residential property; project viability, land acquisition, design, construction and permanent financing, marketing, sales and supervision of construction management.

- Obtained over $25 million in acquisition and construction financing in 18 months.
- Founded a real estate company, mortgage company, and construction division to maximize internal profits.

1985-1989

PROJECT MANAGER - Turner Corporation   Washington, DC
PROJECT MANAGER – Lenmar Corporation
Responsible for: Construction of multiple retail projects from bid through completion; subcontractor and purchase contracts; cost control; liaison with developer, tenant, architect, and engineer; scheduling document submittal/approval.

- Simultaneously managed seven separate projects in three different states on-time and under budget.

EDUCATION

1985

B.S., Civil Engineering, Brown University

DARNEL D. LAYTON

436 Tumbleweed Way
Oklahoma City, OK 19375
Phone: (384) 998-7937   E-Mail DDLAY@AOL

Results-oriented, entrepreneurial leader with extensive experience in full-service commercial real estate development and management. CFO with successful track record in transaction structuring, acquisition, financing, asset management, investment maximization and raising equity.

SELECTED ACCOMPLISHMENTS

Vice President/CFO   2000-Present
Blue Sky Ventures Management, Inc.

Founding principal of $415 million full-service real estate company providing property acquisition, management, leasing, asset management and management consulting services. Portfolio includes office buildings, shopping centers, apartments and industrial facilities.

* Structured real estate investment trust (REIT) including negotiation with investment bankers, overseeing audits on over 15 partnerships, and preparation of prospectus.

* Supervised management of 32 properties owned by Blue Sky Ventures Management, resulting in annual revenues of over $28 million and attaining an occupancy rate of 97%.

* Renovated, repositioned and developed 32 properties.

Vice President/Chief Financial Officer   1996-2000
Branson Partners, Inc.

Real estate acquisition and development company specializing in office buildings.

* Structured real estate syndications involving assets of $72 million, preparing prospectus for investors and closing transactions.

Senior Accountant   1993-1996
Accountant   1990-1993

EDUCATION/CERTIFICATION

University of Oklahoma, 1990
Bachelor of Science in Business and Accounting

VIRGINIA A. KING

12 Bay Vista Road
Berkeley, CA 90714
(206) 696-4071 (Res.)

SUMMARY: Take-charge sales management executive with 12 years of management and marketing experience in the full service brokerage, banking and public sectors.

PROFESSIONAL EXPERIENCE: SAN FRANCISCO NATIONAL BANK, San Francisco, CA (1998-Present)

Vice President - Securities Marketing

Manage 18-member sales team responsible for the active distribution of a diversified investment product menu to clients and prospective customers throughout California. Sales credits increased 130% from $3.1M to $7.1M.

Selected Accomplishments:

- Motivated sales staff members to increase average individual sales performance by 200% from $120,000 in 1999 to $360,000 in 2000.

- Developed and delivered an extensive in-depth internal sales training program, which resulted in the complete acquisition of product knowledge and selling strategies for all new hires.

- Successfully implemented a marketing plan for the introduction of SFNB's California Tax Exempt Income Fund, which, since inception in 1998, has grown to over $60 million.

- Delivered frequent presentations to consumer bank employees to heighten awareness of products and services capabilities. Resulted in significant sales increases.

S.F.N.B. BROKERS, INC., San Francisco, CA (1992-1998)
Vice President - Sales Manager

Directly managed complete development of an eight-brokerage office system. Oversaw all phases which included: construction, outfitting, staffing, budgeting, and development/execution of each respective marketing plan.

SHEARSON LEHMAN/AMERICAN EXPRESS, San Francisco, CA (1989-1992)
Financial Consultant

Provided continuous Financial Management and Portfolio Analysis for a large retail and institutional customer base. Established customer's goals and objectives, then made appropriate product and service recommendations.

EDUCATION: B.A., Finance & Accounting, Oregon State University, 1989

CYNTHIA STONE

4102 Stoney Point Drive
Cleveland, OH 45349
(513) 698-3404

Results-oriented, entrepreneurial leader with proven record of success in start-up, turnaround and growth of profit centers. Skilled relationship builder/manager with extensive experience in rapid and sustained growth of fast-paced, high-pressure businesses. Major strengths include strategic planning/implementation, team building and development new market segments.

WORK EXPERIENCE

BRANCH MANAGER   1999-Present
Armco Financial Services Group, Middletown, OH

Start-up manager for Midwest office of Armco Financial Services Group, one of the largest credit services in the U.S. with annual sales in excess of $225 million.

- Built Midwest operation, hiring and training staff of 50 and producing annual sales **in excess of $90 million** within three years.

- Increased market share of Armco Financial Services Group business from **5% to 50%**, or $2.0 million per month.

- Created innovative competition among collectors, leading first team to exceed Banc One quota by **$30,000 in first month** of assignments.

- Developed and implemented call accounting software, causing **revenue increase of $150,000.**

- Developed office budget and achieved 13% profit by third quarter of operation.

ASSISTANT BRANCH MANAGER   1998-1999
Depository Trust Company, New York, NY

Promoted to help lead turnaround situation for branch office of large, privately-held collection firm with 15 branches and 300 employees.

- Increased branch revenue by **$150,000 per month in 60 days**, making profit for office for first time in six months.

- Recruited and trained personnel, increasing office staff by **50% in 60 days** and turning around morale to pave the way for increased business.

- Set up new system and developed guidelines for monitoring inventories on a daily basis, **increasing productivity** and speeding up collections.

Cynthia Stone Page Two

- Closed **over 48,000 files** which had been inactive to decrease backlog and focus office on most profitable business. Total review was accomplished within 20 days.

- Developed system to insure contract compliance, **increasing compliance rate to 99%** with Citibank, N.A., leading to significantly higher collection rates and an increase in business.

NATIONAL OPERATIONS MANAGER/EASTERN REGION 1993-1998
Sunwest Financial Services, Albuquerque, NM

Primary responsibility included ensuring compliance with company policy by all branch offices in Eastern United States.

- Wrote/implemented weekly inventory tracking system which was reported to top management resulting in hiring of 30 new personnel and increase in **profitability to over 10%.**

- Streamlined monthly review process for senior management, decreasing report of essential information from **200 to 10 pages** and highlighting situations in which special attention was needed.

- Wrote new company training program and set up pilot training sessions which resulted in **25% increase** of average size of payment per collector.

EDUCATION

B.A., Accounting 1993
Kansas State University

KENNETH FITZGERALD
405 Marshallton Street
Boston, MA 02210

(617) 792-4519 *(Home)*   (617) 268-7800 *(Office)*

SUMMARY QUALIFICATIONS

Senior financial services line manager with profit and loss responsibility. Significant results include sales increases, motivational speaking, profitability increases, cost containment, merger/acquisition search and completion and portfolio management. Harvard Business School MBA with Big Six experience.

PROFESSIONAL EXPERIENCE

MIDLANTIC NATIONAL BANK   **2000 – Present**

Midlantic National Bank acquired Liberty Savings & Loan, (see below) at which time I was selected by the CEO to direct the group of banks. The acquisition represented 15% of the resulting company. Seven months later, I undertook three additional acquisitions, adding six banking facilities.

VICE PRESIDENT – REGIONAL SALES MANAGER

- Acquisition returned to profitability through operations in first year. Today, has the highest internal ROA of all regions.

- Changed operations to sell asset products through the individual banks.

- Consolidated three banking facilities, improving customer service and product delivery, and eliminated a production facility.

- Achieved product sales exceeding the historical sales records of the prior company with 50% of the personnel (150/300).

- Performed individual and group sales training and instituted a value added sales program.

LIBERTY SAVINGS & LOAN ASSOCIATION   **1996 – 2000**

Recruited to this $400 million mutual savings and loan association. Attractive due to opportunity to succeed the CEO in a few years.

SENIOR VICE PRESIDENT – CHIEF FINANCIAL OFFICER

- Led capital acquisition search, resulting in four viable candidates and a definitive agreement in six months.

- Managed $100 million investment portfolio. Eliminated external manager and restructured portfolio, achieving yield targets and small trading gains.

- Implemented profitability and cost accounting system. PC-based, internally designed, fully allocated cost and revenue driven system.

- Prepared strategic plan. Identified cost reductions, revenue increases and capital concerns (pre-regulatory change).

KENNETH FITZGERALD
Page Two

MIDLANTIC NATIONAL BANK   1995 – 1996
Successor to First Savings of Massachusetts.

SENIOR VICE PRESIDENT – DATA PROCESSING

- Agreed to remain with successor to complete two primary objectives:

    - Determined data processing direction. Dissolved one major in-house data center and converted three separate companies to a single servicer. Company with servicer today.
    - Negotiated the sale/dissolution of a Georgia joint venture. Recreated the financial records and rebuilt the data base. Locations were Atlanta and Augusta, Georgia.

FIRST SAVINGS OF MASSACHUSETTS   1994 – 1995

CHIEF FINANCIAL OFFICER

- Recruited as Vice President and Controller; made Chief Financial Officer within seven months.

- Negotiated sale of $2.1 billion stock savings bank to successor noted above in 1995. Sale precipitated by dissident shareholder actions. Return to shareholders exceeded 400%.

PRICE WATERHOUSE   1987 – 1994

SENIOR MANAGER – AUDIT

Audit clients included $3.6 billion multinational commercial finance company, $2.3 billion consumer finance company, commercial banks, other consumer finance, diversified holding company and foundry operations. Financial statements issued included annual reports, Forms 10 and various registrations under the 1933 and 1934 acts with respect to acquisitions and security issuances. Instructor for national and regional training and computer audit specialist.

PROFESSIONAL

CPA, State of Massachusetts, 1987
Director, Pioneer Mortgage Service Company, 1994 – 1995
Director, PAR Leasing Corporation, 1994 – 1995

EDUCATION

MBA, Harvard Business School, 1987
BA, Villanova University, 1985

LESTER P. JACKSON

12 Sea Spray Circle
Laguna Beach, CA 90725

Home: (414) 776-9041
Work: (414) 256-8400

E-Mail: LPJAC@AOL

OBJECTIVE Senior executive position with major leader in retail industry

EXPERIENCE

1998 - Present WEST COAST PETROLEUM, INC., Los Angeles, CA
Vice President
Responsible for the overall management of 35 retail stations and eight franchised parts outlets with revenues of $80 million and 295 personnel. Executive Committee member involved in the management of the Company.

- Negotiated and acquired 29 retail sites in three states during a two-year period. Developed and implemented all operating policies and procedures.
- Improved profitability of the division through significant reductions in expenses and effective marketing strategies.
- Administered an $8 millon acquisition and capital expenditure budget. Created and implemented customer service and store-level training programs.
- Reorganized division and introduced new positions and concepts to promote empowerment and reduce overhead.
- Improved sales and volumes by 80%.
- Increased the Division's cash flow by $60 million.

1990 - 1998 TEXACO, INC., White Plains, NY
Marketing Advisor (1994 - 1998)
Led the task force which developed an Automotive Parts Franchise Program for service station dealers.

- Conducted market and consumer research to assess industry direction.
- Developed standards for dealer enrollment.
- Determined training programs, nationwide warranty offer, program compliance mechanism and franchise fee structure.
- Recommended necessary organizational structure.

Marketing Analyst (1990 - 1994)
Evaluated and automated field and staff functions to improve productivity. Directed the design of a management information system for the West Coast marketing region.

EDUCATION Boston University
M.B.A., 1990 Major: Management

University of Massachusetts
B.S., 1988 Major: Marketing

TINA ARNOLD
700 Park Avenue
New York, New York 10021

Residence: (212) 753-3563   Office: (212) 753-4600

SUMMARY

Entrepreneurial success in retail merchandising, including design and product development, planning, marketing, implementation of programs and management. Exceptional problem solving, team building, communication, analytical, strategic planning and negotiation skills. Unique ability to bring people together for accomplishment of common goals and successfully exercise creativity in both merchandising and product development.

PROFESSIONAL EXPERIENCE

BERGDORF GOODMAN INC.   **1985 - Present**
BG Essentials, New York, NY (1999 - Present)

Divisional Merchandise Manager
Responsible for planning, development, advertising and profitability of the Women's Sportswear and Cosmetics areas, which include: Clothing, Leather Goods, Handbags, Gloves, Perfumes and Cosmetics. Directly responsible for the 20 stores of BG Essentials with volume in excess of $35 million.

- Expanded Jones of New York sportswear business from $2.2 million to $5.5 million while maintaining gross margin in excess of 50%.
- Refixtured the entire division with new fixtures from Jones of New York at no cost to the company, a savings of over $175,000.
- Created excitement and enthusiasm and increased sales by negotiating promotional appearances of several well-known celebrities.
- Promoted one buyer to store merchandise manager.

BG Essentials, Stamford, CT (1996 - 1999)

Merchandise Consultant
Responsible for the planning, development, sales promotion and profitability of Women's Sportswear. Supervised three buyers while simultaneously maintaining direct buying responsibilities for small leather goods. Directly responsible for annual volume in excess of $12 million.

- Expanded Dana Buchman sportswear business from $525,000 to $1.75 million with no margin deterioration.
- Promoted three assistants to Group Sales Manager positions within one year and promoted one buyer to a senior-level buying position in Women's Accessories.

Buyer (1989 - 1996)
Managed the planning, development, acquisition, presentation, sales promotion and profitability for the Women's Shoe Department for Bergdorf Goodman's eight stores in the Northeast. Annual volume in excess of $4.5 million.

- Increased volume by over 255% while also maintaining a 255% increase in profits, making the department an important profit center at Bergdorf Goodman.
- Developed all private label programs covering five product labels in four major categories.
- Represented Bergdorf Goodman on a continuing basis in the Far East and Europe as a key member of their Product Development Team.
- Planned and implemented departments in four new Bergdorf Goodman stores and the complete renovation at 17 others.

Prior Buying and Management Experience

BG Essentials, Boston, MA (1985 - 1989)
Progressed through Bergdorf's Training Program and held positions of: Junior Assistant Buyer - Women's Clothing; Sales Manager - Sporting Goods and Toys; Senior Assistant Buyer - Women's Robes and Loungewear, and Group Sales Manager - Women's Sportswear & Cosmetics.

EDUCATION

Bachelor of Science - Marketing, 1985
Fashion Institute of Technology, New York, NY

ALFRED L. NEWMAN
FRANKFORT, GERMANY- 215-679-4359 (U.S. MESSAGE SERVICE)

OBJECTIVE

A high-impact financial position requiring creative and innovative approaches to strategy development, problem solving, and achievement of business and financial goals.

CAREER SUMMARY

Advanced very rapidly to partner after only eight years with an international "Big 6" accounting firm, continuously operating on the leading edge of new practice areas and business trends, as exemplified by Russian assignment. Tax and business advisor with 16 years of heavy transaction-related consulting to rapidly growing businesses, from venture capital financed technology start-ups to large multinationals. Strong finance, accounting, and legal knowledge on many transactional issues has been a key contributor to success. Leader of national efficiency/technology initiatives related to corporate tax return compliance practice.

BUSINESS EXPERIENCE

DELOITTE & TOUCHE   **1986 - Present**

PARTNER, Tax Division – Frankfort, Germany (1999 - Present)

Assumed responsibility for neglected, demoralized, and under-resourced tax practice comprised of eight professionals, six of which had less than six months' tenure, and after seven recent terminations/departures, including predecessor.

- Achieved dramatic improvement in division profitability to $700,000 for FYE December, 1999 (after $155,000 loss for year of arrival). Profit level is fully costed, and after all partner distributions and expatriate allowances and costs. This was one of the higher profit levels in the worldwide tax practice on a per partner basis for the year.

- Built team, net of two more terminations, to 18 professionals by fall 1997, through internal and external recruitment.

- Dramatically improved client service capability, quality, and responsiveness and instituted intensive training program and recruitment effort.

- Quickly developed high degree of personal technical competence in German tax, accounting, legal, and business matters.

- Served over 125 clients from all over the world, including several Fortune 500 companies investigating expansion opportunities in Germany.

Repatriating February, 2000 to Atlanta, GA to assume engagement tax partner responsibility similar to previous position in New York.

ALFRED L. NEWMAN....... **Page Two**

PARTNER – New York, New York (1994-1999)

Engagement tax partner on a variety of primary manufacturing clients providing comprehensive corporate, partnership, individual executive, and employee compensation tax consulting and compliance services, and representation in tax controversies before tax authorities. Clients served included major automobile manufacturers.

- Merger and acquisition coordinator for Southeast Region and member of firm-wide Mergers and Acquisitions Tax Specialty Team.

- Technical specialist in all aspects of LBOs, tax-free mergers, divestitures, takeovers, bankruptcies, restructuring, golden parachutes, joint ventures, leasing, consolidated returns, and other transaction and capital structure-related matters.

- Regular instructor at internal D&T training courses and partner/manager workshops on M&A.

- Sparked early roll-out of national efficiency program to introduce advanced software and reengineered methodologies to corporate compliance practice. Supervised final beta test sign-off by practice offices on internally developed corporate tax software.

- Participated on task force responsible for defining requirements for next generation corporate tax software and for developing the case and strategy for starting a new specialty line aimed at reengineering management practices, especially data management, in large corporate tax departments.

MANAGER – Chicago, Illinois (1986 - 1994)

Joined Deloitte & Touche in 1986, advancing through several junior-level positions until making Partner in 1994.

EDUCATION

MBA, HARVARD BUSINESS SCHOOL, HARVARD UNIVERSITY   **1986**
Finance concentration.

BA, ACCOUNTING, SETON HALL   **1984**
- Graduated summa cum laude.
- Awarded Phi Beta Kappa.
- Passed C.P.A. examination upon graduation.

DIANE MACKEY
23 Strawberry Hill Avenue
Stamford, CT 06990
(203) 435-6832

EXPERIENCE:

JOHNSON & HIGGINS, New York, NY   **1999 to Present**

Lead Associate, Operations Management Group
Direct consulting engagements for various Fortune 100 companies in business strategy,
business process re-engineering, strategic sourcing, manufacturing/operations strategy,
distribution and logistics, strategy and product innovation/technology development.

- Led business re-engineering efforts in several diversified manufacturing, utilities and
  oil transport companies to streamline their manufacturing, distribution and customer
  service delivery processes resulting in $150 - $450 million in cost savings over 3-5
  year periods.
- Rationalized order fulfillment strategy for a global pharmaceutical client resulting in
  40% ($30 million) reduction in overall distribution costs in North America.
- Assisted a global energy and automation client in developing channel strategy and
  customer service improvement resulting in fewer product lines and 30% reduction in
  finished goods inventory.
- Assisted several key clients in developing and implementing Strategic Sourcing
  capabilities which led to $40 to $100 million in cost savings.
- Assisted a leading news and entertainment network in developing long-term
  technology strategy for global expansion.
- Assisted a building materials client with post-bankruptcy profit improvement
  strategy. Reduced corporate overhead by 50%, streamlined sales forces and
  manufacturing operations, resulting in $30 million annual cost reduction.
- Participated in due diligence effort which led to a billion dollar acquisition by a
  venture capital firm.

AMERICAN BRANDS, INC., Greenwich, CT   **1996 to 1999**

Manager, Business Analysis & Strategy Development
Reporting to the CFO, initiated and formulated annual strategic plan, product line P&L
analysis, economic studies of major acquisition and capital investment and special projects in
cost reduction, market expansion and new product development.

- Achieved strategic cost reduction of $6-10 million through shutdown of a major
  production facility, product redesign/positioning and usage of alternative raw
  materials in existing products.
- Counseled top management on strategic issues in product line profitability,
  competitive pricing and cost saving opportunities.

DIANE MACKEY   **Page 2**

Manufacturing Manager
Reporting to Senior VP of Operations, formulated and implemented productivity
improvement strategies through (1) in-depth analysis of manufacturing productivity in 13
operating locations, (2) upgrading of manufacturing technology and (3) improving product
quality through increased employee involvement (EI), and statistical process control (SPC).
Position required hands-on factory floor involvement, supervision of multi-plant activities and
large program/project management.

FREDERICK ATKINS, INC., New York, NY   **1995 to 1996**

Staff Consultant
Managed project teams in developing innovative concepts and systems using state-of-the-art
technologies to improve mail coding, sorting and distribution of US Postal Service.

UNION PACIFIC CORPORATION, Bethlehem, PA   **1988 to 1991**

Project Engineer/Design Engineer
Conducted engineering design works and testing, contract negotiations, vendor selection and
qualifications and project management for mass transit systems in New York City,
Washington, DC and San Francisco.

EDUCATION:

HARVARD BUSINESS SCHOOL, Harvard University, Cambridge, MA

Master of Business Administration   **1994**
Major: Finance and Operations. Minor: Strategic Planning. Tutored undergraduate students
and worked on research projects on distribution and market research with Harvard faculty to
support family.

ROCHESTER INSTITUTE OF TECHNOLOGY, Rochester, NY

Master of Science in Mechanical Engineering   **1988**
Specialized in automation, robotics and human factor studies. Member of Graduate Student
Council.

Bachelor of Science in Mechanical Engineering   **1986**
Specialized in combustion engineering and control theory. Minor: Economics. Member of
national honor societies - Tau Beta Pi and Pi Tau Sigma. Completed degree in 3 years and
was in the top 1% of class.

BRENDA AIKEN

34 East 78th Street
New York, NY 10022
(212) 789-3469

Results-oriented, self-motivated leader with proven record of success in direct marketing and tele-communications.   Recognized manager/team builder and strategic planner with significant P&L responsibility. Extensive experience formulating and implementing policy for fund-raising offices serving multiple, diverse client base.

AREAS OF EXPERTISE

Team Building   *Fund Raising*
Strategic Planning   *Personnel Development*
Relationship Management   *Cost Control*
Marketing/Telemarketing   *Innovative Product Development*

SELECTED ACCOMPLISHMENTS

McKinsey and Company   **1995 to Present**

A political management consulting firm providing business services for non-profit, grassroots environmental and consumer organizations. Services include political consulting, fund raising, list management and development, market research, public education, layout, design, and printing.

DIRECTOR   1999 to Present

- Turned around declining consulting operation with diminishing client base, restructuring operations and implementing plans for potential client growth to make office profitable.

- Cut expenses 15% in $500,000/annum office, reducing payroll from 40% to 303% of revenues and increasing productivity an average of 25% per canvasser.

- Organized/maintained ongoing relationships with entire client base which included weekly client briefings, special liaison relationships, and development of innovative programs for membership management.

- Built and supervised teams in 20-person staff that carried out fund raising and delivery of services to clients, significantly raising morale and increasing employee retention rate.

- Organized/implemented special membership development projects including targeted legislative action alerts, newsletters, and other campaign support.

- Researched/recommended and negotiated deal for state-of-the-art automated call management system which keeps records up to date and helps direct all list management and fund raising efforts for multiple client base.

- Recruited, trained, and developed potential staff leadership. Responsible for growth and promotion of two of McKinsey's highest rated supervisors.

Brenda Aiken

McKinsey and Company (cont'd)

Promoted within 18 months from Fund Raiser.

MANAGER OF FUND RAISING   1996-1999

- Led office to growth of over $825,000 in two years.

- Designed/implemented program of list management and growth for company, achieving $9.50 return per name in market where average is $3.00 per name.

- Trained/supervised staff of 22 canvassers in telemarketing skills, motivating fastest growing office in company to reach highest profits ever.

- Researched and implemented Tele-Direct CAT and EISI Call Management System serving entire client base.

- Created cold calling and direct mail campaign for Friends of the Philadelphia Zoo, resulting in growth from 2,000 to over 10,000 pledged annual contributors in 18 months.

FUND RAISER   1995 - 1996

- Received award for outstanding fund raising results in 1995.

- Developed membership for Crime Victims Association, increasing their overall size by 40% and their revenues by over $1.2MM in one year.

- Planned/conducted numerous public education events and legislative action alerts on behalf of clients in seven states.

- Served as liaison between client and McKinsey and Company, preparing updates on political and legislative activities and other relevant information.

- Traveled extensively to client locations as troubleshooter, fund raiser, and trainer. Built staff in three client-based offices.

EDUCATION

M.B.A., Marketing   1995
American University

Bachelor of Science, Marketing   1993
American University

FRANK GRIFFITH
11 North Ridge Road
Detroit, MI 48226   313-237-6682

EDUCATION

M.B.A., Michigan State University (1981)

B.S., Business Administration, University of Wisconsin (1979)

EXPERIENCE

MICHIGAN STATE UNIVERSITY – East Lansing, MI   (1999 to Present)

CHAIRMAN – DEPARTMENT OF BUSINESS ADMINISTRATION. Responsible for curriculum development, faculty evaluation, community relations and budget supervision. Taught upper level undergraduate/graduate management and marketing courses including: Strategic Management, International Marketing, Human Resources Management, Marketing Management, Production Management, Sales Management, Labor Relations, Marketing Research, International Business and Advertising.

- Developed M.B.A. degree program.
- Provided consulting and implemented specialized training programs to assist local businesses.
- Revised undergraduate business program.
- Recruited faculty.

CLARK EQUIPMENT COMPANY – South Bend, IN   (1997 to 1999)

PRESIDENT of a $20 million manufacturer of industrial equipment. Full profit and loss responsibility for all phases of corporate operation, including: marketing/sales, engineering, accounting and manufacturing. Formulated corporate policy and instituted strategic planning. Installed three-year and annual business plans with budget. Introduced Management-By-Objectives program. Implemented a new product development plan. Initiated sales training. Developed Zero Defects program. Eighty-six person, two-plant organization. Staff directly supervised: Vice-President of Marketing/Sales, Vice-President of Manufacturing, Controller and Director of Engineering as well as Legal Counsel and Advertising Agency.

- Introduced the first sales and labor forecasting system.
- Designed a marketing program for manufacturers' representatives, which increased sales 15%.
- Initiated control programs resulting in 10% reduction in inventory levels.
- Developed completely new product.

HUNT MANUFACTURING COMPANY – Philadelphia, PA   (1993 to 1997)

PRESIDENT of an $8 million manufacturer of capital equipment. Directly responsible for corporation, including manufacturing, sales/marketing, finance, engineering, and accounting. Instituted long-range planning. Developed annual and five-year business plan and budget. Formulated policies and objectives. Designed detailed action plans for all elements of the business. Developed corporate organizational structure. Created a management development program to meet projected needs. Directed the evaluation of acquisitions. Total number of personnel under direction, approximately 125. Directly reporting: Director of Sales/Marketing, Director of Manufacturing, Director of Finance, Director of Engineering, Legal Counsel and outside Auditors. Also various consultants.

FRANK GRIFFITH   (2)   RESUME

- Doubled sales first year by developing international markets.
- Completed major profit turnaround of company in first year.
- Developed new, fully integrated marketing programs resulting in a 50% increase in market share.
- Reduced labor cost by 23%.

FOUR SEASONS FIREPLACE, INC. – Philadelphia, PA   (1990 to 1993)

VICE-PRESIDENT AND GENERAL MANAGER of a $4 million manufacturer of fireplace tools and accessory products. Responsible for corporate operation including sales/marketing, production and finance. Developed annual business plan and budget. Established and maintained a system of controls of a financial and operational nature that assumed timely management information of performance versus plan. Oversaw the activities of 120 employees. Direct reports: Sales Manager, Manufacturing Manager, Controller, Auditors and Legal Counsel as well as Engineering, Design and Training Consultants.

- Increased sales by 17%.
- Introduced brand differentiation which increased customer loyalty.
- Defeated unionization attempt by Steel Workers.
- Installed new system of warehousing and inventory control which reduced shipping time 30%.

SCM CHEMICALS – Baltimore, MD   (1985 to 1990)

DIRECTOR OF MARKETING for a $6 million manufacturer of specialty chemicals. Responsible for management of the total marketing effort and the formulation of marketing plans. Directed all marketing activities to achieve profit objectives. Developed marketable product lines. This responsibility encompassed the full range of marketing strategy and tactical execution, including such areas as pricing, selection of market segments for special emphasis and specifying the necessary product characteristics. Supervised three Product Managers, Advertising Manager, Sales Training Manager, Marketing Assistant and Staff.

- Increased overall sales by 78% and profits by 37%.
- Assisted in major profit turnaround of company in first year.
- Developed and introduced three complete product lines resulting in increased volume and profitability.
- Developed a three-dimensional direct mail program which was a key factor in increased sales.

NOVA CHEMICAL CORPORATION – Baltimore, MD   (1981 to 1985)

SENIOR MARKET ANALYST (1984 – 1985)
SALES REPRESENTATIVE (1981 – 1984)

3

Sample Resumes—For Recent College Graduates

In this chapter, you will find 50 carefully-selected sample high-impact resumes of recent college graduates. In contrast with the resumes provided in Chapter 2, the resumes contained in this chapter represent individuals who have little or no professional-level experience. Most, in fact, are seeking their first full-time, professional position in their chosen career field.

Although these are actual resumes of employment candidates, they have been altered in the same ways as the previous resumes, to conceal the identity of the authors.

Careful review of these resume samples will provide some excellent ideas for preparing an effective entry-level resume for use in your first professional job-hunting campaign.

To locate those sample resumes that most closely correspond to your own job-hunting objectives, you may want to refer to the Contents (see page x). In reviewing the Contents, you will note that the resume samples contained in this chapter have been conveniently grouped into 13 occupational categories, allowing easy identification of those resumes most related to your own career interests and objectives.

Jennifer Fulton

Present Address

3 State Street Dorm #15
Corvallis, OR 98432
(503) 238-5782

Permanent Address

24 River Walk Drive
San Antonio, TX 74389
(713) 952-8212

OBJECTIVE

To obtain a permanent position with a company that utilizes my previous work experience, interpersonal skills, and leadership ability.

EDUCATION

Oregon State University: Corvallis, OR
B.S. in Accounting, May 1999
Cumulative GPA: 3.42/4.0; Major GPA: 3.38/4.0; Dean's List (2)

WORK EXPERIENCE

Valero Energy Company   San Antonio, TX
Accounting Clerk (GL, AP)   Summers '96 & '97
· handled petty cash box which contained $1000.
· managed four accounts and set up billing of lessees, researched problem accounts and made adjusting entries.
· performed reconciliations of general ledger accounts.
· oversaw daily inventory and input control.
· rehired repeatedly for summers and holidays.

Luby's Cafeteria   San Antonio, TX
Waitress   6/92-12/94
· performed responsibilities of cashier and hostess when needed.
· trained new employees.
· received Employee of the Week award.

ACTIVITIES

Phi Gamma Nu Professional Business Fraternity
· served as Pledge Class Treasurer.
· involved with Financial Affairs and Philanthropy committees.
· raised funds: Oregon State Dance Marathon (largest student philanthropy in U.S.).

Student Advisor - College of Business Administration
· helped incoming students with transition to college.

Red Cross Club & Special Olympics Club
· volunteered 10-15 hours per semester.

COMPUTER SKILLS

Systems: IBM, Tandy, MacIntosh
Packages: Lotus 1-2-3, Excel, Professional Write, Dbase III+, Pascal, Minitab, MacWrite II

LISA FOXWORTH

School Address
West End Hall, Room 36
Saint Joseph's University
Philadelphia, PA 19341
(215) 648-3494

Permanent Address
78 Oak Brook Drive
Chicago, IL 60666
(312) 638-8934

OBJECTIVE

To obtain an entry level position in a business firm which will utilize my educational background and allow development of my abilities to their fullest potential.

EDUCATION

1996-present

Saint Joseph's University, Philadelphia, PA
Accounting Major; Dean's List 2nd, 3rd, and 4th semesters; present grade point average 3.60/4.0; will graduate May 2000.

1992-1996

Central High School, graduated in the top 10% of the class from the Excel Program which included advanced classes in Science, Math and English.

EXPERIENCE

August 1997
to July 1998

Accounting Clerk, Fleer Corporation, Philadelphia, PA
Responsibilities include: handling of multiple company payroll, processing of accounts payable, assisting the Controller in monthly closing activities, updating selected general ledger accounts, handling cash receipts, filing, phones, preparing bank reconciliations and analysis reports.

March 1997
to Aug. 1997

Office Clerk, Geriatric Medical Services, Malvern, PA
Responsibilities include: preparation and follow up of Medicare Reviews, processing orders for medical supplies and equipment, preparing invoices for insurance companies and customers, preparation of billing and inventory books on a monthly basis, coordinating letters to insurance companies and customers, filing, phones.

September 1996
to March 1997

Assistant to Bookkeeper/Cashier, Rite Aid Pharmacy, Philadelphia, PA
Responsibilities include: preparation of charges for pick up, handling of register, verification of incoming inventory, stocking of shelves, filing, phones.

August 1994
to Dec. 1996

Cashier, Kelly Sports, West Chester, PA
Responsibilities include: handling of register, assisting manager in all aspects of store opening and closing, verification of inventory, making of bank deposits, assisting in floor moves, phones.

ACHIEVEMENTS

Awarded Wayne Scholar
Member of Golden Key National Honor Society

REFERENCES

Available upon request

ELIZABETH KIMBROUGH

Permanent Address
305 Firethorne Drive
West Chester, PA 19382
(610) 793-3905

Local Address
45 University Hall
American University
Washington, DC 22459
(301) 341-6436

OBJECTIVE: To obtain an entry level position in Accounting.

EDUCATION: Bachelor of Science in Accounting, May 1999
American University
GPA: 3.29/4.00   Major GPA: 3.41/4.00

Relevant Courses:

Financial Accounting I, II	Corporate Finance
Managerial Accounting	Business Law
Federal Income Taxation	Int'l Business Operations

HONORS:
Golden Key National Honor Society
Phi Eta Sigma Freshman Honor Society
Dean's List - 2 semesters

WORK EXPERIENCE:

Clerk - American University Athletic Department   6/97 - 8/97
- organized and developed football tickets
- receptionist for athletic director

Secretary – Claymont High School   5/96 - 8/96
- developed and implemented the scheduling, billing and grading procedures for the computer
- responsible for efficient functioning of the office

Secretary – Segal, Jones & Narberth   5/95 - 8/95
- prepared legal documents
- filed employee wages, documents and research

ACTIVITIES:
The College of Business Administration
- Overall Steering Committee Advising Program
- Student Advisor
Order of Omega
Gamma Phi Beta Sorority
- Panhellenic Delegate
- Assistant Membership Chairman
Panhellenic Council - Assistant Rush Coordinator
IFC/Panhellenic Dance Marathon Morale Team - 2 years
IFC/Panhellenic Spring Week Skits Committee
Beta Alpha Psi Accounting Honors Fraternity
Business Student Council

REFERENCES: Available upon request.

ELIZABETH DAVIDSON

HOME ADDRESS:
8 Vancouver Street
Minneapolis, MN 55433
(612) 348-3486

SCHOOL ADDRESS:
Seton Hall University 5E-206
South Orange, NJ 08845
(908) 948-4557

OBJECTIVE: To obtain a position in the accounting department of a large corporation and progress within the organization

EDUCATION: Seton Hall University, South Orange, NJ
- Candidate for Bachelor of Science, Accounting - May 2000
- Cumulative GPA 3.25; Accounting GPA 3.39

RELEVANT COURSES:

Intermediate Acctg I & II	Financial Acctg	Business Writing
Managerial Acctg I & II	Corporate Finance	Business Logistics
Federal Income Taxation	Computer Science	Business Law
Quantitative Business Analysis	Micro & Macro Economics	MIS

PROFESSIONAL EXPERIENCE:

Accounting Clerk, South Orange Community Bank (2/96 - Present)
- Daily maintenance of the general ledger system.
- Reconcile branch settlement to currency and coin account.
- Balance official checks.
- Prepare accounts payable checks to be remitted on a weekly basis.
- Prepare ATM, Loan, CD, and Investment monthly reports.

Cashier, J. Crew (5/95 - 9/97)
- Managed problems and complaints for customer sales and returns.
- Trained new cashiers.
- Performed opening and closing procedures.

ORGANIZATIONS: Beta Alpha Psi, Honorary National Accounting Fraternity

Vice President Finance, Kappa Kappa Alpha Sorority
- Prepare yearly budget
- Control disbursements of a $40,000 account

Purchase Fund Chairman Kappa Kappa Alpha Sorority
- Responsible for a $5,000 account.

Financial Committee, Seton Hall University Dance Marathon
- Billed and collected $745,000 in donations

Homecoming Committees, Seton Hall University
- King and Queen, 1998
- Student Relations, 1997

ACHIEVEMENTS: Dean's List – Seton Hall University, Spring, 1998
South Orange Community Bank Scholarship

TECHNICAL SKILLS: Experience with Lotus 123, dBase, Microsoft Word and PASCAL

ANNETTE MILLER

Local Address:
34 East 72nd Street
New York, New York 10023
(212) 789-4375

Permanent Address:
12 Hemlock Street
Greenwich, Connecticut 06909
(203) 674-8326

Objective: To gain a challenging entry level accounting position with a company in corporate accounting.

Education: Manhattan College, New York, New York
B.S. in Accounting. Degree expected: December, 1999
Overall GPA: 3.49/4.0; Major GPA: 3.61/4.0

Work Experience: ITT CORPORATION, New York, NY
Accounting Intern, January 1998 - July 1998
- Facilitated recording of charges between ITT US & ITT UK
- Communicated with UK to improve billing process
- Acquired knowledge of intercompany accounting
- Developed professional and communication skills
- Trained incoming interns

CRANE COMPANY, Stamford, CT
Secretary, February 1997 - August 1997
- Organized office and daily schedule
- Typed financial reports
- Scheduled appointments
- Completed tax forms and reports

BIG K-MART, Stamford, CT
Office Clerk, February 1995 - August 1995
- Accounted for the cash and checks from front end to the office
- Deposited large sums of cash and checks
- Satisfied customer needs
- Worked in video department

Campus Activities:
- Beta Alpha Psi - National Accounting Fraternity 1997 - present
- Golden Key National Honor Society 1997 - present
- Dean's List - 1996, 1997, 1998
- Society of Business Interns 1998 - present
  - Secretary 1999
  - South Campus Committee Chairperson - 1999
- Resident Assistant Candidate - 1999

Interests:
- Physical Fitness, Traveling, Reading

Jonathan Hazlett

Present Address:
800 St. James Street
Apartment 3-A
Harrisonburg, VA 23843

Home Address:
843 Dilworthtown Road
Baltimore, MD 23210
(301) 675-3487

OBJECTIVE: To apply my knowledge and experience to a public accounting position.

EDUCATION: **JAMES MADISON UNIVERSITY**
Harrisonburg, VA
B.S. in Accounting, May 2000
Overall GPA: 3.51
Related Course Work:
· Advanced Financial Accounting
· Advanced Business Law
· Business Policy Management

RELATED WORK EXPERIENCE: LANDMARK COMMUNICATIONS, Norfolk, VA   May 1998 - Present
Assistant Accountant and Financial Analyst
· Assisted in day-to-day payroll activities
· Responsible for daily production output analysis reports
· Prepared monthly operations reports
· Assisted in random financial report preparation
· Actively participated in long-term corporate goal research project

OTHER WORK EXPERIENCE: JAMES MADISON UNIVERSITY, Harrisonburg, VA   Feb. 1999 - Present
Tutor
· Tutored students in accounting, computer science, and psychology

UNDER FOOT CARPET CARE, Richmond, VA   May 1995 - Sept.1997
Floor Specialist Custodian
· Professional carpet cleaning, floor refinishing and buffing
· Basic custodial responsibilities

GUINTA'S MARKET, Baltimore, MD   June - Sept.1994
Stockperson
· Assisted customers in various capacities
· Stocked shelves

SELF EMPLOYED ($100+/wk)   1992 - Present
Extensive work in areas of:
· Lawn care, snow removal, driveway sealing

ACTIVITIES: Beta Alpha Psi, National Accounting Fraternity
Accounting Club
James Madison University Marching Band
Various Intramural Sports - softball, basketball, volleyball
Varsity Crew Team

PATRICIA LONG

Home Address:	89 Main Street Kennett Square, PA 19382 (610) 348-1758	School Address:	14 Peach Street, A-206 Durham, NC 28945 (513) 773-4579

OBJECTIVE: To be able to utilize my leadership and interpersonal skills in a full-time position within the field of Business Logistics.

EDUCATION: **DUKE UNIVERSITY**, Durham, NC
B.S. Degree in Business Logistics expected May 2000
Cumulative GPA: 3.7/4.0; Major GPA: 4.0/4.0

COMPUTER EXPERIENCE:

Microsoft Word	MacWrite	Lotus 1-2-3	Minitab
dBase III+	Turbo Pascal	BASIC	

WORK EXPERIENCE:

Catering to You, Kennett Square, PA   May 98 - Aug. 98
Assistant Chef
* Planned and prepared daily menus and elaborate catering trays.
* Responsible for inventory, ordering of all supplies, and logging of bills.
* Successfully implemented new inventory system to limit stock and prevent stockouts.

Chadds Ford Inn, Chadds Ford, PA   May 97 - Jan. 98
Waitress
* Efficiently and skillfully served food and beverage to customers.
* Responsible for correctly billing and collecting payment from patrons.
* Trained new employees after only two days of employment.

Patty's Play Pals, Malvern, PA   May 96 - Aug. 96
Painter/Craftsman
* Prepared and assembled wooden, collector's item dolls for painting.
* Skillfully painted and stained detailed dolls which carry my signature.
* In charge of training new painters.

Highland Marketing Group, Malvern, PA   June 95 - Nov. 95
Filing Clerk
* Filed, obtained, and destroyed outdated case files.
* Responsible for updating filing system, client relations, and all mailings.

HONORS: Marsha Lewis Memorial Scholarship
Council of Logistics Management's College Bowl Challenge, 2nd place, Captain
Golden Key National Honor Society
Phi Eta Sigma National Honorary Fraternity
Dean's List (4 out of 5 semesters)

ACTIVITIES: ALPHA KAPPA PSI Professional Business Fraternity
- President
- Treasurer
- Pledge Selection and Dance Marathon Committees
- Chapter Delegate, National Convention
President, Residence Hall Floor
Duke University Marketing Association
- Company Seminar and Career Night Committees
Logistics Association
Freshman Orientation Leader
Intramural Volleyball, Basketball (Champions), Softball, Co-ed Football

FELICIA NEWCOMB

College Address: Home Address:
56 Naamans Road, Apt. 2   16 Pellbridge Drive
Wilmington, DE 19872   Poughkeepsie, NY 12467
(302) 886-4356   (914) 368-5685

OBJECTIVE

A full-time position in Business Logistics with special interests including but not limited to purchasing, warehousing, and traffic management.

EDUCATION

University of Delaware, Wilmington, DE
Bachelor of Science in Business Logistics expected in January 1999.
Current GPA: 3.9
Relevant coursework:

Business Logistics Management	Transportation
Purchasing & Materials Management	Traffic Management
Warehousing & Physical Distribution	Highway Engineering

Villanova University, Villanova, PA
College of Business Administration

EXPERIENCE

Project Support Services Expeditor: SSI, Inc.   6/97 - 1/98
Responsibilities: liaison between suppliers and end users; handling details of purchase orders; expediting orders; establishing relationships and maintaining regular contact with suppliers; troubleshooting for engineering; customer service; purchasing; supplier visit; attended supplier trade show; project team meetings; trained successor.
Special Projects: developing execution plans for field coordination teams on major construction projects; developing orientation manual; producing organizational charts, overheads, and flow charts on Freelance software; presentation to supervisor and department managers; autofaxing purchase orders to suppliers.

Salesperson: Nordstrom's, Christmas 1996
Receptionist: Express Personnel Services, Summer 1996
Waitress: Cuisine's Restaurant, Summer 1995
Clerical Assistant: Villanova University, 9/94 - 4/95

HONORS AND ACTIVITIES

Teaching Assistant for Business Logistics Management
Transportation Research
University of Delaware Logistics Association Chairman: Interaction Committee
University of Delaware Marketing Association
University of Delaware Concert Choir
Zeneca Scholarship in Business Logistics - 1996
Traffic Club of Poughkeepsie Scholarship - 1997, 1998
The Honor Society of Phi Kappa Phi
Golden Key National Honor Society
Dean's List: All semesters

HOBBIES

Aerobics, reading, fishing, weight lifting, waterskiing, and singing

JACK TALBERT

School Address:
Hampton Hall, B-304
Orono, ME 17436
(261) 793-4381

Permanent Address:
12 Stoney Creek Road
Boston, MA 02231
(208) 343-8355

OBJECTIVE: To obtain a permanent position related to the field of Business Logistics.

EDUCATION: B.S. in Business Logistics, May 2000
University of Maine   GPA 3.51

HONORS: Dean's List 3 of 5 semesters
Golden Key National Honors Society

WORK EXPERIENCE:

Housing and Food Services   9/98-Present
University of Maine
- Worked as a cook, busboy, and dishperson
- Handled materials and equipment as well as customers

Career Development and Placement Services   8/97-5/98
University of Maine
- Answered student and recruiter questions about CDPS
- Stocked shelves, kept library presentable
- Performed some clerical duties

Landscaping and Contract Work   Summers 95,96,97,98
- Worked as a laborer
- Collected fees and discussed bids with clients
- Supervised other employees

Alpha Scientific   Winter/Spring Break 97, 98
- Worked as a packer
- Assembled, packaged, and wrapped finished product for shipment

OTHER EXPERIENCE:
Boston Parks and Recreation
Joseph Klaus Bricklayer
Intramural Volleyball Official

ACTIVITIES:
University of Maine Volleyball Club
-   Vice President, member USVBA, USVBA official, Team Representative
University of Maine Business Logistics Association
-   Active Member
Intramural Sports
St. John's Church
-   Active leader of activities

STANLEY COLLINS

CURRENT ADDRESS:	PERMANENT ADDRESS:
309 Federal Street	9012 Allegheny Drive
Richmond, VA 23733	Wilmington, DE 19855
(415) 903-3389	(302) 774-7487

EDUCATION: University of Virginia, Richmond, VA

B.S. in Economics (May 2000)
Major GPA: 4.00/4.00; Cumulative GPA: 3.92/4.00

Crosslands High School, Newark, DE
Graduated June 1996; Cumulative GPA: 3.93/4.00
Gifted/High Potential Classes

AFFILIATIONS/ACTIVITIES:

Economics Association	1999
Beta Gamma Sigma	
- Honor Society for Collegiate Schools of Business	1999
The Honor Society of Phi Kappa Phi	1999
Golden Key National Honor Society	1998-Present
Phi Eta Sigma Honor Society	1997-Present
Intramurals: Basketball, Football	1996-Present
High School National Honor Society	1994-1996
Who's Who Among American High School Students	1993-1994
Varsity Basketball Team	1993-1996
- All-Star Conference - Senior Year	
Varsity Golf Team	1992-1996
- All-Star Conference - Senior Year	

WORK EXPERIENCE:

Delco Township	May-August 1998
700 Street Road, Newark, DE	
Laborer - involved in operations concerning township maintenance	
Brinkman Landscaping Service	Summers 1996, 1997
9 Oakland Road, Newark, DE	
Landscaper - performed general landscaping duties	
White Glove Car Wash	March-May 1996
134 Westside Drive, Wilmington, DE	
Car Wash Attendant - supervised operations in owner's absence	
Self-Employed Lawn Service	Summer 1994

- REFERENCES AVAILABLE UPON REQUEST -

BRUCE LIVINGSTON

Temporary Address
440 Swedesford Road
East Lansing, MI 54437
(618) 855-6632

Permanent Address
5 Winston Court
Columbus, OH 45318
(312) 991-3376

OBJECTIVE: To obtain a full-time position in the field of securities analysis and financial management.

EDUCATION: MICHIGAN STATE UNIVERSITY, East Lansing, MI

B.S. in Economics (May 1999)
College of Business Administration
Cumulative G.P.A.: 2.91/4.00

Relevant Coursework:
- Industrial Organization
- Money and Banking
- Intermediate Microeconomic Analysis
- Intermediate Macroeconomic Analysis
- International Economics
- Public Finance
- Corporate Finance
- Financial Accounting
- Managerial Accounting
- Lotus 1-2-3, dBase III+, Minitab, PASCAL

WORK EXPERIENCE:

Birmingham Township, Columbus, OH
Clean Community Supervisor   5/97-8/97 & 5/96-8/96
- managed community volunteer groups in roadside clean-ups
- approved refuse for recycling
- conducted searches for future clean-up sites

Birmingham Township, Columbus, OH
Road Department Employee   6/94 - 8/94
- repaired township roadways
- assisted in overall maintenance of township grounds and facilities

ACTIVITIES: MSU Economics Association
MSU Financial Management Club
MSU Intramural Basketball and Softball

SANDRA SLADE

CURRENT ADDRESS
345 E. Lancaster Avenue, Apt. C-3
Lancaster, PA 17752
(717) 393-4586

PERMANENT ADDRESS
9803 Standish Court
Athens, GA 34548
(404) 267-1932

OBJECTIVE   To obtain an entry level position in marketing research. Special area of interest is international markets.

EDUCATION   Franklin and Marshall College, Lancaster, PA
Will receive a Bachelor of Science degree December 1998
   Major: Economics and International Business
   Minor: French

HONORS
· Golden Key National Honor Society
· Delta Phi Alpha French Honor Society
· Dean's List (4 semesters)
· G.P.A. of 3.51/4.0

RELATED COURSES

International Economics (3 Cr.)	Introductory Marketing (3 Cr.)
Adv. International Economics (3 Cr.)	Global Marketing (6 Cr.)
International Business Policies (3 Cr.)	

STUDENT ACTIVITIES
· Studied abroad in Paris, France (Spring 1997)
· Secretary of the International Business Association
  - Managed all correspondence and records and performed other duties assigned by the IBA
· French tutor on campus (Spring 1996)
· Little Sister at Delta Upsilon Fraternity

EXPERIENCE

F&M Dining Hall   Fall 1996, Fall 1997, Spring 1998
Performed various food preparation, dishroom, and customer services.

Interim Temporary Services   Summer 1997
Performed various secretarial duties.

Dell Publishing   Summers 1995, 1996
Worked with computers in processing returned books.

REFERENCES   Available upon request

JOSEPH ALFONSE

Permanent Address:
72 Bridge Street
Seattle, WA 98115
(206) 921-3424

Temporary Address:
967 Broadway, Apt. 3
Stillwater, OK 78451
(918) 599-8902

EDUCATION:
Oklahoma State University, Stillwater, OK
Bachelor of Science in Finance, December 1999
Overall G.P.A.: 3.32/4.0

Relevant
Coursework

Managerial Accounting
Financial Accounting
Intermediate Financial Accounting
Speech Communications

Corporate Finance
Financial Management
Commercial Bank Management
Effective Business Writing

WORK EXPERIENCE:

Flint Industries   6/98-1/99
Pre-Professional Tax Analyst   Tulsa, OK

- Filed monthly sales tax returns
- Audited monthly exception reports
- Interpreted tax laws for branch offices
- Determined tax exempt status of customers
- Daily work required extensive knowledge of Lotus 1-2-3

Capital Group, Inc.   12/97-5/98
Sales Associate   Tulsa, OK

- Initiated marketing strategy for new fund, LINC
- Developed skills in prospecting and presenting
- Managed spreadsheet data base on Lotus 1-2-3

The Gap   8/95-1/98
Stock Clerk/Salesperson   Stillwater, OK

- Worked 30-40 hours a week while full-time student
- Coordinated inventory flow
- Assisted customers

ACTIVITIES & INTERESTS:

Boy Scouts, Earned Eagle Scout Award (1995)
- Held numerous leadership positions
- Organized and coordinated over 200 man hours for renovation of campsite
  at Allegheny Portage R.R. National Historic Site
Economics Association of Oklahoma State
Peer Tutor (Calculus and Quantitative Business Analysis)
Intramural Softball and Football

REFERENCES: Available Upon Request

JEREMY PRICE

Home Address:
5 Valley Drive
Aston, PA 19352
(610) 459-3412

Campus Address:
92 Campus Lane, #3C
Villanova, PA 19742
(610) 348-6778

EDUCATION: Villanova University, GPA: 3.22/4.0
B.S. Degree in Finance, December 2000

Relevant Coursework:

Corporate Finance	Introductory Financial Accounting
Financial Management	Introductory Managerial Accounting
Investment Valuation	Intermediate Financial Accounting
Money and Banking	Intermediate Macroeconomics

Current: Intermediate Financial Accounting II, Capital Budgeting, Speculative Markets

WORK EXPERIENCE:

Eastman Kodak Company, Rochester, NY
Fixed Asset Accounting   June 1999-December 1999

- Cooperative assignment where I was responsible for insuring that proper controls existed to track and maintain all capital fixed assets
- Major duties included RAID (Rental Asset Inventory & Depreciation) RNB/BNR reconciliation, performed tool audits/tracking, System/Table Access Security, and provided financial approval for expense purchase requisitions

Waterview Swim Club, Goshen, PA
Lifeguard   January 1995-August 1998

- Responsible for the safety and well-being of swimmers
- Enhanced my decision-making skills and improved judgement skills
- Pool maintenance

Concord Country Club, West Chester, PA
Camp Swim Instructor/Lifeguard   Summer 1995-Summer 1998

- Taught Red Cross approved swimming techniques to campers
- Presented water safety instruction to advanced swimmers

ACTIVITIES & INTERESTS:

- Vice President and Treasurer of Bistro House (1997 & 1998)
- Brother of Delta Chi Alpha, Professional Business Fraternity
- Member of The Financial Management Association National Honor Society
- Society of Business Interns
- Proficient user of Lotus and PASCAL
- Certified in CPR
- Certified in Advanced Lifesaving and Water Safety
- Intramural Athletics

REFERENCES: Available upon request

RICHARD FISHER

School Address
8903 Winding Road, Apt. 8B
San Francisco, CA 98113
(919) 764-8320

Home Address
42 Eastbridge Drive
Seattle, WA 93589
(798) 323-6745

OBJECTIVE   Challenging position in finance, accounting, or management.

EDUCATION   San Francisco State University, San Francisco, CA   1996-2000
                   B.S. In Finance; Cum GPA: 3.4

RELEVANT   Corporation Finance   Business Computer Applications
COURSEWORK   Investment Valuation   Lotus 1-2-3, Basic, Pascal
                   Financial Management of   Business Policy Formulation/Control
                     the Business Experience   Basic Managerial Concepts
                   Commercial Bank Management   Real Estate Fundamentals
                   Speculative Markets   Risk and Insurance
                   Financial Markets   Property and Casualty Insurance
                   Money and Banking   Industrial Organization
                   Monetary Theory and Policy   Principles of Marketing
                   Managerial Accounting   Public Speaking
                   Financial Accounting   Business Writing

RELATED   **COLE & WEBBER, Seattle, WA**   1997-1998
EMPLOYMENT   Provided staff support for a family-owned CPA firm which maintains a large
                   number of small business and individual accounts. Handled account updating,
                   organization of data for quarterly returns, bank reconciliations, time/billing, and all
                   related computer entries. Worked F/T, Summer of 1997, and P/T during college
                   breaks as needed.

                   WILSON LEATHER, San Francisco, CA   1996-Present
                   Given sole responsibility for business operations during assigned shift with a
                   specialty shop (City Mall). Gained extensive experience in direct sales,
                   opening/closing, daily reporting, and making deposits. Worked up to 35 hours/
                   week during the summers and holiday vacations.

STUDENT   **Chi Delta Alpha Fraternity**   1996-2000
LEADERSHIP   · *Treasurer* - Manage house budget of $45-50K/semester. Served on Executive
                     Board; worked with Alumni Board Treasurer.
                   · *Ticket/Admissions Chairman* - In charge of ticket sales and admissions for a
                     major cancer fund-raiser (13,000+ participants).
                   · *Athletic Chairman:* - Recruited, screened, selected, organized, and scheduled
                     teams for 10 sports. Finished with Top 5 ranking.

                   Undergraduate Student Government, Department of Control   1998

                   Interfraternity Council, Department of Control   1999

HIGH SCHOOL   Graduated with 3.7 GPA, College Preparatory; National Honor Society;
BACKGROUND   Student Government (Delegate); Varsity Tennis Team (Captain).

REFERENCES   Available upon request.

JOSEPH BECKER

Temporary Address
708 South Orange Road
New Brunswick, NJ 08845
Phone: (908) 889-3478

Permanent Address
14 Old Greenwich Road
Greenwich, CT 06692
Phone: (203) 668-8856

EDUCATION

Rutgers University, New Brunswick, NJ
B.S. in Finance (May 2000)
Overall G.P.A. 3.34/4.00

RELEVANT COURSEWORK

Corporation Finance
Microeconomic Analysis
Money & Banking

Intro to Financial Accounting
Macroeconomic Analysis
Intro to Managerial Accounting

CURRENT

Investment Valuation
Strategic Management

Financial Management of Business
Intermediate Macroeconomic Analysis

WORK EXPERIENCE

Greenwich Savings Bank, Greenwich, CT
Teller   May 1998 - August 1998
· managed a cash drawer containing up to $10,000
· coordinated electronic fund transfers
· conducted random audits of both mine and fellow employee's vaults
· updated customer records on a daily basis

Precious Petals, Rahway, NJ
Cashier/Delivery Person   May 1997-August 1997
· operated cash register
· monitored inventory and processed merchandise orders
· delivered orders of flowers and trays

Happy Harry's, Stamford, CT
Cashier/Rx Clerk   January 1996 - December 1996
· monitored inventory and processed merchandise orders
· updated computer data base containing customer files
· cross-referenced customer records in order to avoid dangerous combinations of drugs
· processed and recorded prescription orders

Sally's Kitchen, Stamford, CT
Cashier/Cook   November 1994 - December 1995
· operated cash register and prepared food
· earned 5 star employee status

ACTIVITIES

Campus: 1997 Dance Marathon Security Team member, 1998-99; Interfraternity Council
Board of Control Housechecker, 1999; Greek Mixer Physical Plant SubChair, Summer 1999;
Give Your Share Volunteer.

Fraternity: Member, Delta Chi, Fall 1997; House Manager, Spring 1998; Assistant Pledge
Master, Fall 1998; Pledge Master, 1997 & 1998; Spring Week Co-Chairperson; Intramural
Softball.

REFERENCES

Furnished upon request

BRADLEY OSBOURNE

LOCAL ADDRESS:
56 Indian Lake Drive, 4A
Tallahassee, FL 32346
(707) 775-4577

HOME ADDRESS:
12 Lisa Lane
Troy, NY 12568
(568) 689-4114

EDUCATION:

FLORIDA STATE UNIVERSITY, Tallahassee, FL
B.S. in Finance, December 1999
GPA: 3.43/4.00
Dean's List four semesters
Business Logistics Minor
Accounting: Two Financial and Two Cost Accounting Courses

WORK EXPERIENCE:

Central Telephone Company, Tallahassee, FL
<u>Pre-Professional Accountant</u>, January 1998 - June 1998
- Used computers (Lotus) to do accounting transactions.
- Dealt with many facets of fixed assets.
- Gave formal presentations to upper management.

P & C Food Markets, Rochester, NY
<u>Area Supervisor</u>, January 1996 - September 1996
- Supervised staff of over 150 employees.
- Ordered food on a daily basis.
- Called repairmen and suppliers when needed.

<u>Supervisor</u>, January 1995 - December 1995
- Enforced company policies.
- Calculated daily sales.

<u>Line employee</u>, May 1993 - December 1994
- Operated cash registers.
- Prepared food and sold it to customers.

CAMPUS ACTIVITIES:

Financial Management Association, 1997 - 1999
- Actively participated in functions and meetings.

Economics Association, 1997 - 1998
- Attended functions outside of school and went to seminars.

Intramural Tennis, 1995 – 1999
- Played singles and doubles.

REFERENCES: Available upon request

ELIZABETH DANIELS

Permanent Address
87 Ocean Drive
Atlantic City, NJ 08203
(609) 554-9840

Temporary Address
422 South Street, Apt. 3
Philadelphia, PA 19344
(215) 834-8992

Education

University of Pennsylvania
Major: Business Management; **Minor:** German
B.S., December 1998
Overall GPA: 3.42/4.0 Major GPA: 3.61/4.0

Experience

Geriatric and Medical Centers, Inc. – Philadelphia, PA
Financial Analyst Intern - 1997
- Assisted in the reconciliation of 7 G&M Pharmaceutical expense ledgers
- Researched G&M costs and decided whether covered in the service contracts
- Created a procedures manual on the service contract reconciliation process
- Trained personnel on computer systems and the service contract reconciliation
- Researched expenses for G&M account owners as a member of a "hotline"
- Made presentations to management on status of projects and related accomplishments

Ocean National Bank, Atlantic City, NJ
Accounts Payable Clerk/Receptionist - Summer 1996
- Assisted various Vice Presidents at Corporate Headquarters
- Posted transactions into accounts payable ledgers
- Typed, examined and verified payments
- Operated communication network

Teller - Summer 1995
- Responsible for up to $35,000+ daily
- Opened various accounts including money market and certificate of deposit accounts
- Sold and redeemed U.S. Savings Bonds
- Transacted money on an on-line computer system and proved cash daily

The National State Bank, Elizabeth, NJ
Teller - 1994
- Handled large sums of money from the Federal Depository
- Transacted and verified cash daily
- Performed data entry on an off-line computer system
- Maintained good customer relations

Honors &
Activities

Dean's List (2 Semesters)
Geriatric and Medical Center Achievement Award
Management Club
Blood Drive Volunteer
Singer/Performer

References

Available Upon Request

BEATRICE CORNWALLIS

Current Address
505 Snelling Street, Apt. #1
Princeton, NJ 08843
(908) 889-3487

Permanent Address
33 Village Road
Rochester, NY 12458
(238) 459-0072

OBJECTIVE: To obtain a position in a management training department.

EDUCATION: Princeton University, Princeton, NJ
B.S. in **Management**--expected in May 2001
Emphasis in Industrial Organization Psychology
Major GPA 3.12/4.0

WORK EXPERIENCE:

Princeton Business School   8/99-Present
Computer Lab Supervisor
Work an average 20-24 hrs/week maintaining IBM, Hewlett Packard, and Macintosh hardware, training students and faculty in the general use of computer hardware and software, and monitoring and troubleshooting several local area networks.

The Home Shopping Channel   Summers 1999, 1998
Jewelry Rebuyer Assistant
Entered orders into inventory system and maintained current order data. Reorganized and updated information in the filing system. Learned Paradox database program.

Returns and Surplus Assistant/Department Assistant
Requisitioned merchandise for sale and distributed returns and surpluses to outlet stores. Took the initiative to learn computerized inventory system to accurately pinpoint location and quantity of merchandise on order and to significantly reduce the time to requisition goods and distribute returns and surplus. Developed a department procedures manual and used it to train permanent employees.

Acme Supermarkets, Inc.   11/94-8/97
Customer Service Cashier
Assisted with customer service. Maintained balanced cash control. Helped train new cashiers and assisted them in solving customer complaints.

OTHER EXPERIENCE:

The Princeton Press, Philadelphia, PA   1/98-12/99
Office Representative
Trained new office representatives and solved customer complaints. Designed over--the-counter advertising. Required 7 hrs per week.

COMPUTER KNOWLEDGE:

DOS; Microsoft Word (IBM & Mac); Word for Windows; PC-Write; Harvard Graphics; Mac Paint; Mac Draw; Lotus; dBase III +; Paradox; Minitab; Ready, Set, Go; and Pascal.

ACTIVITIES:

Alpha Kappa Psi, Professional Business Fraternity:
- Chairperson for Public Relations & Bylaws Committees, Pledge Selection Committee.

Princeton University Marketing Association

MARK ALEXANDER

PRESENT ADDRESS
College Avenue Dorm, #3-B
Milwaukee, WI 53202
(414) 271-8335

PERMANENT ADDRESS
16 Honebrook Drive
Lancaster, PA 17752
(717) 794-7541

EDUCATION

Marquette University, Milwaukee, WI
B.S. Business Management, August 2001
G.P A. (3.2/4.0)

EXPERIENCE

Marquette University   2000-Present
Proctor, Basic Management Concepts Course
Distributed, collected and sorted exams and answer sheets.
Responsible for insuring an acceptable testing environment.
- Gained leadership and communication skills.

The Borough of Chester   2000-2001
Road Crew and Parks Crew, Department of Public Works
Prepared daily fuel, work and time schedule reports.
- Gained communication skills and demonstrated responsibility.

Burger King   1999-2001
Cook, Customer Service
Responsible for analyzing and ordering inventory.
- Gained communication and leadership skills.

Wawa Food Market   1997-1998
Deli Attendant, Customer Service
Responsible for handling cash receipts at end of the business day.
- Gained communication skills and demonstrated responsibility.

Sam's Diner   1996-1997
Cook, Customer Service
- Gained communication skills and demonstrated responsibility.

HONORS/ ACTIVITIES

Dean's List - One Semester
Active Member of the Marquette University Marketing Association
- Fund Raising Committee
- Company Seminars Committee
Varsity Baseball,1997 - 1999

COMPUTER SKILLS

Lotus 1-2-3, WordPerfect, dBase III +, MiniTab, MacWrite,
PASCAL

REFERENCES PROVIDED UPON REQUEST

DAVID BARTON

Current Address:
102 South 10th Street, Apt. 8
College Park, MD 21224
(410) 558-7428

Permanent Address:
1715 Westheimer Road
Houston, TX 75717
(713) 692-9112

OBJECTIVE

To obtain an internationally focused position which utilizes my knowledge of Management and International Business.

EDUCATION

B.S. in Management/International Business, December 2000
Minor in Labor Studies
University of Maryland
Overall GPA: 3.32/4.0; Major GPA: 3.81/4.0

WORK EXPERIENCE

Intern – B. Green & Company, Baltimore, MD   1998-1999
-- Processed shareowner stock repurchases
-- Updated on-line stock management system
-- Researched and prepared special projects
-- Prepared routine reports on Lotus program

Carpenter – Ryan Homes, Inc., Baltimore, MD   1997
-- Designed and built interior/exterior fixtures
-- Solicited customers
-- Purchased and delivered materials
-- Met precise deadlines

Machine Operator – Delmar Avionics, Baltimore, MD   1996
-- Manufactured aircraft parts for U.S. government contracts
-- Produced extremely detailed components
-- Granted low security status

HONORS

Attended University of Melbourne, Australia   Spring 1999
Accepted into highly competitive International Business major
Dean's List (3 semesters)
Sigma Iota Epsilon National Honorary Management Fraternity

ACTIVITIES

Alpha Kappa Psi Professional Business Fraternity
-- Business Fraternity Council Representative
-- Social Committee Chairman
Vice President, International Business Association
Total Alcohol Awareness Program Director (TAAP)
Teaching Assistant for Introductory Business Course (BA 103A)
Student Blood Coordinator for Red Cross Club

SKILLS

Basic German
Lotus 1-2-3, Aldus Freehand, Harvard Graphics, WordPerfect, Wordstar, Microsoft, dBASE III +

SALLY ANN ROGERS

Current Address:
823 Bolmar Street
State College, PA 16342
(814) 992-6901

Permanent Address:
661 New Street
Akron, OH 44332
(216) 798-3443

OBJECTIVE   A position as a Computer Programmer or a Systems Analyst.

EDUCATION   Pennsylvania State University, University Park, PA
B.S. Degree in Business Administration, May 2001
Major in Management Information Systems
Cumulative G.P.A. 3.42

Relevant Courses:

Information Processing Systems	Cobol
Accounting Information Systems	Business Writing
Managerial Accounting	Speech Communications
Financial Accounting	Risk and Insurance

EXPERIENCE   PENN STATE UNIVERSITY   January 2001-Present
Lab Attendant - Center for Academic Computing

Duties include maintaining computer hardware and assisting users on
Macintosh, IBM PS/2, IBM AS/400, and IBM VWCMS with various
software packages.

OLSTEN TEMPORARY SERVICES   May 2000-August 2001
Administrative and Clerical Worker
Assignments included USX Cyclone Fence and GMAC.
Duties included quoting proposal bids, preparing purchase
order forms, and office administrative duties.

PARKWAY DRY CLEANERS   May 1999-August 2001
Customer Service Worker
Duties included serving customers in a computer automated
environment.

BAGELS & BUNS   April 1997-January 1999
Crew Leader
Duties included supervising crew and managing the daily operations of
the bakery.

HONORS   Scholarship of the Metals & Mining Industry
College of Business Administration Scholarship
Golden Key Honor Society
Alpha Lambda Delta Honor Society
Dean's List

REFERENCES   Furnished upon request.

NICOLE BRUNETTI

Temporary Address
900 Pennsylvania Avenue, Apt. 8
Washington, DC 22001
(202) 333-3792

Permanent Address
4215 Wylie Road
Boston, MA 02105
(617) 774-0028

EDUCATION:
American University, Washington, DC
B.S. in Management Information Systems (May 2001)
Minor: Legal Aspects of Business
Overall G.P.A.: 3.49/4.00
G.P.A. in major: 4.00/4.00

RELEVANT COURSEWORK:
Introduction to Management
  Information Systems
Business Program
  Applications: LOTUS, DOS
Introduction to Management

Managerial Accounting
Quantitative Methods
Macroeconomics
Legal Environment
  of Business

CURRENT COURSEWORK:
Accounting Information Systems
Business Information
  Processing Systems

Corporate Finance
Introduction to Operations
  Management

WORK EXPERIENCE:
The Gillette Company, Boston, MA
<u>Packaging Operator</u>   June 1999-August 1999
· ensured accuracy of incoming materials
· performed quality inspections on finished products
· developed strong interpersonal skills

Stop & Shop Supermarket, Boston, MA
<u>Cashier/Salesclerk</u>   June 1998-August 1998
· recorded and processed customer sales
· managed customer relations
· developed use of supervisory skills
· performed daily inventory analysis

ACTIVITIES/ HONORS:
Sigma Iota Epsilon (Management Honor Society)—President ('00-'01)
Residence Halls Advisory Board of AU—Secretary (1999)
Phi Mu Delta Little Sister—Fund Raising Chairman (1999)
Information Systems Association—Membership Committee ('99-'00)
Phi Eta Sigma—Distinguished Freshman Honor Society
Gillette Company—Outstanding Employee Award

REFERENCES:
Available Upon Request

RYAN PETERSON

Home Address
12 Honeysuckle Street
Louisville, KY 40223
(502) 581-4298

School Address
1472 Schoolhouse Road, #1
Stillwater, OK 73489
(918) 337-3381

OBJECTIVE: To obtain a position with a dynamic company that will utilize both my computer skills and business background.

EDUCATION: **Management Information Systems Major**
Oklahoma State University
Graduation: December 2000
GPA: 3.68/4.00

RELEVANT COURSEWORK: Honors: Macro Economics, Corporate Finance, Strategic Management, Marketing Principles, Accounting Ethics

MIS: Accounting Information Systems, Decision Support & Expert Systems, Business Information Procedures, Systems Analysis Design

Computer Languages: dBase III+, R:Base, Lotus 1-2-3, Cobol, Hpaccess

HONORS & ACTIVITIES: University Scholars Program
Golden Key National Honor Society
Alpha Delta Lambda National Honor Society

WORK EXPERIENCE: The Jordan Company   5/99 - 12/99
Accounting and Information Systems Co-op

· As we changed from a functional to a Business Unit organization, I worked with others developing reports to determine each product's profit margin. This project provided management with an essential tool to change the way they do business.

· My supervisor at Jordan completed the evaluation of my work for Oklahoma State. He gave me an "A" for the credits I received, and stated that he would go to "extraordinary lengths" to hire me again. A copy of this evaluation is available upon request.

I enjoy traveling and am willing to relocate

Colin Sebastian

Present Address
1235 Commons Boulevard, Apt. #4-B
Boston, MA 02214
(617) 292-3445

Permanent Address
3 Rosewood Drive
Alexandria, VA 12351
(312) 443-7893

EDUCATION

Boston University, Boston, MA
MAJOR: Management Information Systems
DEGREE: B.S., 2001
GPA: 3.68 (4.0 in major)

HONORS/ACTIVITIES

- Deans List (Boston University)
- Golden Key National Honor Society
- University Scholars Program
- Phi Sigma Pi National Honor Fraternity
- Information Systems Association
- Boston University Men's Bowling Team
- National Honor Society (high school)
- Who's Who Among American High Schools

WORK EXPERIENCE

Summer 2000
and
Summer 1999

SHORE POINTS POOLS & SPAS, Virginia Beach, VA
(full-time) Swimming pool water analysis and technical/
operational support; chemical manufacturing and blending.

1/95 - 8/98

UNIVERSITY BOWLING LANES, Boston, MA
(part-time and full-time) Pinsetter
- maintenance and mechanical repair; bowling lessons; customer
  service and counter help.

COMPUTER SKILLS/ABILITIES

Computer Language and Software Experience
- COBOL
- Turbo Pascal
- Lotus 1-2-3
- WordPerfect
- IBM DOS
- Harvard Graphics

Computer System Experience
- IBM PCs
- IBM 3090 VM/CMS
- IBM AS/400

REFERENCES

Upon request

JEREMY BARBER

School Address
9 Beachwood Road, Box 340
Tallahassee, FL 33481
(813) 942-8856

Permanent Address
18 Kimberly Lane
Downingtown, PA 19742
(610) 648-3778

OBJECTIVE: To obtain an entry level position that will enable me to utilize and further develop my analytical and interpersonal skills.

EDUCATION:

Florida State University
Candidate for Bachelor of Science in Marketing
Minor in Economics

August 1996 - Present
December 2000

WORK EXPERIENCE:

Claire's Stores Inc., Tallahassee, FL
Sales Representative

August 1999 - Present

- Prospected potential customers.
- Performed financial and collection responsibilities for clientele.
- Conducted new product demonstrations resulting in increased sales.

Florsheim Shoe Company, Exton, PA
Assistant Store Manager

May 1999 - August 1999

- Performed all management functions in a store with monthly volume of $30,000 including sales, market targeting, order processing, accounts receivable, handling of returned merchandise and payroll.

Stanley Auto Parts Inc., Tallahassee, FL
Delivery Person

August 1998 - May 1999

- Responsible for the efficient delivery of parts to local service establishments.
- Emphasis in opening and closing procedures, receiving and inventory maintenance.

HONORS & ACTIVITIES:

Dean's List, Fall 1999
Florida State University Marketing Association Member
Phi Kappa Sigma National Fraternity
- House Manager: Spring 1998 and Fall 1998
- Executive Board Committee
- Centennial Celebration Planning Committee
- Intramural Sports
Special Olympics Volunteer

REFERENCES: Available upon request.

MITCHELL HORTON

CAMPUS ADDRESS (until 5/8/99)
5 Cayuga Road, Apt. 17
Orlando, FL 33481
(313) 892-7892

HOME ADDRESS
1 Ivy Road Lane
Princeton, NJ 08934
(908) 442-5653

OBJECTIVE
To obtain an entry-level position in marketing; special interests in retailing, customer service and public relations.

EDUCATION
UNIVERSITY OF CENTRAL FLORIDA
Bachelor of Science in Marketing, expected December 1999
3.43/4.0 overall GPA; 3.46 in major

INTERNSHIP
EXHIBIT REPRESENTATIVE   June 1998-January 1999
Walt Disney World/General Motors, Orlando, FL
* Represented General Motors and Walt Disney World
* Greeted and assisted guests at World of Motion
* Coordinated Technical Information Reports
* Conducted surveys and developed training program revisions
* Researched information and attained knowledge of car industry
* Monitored and maintained show quality

EMPLOYMENT
ASSISTANT TO THE MANAGER   Summers 1996-1998
Tech Data Corporation, Clearwater, FL
* Handled computer applications and conducted inventory checks
* Filled customer orders and prepared shipments
* Restocked shelves and mixed paint

ACTIVITIES
* **AMERICAN MARKETING ASSOCIATION**
* **UCF MARKETING ASSOCIATION**
    Marketing Services and Advertising Committees
    Achieved Award for Outstanding Membership
* **UCF TRACK CLUB**
    Budget Director, Spring 1997
* **STUDENTS AGAINST DRIVING DRUNK**

HONORS
* **DEAN'S HONOR LIST**
    Spring 1997; Spring 1998
* **GOLDEN KEY NATIONAL HONOR SOCIETY**
* **PHI ETA SIGMA NATIONAL HONOR SOCIETY**
* **MARY WALKER MEMORIAL SCHOLARSHIP**

REFERENCES
Available upon request.

CALVIN SIMPSON

Temporary Address	**Permanent Address**
54 Riverfront Road	689 Grant Street
Philadelphia, PA 19762	Pittsburgh, PA 15291
(215) 358-3189	(412) 433-1789

OBJECTIVE: To obtain an entry level position with a dynamic company that will allow me to utilize my education, interpersonal skills and work experience.

EDUCATION: Drexel University
Bachelor of Science in Marketing, Anticipated December 2001
Emphasis: Sales and Sales Management
GPA: Major 3.63/4.00; Cumulative 3.23/4.00
Dean's List - Fall 1999, Spring 2000

WORK EXPERIENCE:

Shearson Lehman Brothers, Inc.   1/01 - Present
- Client account analysis and evaluation
- Developed direct mail marketing plan
- Stock research and evaluation
- Managed $100,000 paper portfolio

Self-Employed Painter   1994 - Present
- Owner-operator, placed bids and negotiated contracts
- Recruited and hired employees each summer
- Monitored project progress to ensure highest quality job completion
- Followed up with customers to ensure satisfaction

Field House Attendant   9/98 - 10/99
Drexel University Indoor Sports Complex
- Responsible for monitoring activities and locking up field house

ACTIVITIES:

Division of Undergraduate Studies Advisory Board
- Serve on a committee to improve the interaction of the Drexel administration with the undergraduate community
- Student-to-Student Subcommittee, greeted and conferred with incoming Division of Undergraduate Studies students

Chi Alpha Sigma
- House Manager
- Social Chair
- House Cook

Drexel University Student Recruitment Task Force
- Represented Drexel University to home area high schools in order to attract qualified individuals to the University.

REFERENCES: Available upon request

CHARLES CROWLEY

833 Country Club Drive
Teaneck, NJ 07666
(201) 837-1949

OBJECTIVE: To use my marketing and advertising skills in a position involving public relations and promotions.

EDUCATION: **Fairleigh Dickinson University**, Teaneck, NJ
B.S. in **MARKETING** — expected in May 2000
Emphases: promotions, international marketing
Major GPA 3.12/4.0

The Center for European Studies, Maastricht, The Netherlands
University of Limburg — 8/99-12/99
Relevant Courses:
Economics of European Integration
The European Political and Legal Environment
Management in an International Environment
Multinational Marketing Strategy
German

WORK EXPERIENCE: The Collegian Times, Teaneck, NJ

1/99-5/99 **Marketing Specialist**
- Re-designed and updated look of marketing report
- Formulated questions for telephone survey
- Assisted Marketing Manager in on-going activities

1/98-12/98 **Advertising Sales Representative**
- Generated sales exceeding $29,000 from 6/98 - 12/98
- Serviced and maintained 12-25 local accounts daily
- Created advertisements on graphics computer system
- Managed all contracts, payments, and billing for clients
- Developed interpersonal and time-management skills

INTERESTS & ACTIVITIES:
- The Collegian Times, Merit Scholarship Recipient
- Public Relations Co-Chairperson, Alpha Kappa Psi Professional Business Fraternity
- Fairleigh Dickinson University Marketing Association
- Orientation Leader, Fall 1997
- French and German languages
- International travel, music, ballroom dance

EMILY CRANSTON

Local Address

23 Indiana Avenue
Frankfort, Kentucky 40278
(512) 267-2278

Permanent Address

1024 Oceanfront Drive
San Diego, California 92112
(619) 594-1299

OBJECTIVE: To obtain an entry level position in the field of marketing that utilizes my sales, leadership, and business background.

EDUCATION: Kentucky State University, Frankfort, Kentucky
BS Degree in **Marketing** with an emphasis in <u>Psychology</u>, May 2000
Cumulative GPA: 3.38; Major GPA: 3.45

RELATED COURSEWORK:

Introduction to Marketing	Introduction to Financial Accounting
Introduction to Management	Buying Behavior
Introduction to Managerial Accounting	Introduction to Psychology
Marketing Research	Computer Science
Corporate Finance	Sales Management
International Business	Business Logistics

EXPERIENCE: KENTUCKY STATE UNIVERSITY MARKETING ASSOCIATION
Director of Fundraising 4/99-4/00
- Responsible for overseeing and motivating committee members
- In charge of organizing and creating new fundraising activities to help support KSUMA

UNION UNDERWEAR COMPANY, Bowling Green, KY
Assistant Manager and Salesperson 6/97-1/99
- Gained experience in the retail industry by participating in sales, payroll, and supervision of employees
- Assisted in merchandising and helped coordinate advertising campaigns and sales promotions

FILENE'S DEPARTMENT STORE, Bowling Green, KY
Salesperson 8/95-8/96
- Assisted in merchandising and maintaining inventory control
- Sharpened interpersonal skills through various sales transactions
- Responsible for opening and closing transactions each day

THE GAP, San Diego, CA
Sales Associate 6/95-1/95
- Top salesperson for five consecutive weeks
- Winner of store-wide sales contest for highest cumulative sales
- Assisted in training new employees
- Prepared eye-catching displays

ACTIVITIES: Dean's List
Kentucky State University Marketing Association
Orientation Leader for Incoming Freshmen
Morale Committee - IFC Dance Marathon
Business Student Council
Football Recruiting Hostess
Staff Member - Regatta Philanthropy
Dorm Complex Representative

MARILYN JASPER

Present Address
303 Pratt Street
Phoenix, AZ 85903
(602) 272-6671

Permanent Address
1 Post Oak Road
Albuquerque, NM 98215
(505) 765-3465

OBJECTIVE: A position involved with planning and implementing marketing strategy for a company.

EDUCATION: **Arizona State University**
B.S. in Marketing, December 1996
GPA 3.48/4.00
Dean's List past four semesters.

RELATED EXPERIENCE:

<u>Development Intern</u>   January-August 2000
The Circle K Corporation, Phoenix, AZ
- Created and implemented a volunteer incentive and evaluation program.
- Reviewed/approved daily and weekly Telefund reports.
- Conducted yearly prospect research; updated database.
- Distributed donor benefits; helped plan events.

<u>Sales Associate</u>   Summers 1998, 1999
American Eagle Outfitters, Albuquerque, NM
- Assisted customers locate and select merchandise by serving as a personal consultant.
- Displayed merchandise; controlled inventory.
- Named a Top Sales Associate for June 1998.

<u>Accounts Receivable Assistant</u>   Summer 1997
Diagnostek, Inc., Albuquerque, NM
- Researched delinquent accounts to determine cause of nonpayment.
- Facilitated payment by serving as an information link between company and client.

<u>Telemarketer</u>   November 1996-March 1997
PhoneMate Marketing, Inc., Albuquerque, NM
- Conducted direct marketing calls to selected customers, persuading them to renew their magazine subscriptions.

ACTIVITIES:

Alpha Kappa Psi Professional Business Fraternity   1999-present
- Executive Committee: planned activities, oversaw three committees, conducted ceremonies.
- Fundraising Chairman: achieved $2,000 fundraising goal.
- Alumni Communications, Pledge Selection Committees.

Arizona State University Marching Band   1998-present
- Also participated in Basketball Pep Band and Concert Band.

Randy Barnsworth

School: 874 Franklin Avenue, Philadelphia, PA 19105   (215) 931-7825
Home: 9 Clifton Avenue, Clifton, NJ 07715   (201) 837-4503

EDUCATION

St. Josephs University, Philadelphia, PA
B.S. in Operations Management, December 1999
Minor in Business Logistics

ACHIEVEMENTS

Overall Grade Point Average: 3.42
Golden Key National Honor Society member

EXPERIENCE

McNeil Consumer Products Co., Fort Washington, PA
(A Johnson & Johnson subsidiary; producer of the Tylenol® family of products)

1/99-7/99

Planning Coordinator, Fort Washington Planning Department
- Planned material requirements for over 150 components and finished goods using AMAPS and communicating with manufacturing floor
- Managed on-line information database (FOCUS) for Fort Washington Planning
- Assisted in reducing company back orders by $0.4M within one month through careful attention to material management and customer service issues
- Initiated implementation of Finite Capacity Scheduling System software
- Developed comprehensive manual for Tactical Purchasing functions

6/97-1/98

Tactical Buyer, Chemical Purchasing Department
- Placed $1M in purchase orders daily using Cullinet system
- Reduced delivery non-conformances by 80% through effective communication and correspondence with over 70 external chemical suppliers
- Introduced EDI order placement by coordinating with suppliers
- Trained new Buyer in Chemical Department
- Developed comprehensive manual for Tactical Purchasing functions

St. Josephs University, Philadelphia, PA
8/96-5/97   Student Security Assistant; night watchman
8/96-5/97   Research Lab Assistant

St. Josephs Press, Philadelphia, PA
5/96-1/97   Office Representative

COMPUTER SKILLS

IBM PC (including Windows), Macintosh and mainframe environments.
Languages: Basic, Focus, Fortran-77, Pascal, Siman
Business Systems: AMAPS (MRP), Cullinet (Purchasing), FOCUS
Applications: AutoCad, dBase, Lotus, Minitab, STORM, various word processing packages

ACTIVITIES

Delta Sigma Pi, Professional Business Fraternity
Society of Business Interns, founding member
American Production & Inventory Control Society, student member
St. Josephs University Ski Team
St. Josephs University Racquetball Club

NELSON E. CLAYTON

SCHOOL ADDRESS
99 Bradbury Road
Athens, GA 30033
(325) 835-9095

PERMANENT ADDRESS
1931 Colonial Drive
Williamsburg, VA 20212
(809) 671-8102

OBJECTIVE: Obtain an operations management position in a production facility.

EDUCATION: **University of Georgia,** December 2000
- B.S. in Operations Management
- **Financed 95% of education**
- Dean's List (Spring 1999)
- Overall GPA 3.3/4.0
- Major GPA 3.5/4.0

Relevant Coursework
- Facilities Management
- Operations Planning and Control
- Materials Management
- Quality Assurance
- Computer Science
- Effective Speech
- Business Writing
- Business Logistics

In-company Research Project with Bergen Mills
- Redesigned a warehouse and worked on warehouse efficiency
- Worked on transportation of goods to the distribution center
- Incorporated a FIFO inventory system in the distribution center
- Worked with ABC classification in a warehouse

WORK EXPERIENCE: **Park Corporation,** Williamsburg, VA
Inventory Auditor   Summers 1994-1999
- Redesigned and inventoried auto parts room
- Placed orders and expedited for government contracts
- Received and checked orders

B & B Liquors, Athens, GA
Liquor Store Clerk   Winters 1995-1999
- Maintained inventory for store
- Received shipments and stocked shelves
- Assisted customers in finding products
- Performed cashier and check-out duties

ACTIVITIES: **Delta Epsilon Phi Fraternity**
Executive Board Member   Spring 1997-2000
- Rush chairman, responsible for building membership
- Secretary, responsible for corresponding with headquarters
- Alumni Liaison, responsible for corresponding with the alumni
- Kustos, Advisor to the executive board committee

REFERENCES: Available Upon Request

MARILYN A. PARKER

43 State Street
Ithaca, NY 12151
(231) 382-7418

EDUCATION

Cornell University
B.S., Operations Management with Honors, May 2000
Minor: Business Logistics
G.P.A.: 3.73/4.00; Major: 3.81
Honors Thesis: Total Quality Management

RELEVANT COURSES

Operations Management	Quantitative Business Analysis I & II Honors
Quality Assurance Honors	Management Honors
Simulation	Advanced Calculus I and II

CURRENT

Intro to Business Logistics	Facilities Management
Transport Systems	Business Logistics Management
Traffic Management	Operations Planning and Control
Materials Management	Management Information Systems

PROFESSIONAL EXPERIENCE

Credit Office/Sales Associate   6/95-1/98
Noland Company, Ithaca, NY
· Assisted customers and registered sales
· Checked and placed stock
· Took inventory
· Counted, balanced, and deposited store monies
· Monitored outgoing and incoming calls
· Handled credit payments and questions

Data-Entry   Summer 1997
Lord Corporation, Ithaca, NY
· Updated files using the company's mainframe
· Entered data into Lotus spreadsheets
· Did small-scale data collection and compilation projects

Temporary Clerical   Summer & Winter 1998
Pratt Company, Ithaca, NY
· Made collection calls on delinquent accounts
· Researched customer problems
· Prepared bills
· Balanced books
· Opened mail and prepared payments for processing

COMPUTER SKILLS

Hardware:	IBM PC, Macintosh, Cornell University Mainframe
Software:	Lotus 1-2-3, dBase III+, Siman IV, Minitab, Q&A, Pascal, MacWrite, WordPerfect

HONORS & ACTIVITIES

Dean's List, University Scholars Program, Golden Key National Honor
Society, Woman's Chorus, Keynotes, University Choir

ASHLEY BANKS

Current Address
53 Johnson Avenue, #1
Wilmington, DE 19898
(315) 644-9829

Permanent Address
758 Berkeley Avenue
Allentown, PA 17503
(610) 459-3781

OBJECTIVE: To obtain an entry level position in Management Science/Operations Research or Management Information Systems.

EDUCATION: University of Delaware
Bachelor of Science in Quantitative Business Analysis
Minor in Business Law
Graduation August 2000
Cumulative GPA: 3.25/4.00; Major GPA: 3.64/4.00

RELEVANT COURSES:

Forecasting
Simulation
Statistical Methods

Linear Programming
Operations Management
Business Writing and Public Speech

COMPUTER SKILLS: In both Mainframe and PC environments: SIMAN, SAS, Q&A, FORTRAN, LINDO, Lotus 1-2-3, Minitab, deBase III+, MEMO, DOS, Excel, Paradox, Turbo Pascal and various word processors.

RELATED EXPERIENCE:

UNIVERSITY OF DELAWARE, Wilmington, DE
School of Hotel Management, Spring 2000
- Forecasted future statistics for a local restaurant from actual data
- Used Box Jenkins methods as well as Exponential Smoothing

DELAWARE TRUST, Wilmington, DE
University of Delaware Extern Program, 1/5/00 -1/10/00
- Received hands-on experience in customer contact areas
- Learned various aspects of the student segment of Delaware Trust's portfolio
- Developed ideas for University of Delaware account acquisition, retention and control

CENTOCOR, INC., Malvern, PA
MIS/Telecommunications Intern, Summer 1999
- Developed statistical reports using SAS
- Maintained and created databases using Q&A
- Trained coworkers in specific database usage for billing purposes
- Updated form programs previously created in MEMO

OTHER WORK: **THE WEST COMPANY,** Holidays
PRESTON CORPORATION, Summer 1998
HECHT'S DEPARTMENT STORE, Summer 1997
PIZZA HUT, 8/95 - 4/96

HONORS/ ACTIVITIES:

Early college admission
Dean's List 7th semester
Management Science Club

Alpha Chi Delta
Certified SCUBA diver
Modeling

References available upon request

Melissa R. Boerner

School Address:
89 Holland Avenue, Apt. 3-B
Raleigh, NC 28656
(919) 651-4599

Home Address:
11 Conestoga Road
Atlanta, GA 30302
(404) 526-6528

Objective

An entry level position as a management consultant or systems analyst

Education

NORTH CAROLINA STATE
B.S.in Quantitative Business Analysis, expected May 2001
Major GPA - 3.41   Overall GPA - 3.38   Dean's List - 2 semesters

Related Courses: Statistical Methods for Business Decisions, Simulation of Management Systems, Advanced Business Statistics, Management Information Systems, Computer Programming with Business Applications, Data Processing, Calculus, Linear Algebra

Work Experience

Mathematics Aide, DEPARTMENT OF THE NAVY   Summer 1999
- Wrote up program specifications
- Worked on a special project team
- Tested data and debugged COBOL programs

Service Representative, MOVIE KING   Summers 1998, 1999
- Served customer needs
- Controlled cash transactions

Sales Representative, Receptionist, MARKETING SOLUTIONS, INC.   Summer 1998
- Performed door-to-door sales
- Filed order forms as they were received
- Explained job responsibilities to prospective employees

Crew Trainer, Crew Chief, BURGER KING   June 1995-August 1997
- Managed daily receipts and grill area
- Trained new employees and opened the store in the morning

Honors and Activities

- Delta Delta Gamma sorority (elected to pledge chairperson 1998-1999)
- Alpha Lambda Delta national honorary sorority (inducted 1998)
- Business Student Council (programming committee, resume book committee)
- Management Science Club
- Inducted into *The Dean's List* (1998)

LAUREN WRIGHT

Permanent Address
21 Garden Road
Woodbridge, NJ 08854
Telephone: (908) 833-4505

Temporary Address
Union Hall, #5, Ohio University
Athens, OH 44013
Telephone: (216) 997-9342

OBJECTIVE: To obtain an entry level position that utilizes my statistical and analytical educational background.

EDUCATION: BS in Quantitative Business Analysis
Legal Environment of Business Minor
Ohio University
Expected graduation May 2000

Major GPA 3.3/4.0; Cumulative 3.15/4.0

Relevant Courses
Quantitative Business Analysis
Elementary Business Statistics
Statistical Programming Packages

Survey and Sampling
Business and Society

SKILLS: Computer: Basic, Cobol, Pascal, dBase III+, Lotus, WordPerfect, SAS, Minitab, SPSS, Fortran, Siman

Foreign Language   Four years Spanish; One semester German

EXPERIENCE: Peer Tutor, Ohio University Writing Center   1998-1999
- Tutored during drop-in hours
- Advised individuals on various written works

Terminal Operator, Armstrong Corporation   Summer 1997
- Made decisions based on issuing credit reports
- Solved customer problems and responded to inquiries

Collector, National Bank of Ohio   Summer 1996
- Handled 30, 60-day delinquent credit card accounts
- Answered limited customer service inquiries

ACTIVITIES & HONORS: President, Phi Chi Theta Professional Business Fraternity   1998-1999
- Oversaw all fraternity activities
- Presided over the Executive Council

Founding Sister, Kappa Delta Chi Sorority   Fall 1997
- Pride Leader: Group leader acting as liaison to Executive Council
- Gift Mart Chairman: Ordered Kappa Delta Chi items through national organization
- Risk Management Committee

Business Student Council

Spring Week Special Events and Activities Overall Committee
- Scheduled acts for performances on campus
- Organized and oversaw contests and competitions

Dean's List 3rd Semester

JOHN LUNDEN

Local Address:
92 Highland Avenue, #7
Syracuse, NY 15430
(213) 979-3348

Permanent Address:
400 Eighth Avenue
Chicago, IL 60063
(613) 438-6144

EDUCATION
SYRACUSE UNIVERSITY
B.S. in Quantitative Business Analysis; Emphasis in Operations Management
G.P.A. in major: 3.48/4.00; G.P.A overall: 3.05/4.00
Graduation: December 1999

SIGNIFICANT COURSEWORK
MATERIALS MANAGEMENT In-company project
- analyzed inventory control consequences of a paper machine for the Fulton Company

FACILITIES MANAGEMENT Case study
- analyzed facility location, facility layout and capacity planning problems using past history of companies

SIMULATION OF MANAGEMENT STUDIES Individual project
- designed computer program to simulate present sorting production line at U.S. Post Office in Syracuse, then altered program to represent future technological innovations and evaluated the expected effects

COMPUTER SKILLS
- SIMAN Simulation Programming
- LINDO Linear Programming
- STORM Software Package
- PASCAL

- Lotus/Symphony
- Minitab
- Microsoft Word
- WordPerfect

WORK EXPERIENCE
Operations Management
RESEARCH ASSISTANT TO PROFESSOR STEVEN WOOD   August 1997 - May 1998
- acquired and outlined research material on Computer Aided Design and Quality in Manufacturing
- evaluated books from student's perspective to aid in Professor Wood's textbook writing
- graded homework and quizzes for computer simulation class

Research Support Center
LIBRARY AIDE   August 1998 - Present
- helped patrons use business indexes and reference guides

The Bakery
SALES ASSISTANT   July 1997 - Present
- handled money and communicated with the public when selling bakery products

ACTIVITIES
- Orientation Leader for Freshmen
- Intramural Sports Chairperson

- Red Cross Volunteer
- Dormitory Social Historian

BRADLEY HARRINGTON

Current Address:
52 Hobart Street, 1-C
Washington, DC 20036
(202) 499-4589

Permanent Address:
303 Finch Lane
Annapolis, MD 12503
(303) 576-7622

OBJECTIVE: To utilize my knowledge and skills in Finance, Economics, and Real Estate in a Financial Management position.

EDUCATION: AMERICAN UNIVERSITY
Washington, DC
Bachelor of Science, December 2000
Major: Real Estate with an emphasis in Finance
Minor: Economics

RELEVANT COURSES:

Investment Valuation
Financial Management
Strategic Management
Management Concepts
Valuation of Real Property
Real Estate Finance and Investment

Speculative Markets
Corporation Finance
Money and Banking
Capital Budgeting
Business Law

EXPERIENCE: PACE MEMBERSHIP WAREHOUSE   1998-Present
· Chosen to represent Pace at different stores and sell memberships
· Helped coordinate the customer service department at the new store
· Handled returns and complaints; issued new membership cards
· Ordered inventory; arranged displays

MAKRO MEMBERSHIP WAREHOUSE   1995-1998
· Provided customer service; handled complaints; took returns; issued "Makro passports"; cashiered
· Took inventory and made sales at the jewelry counter
· Helped transfer stores from Makro to Pace

ACTIVITIES: Finance Club
Real Estate Club
1999 Intramural Softball Champions
Intramural Racquetball

REFERENCES: Available upon request.

THOMAS HARPER

701 Cactus Street   Telephone: (701) 866-6153
Phoenix, AZ 74513

OBJECTIVE: To obtain an entry-level position in the Real Estate and/or Finance field.

EDUCATION: Arizona State University
B.S. Candidate College of Business Administration,
Real Estate Major, Degree Expected December 1999.

Relevant Courses:

Real Estate	Urban Geography	Management	Finance
Economics	Business Law	Marketing	QBA
Computers	B Log	MIS	Int'l Bus.

MILITARY: Disbursing Clerk, United States Navy   5/94-5/96
- Traveled extensively in Bahrain, United Arab Emirates, Saudi Arabia and Oman.
- Provided customer service for personnel concerning disbursing questions, processed numerous pay accounts for payrolls and special payrolls, assisted in processing monthly financial returns.

Disbursing Clerk, United States Navy   11/97-4/98
- Activated under Operation Desert Shield/Storm

WORK EXPERIENCE: Assistant Rental Consultant, Sun Real Estate Group   1/99-pres.
- Worked in Apartment Store Office under Property Mgr., assisted in showing of apartment buildings, approval of prospective tenants and processing of leases; searched for new tenants and performed various other duties.

Carpenter, Grainger Construction   Summer 96-98
- Constructed homes according to blueprint, remodeled homes and commercial properties and became familiar with structural defects.

ACTIVITIES: Real Estate Club, Arizona State University
International Association of Corporate Real Estate Executives
Habitat Program Volunteer, Phoenix Area
Racquetball Club, Arizona State University

PETER McALLISTER

SCHOOL ADDRESS
8101 Seminole Boulevard
Tallahassee, FL 30023
(272) 888-1641

PERMANENT ADDRESS
295 Logan Street
Albany, NY 12356
(243) 459-6219

PROFESSIONAL OBJECTIVE:

To contribute in a professional environment where my strong communication skills, coupled with a sincere desire to learn, may make duties productive and enjoyable for myself and my employer.

EDUCATION:

Florida State University
Bachelor of Science in Real Estate
Anticipated Graduation: May, 2000
Cumulative Grade Average: 3.17

RELATED COURSEWORK:

Accounting	Calculus	Quantitative Business Analysis
Economics Finance	Business Logistics	International Business
Management	Real Estate	Computer Programming
Marketing	Business Law	

COMPUTER SKILLS:

BASIC, Pascal, Lotus 1-2-3, DBase III+, Minitab, MacWrite, MacDraw, and Word Perfect

ACTIVITIES:

Sophomore Business Enterprise Teaching Assistant
Appointed Junior Business Enterprise Teaching Assistant
Member Florida State Real Estate Club
Member 1994 Florida State Boxing Club
Captain of various Intramural sports teams
Member of Florida State University 1997-98 National Club Championship Ice Hockey Team

RELEVANT WORK EXPERIENCE:

1996 - Present	Self Employed (T-shirt distribution business)
Summer 1998-99	Brookstone & Sullivan, P.C., Albany, NY (Administrative duties in a corporate law firm)
Summer 1997	Infinity Broadcasting, Albany, NY (Developed radio advertising)

REFERENCES: Furnished upon request

Montgomery Burns

98 Evergreen Road
Ruston, LA 41221
(319) 661-7883

EDUCATION

Louisiana Tech University, Masters in Business Administration, emphasis in marketing, finance, and land development, expected August 2001

US Military Academy, West Point, Bachelor of Science, Engineering, May 1992

EXPERIENCE

Construction Superintendent, Bethel Construction Company -- Responsible for all facets of construction including scheduling, coordinating, and supervising the work of all subcontractors; and approving monthly fund distributions. Took over as superintendent of a 92-unit, $10M condominium complex after 3 months as an assistant superintendent. Successfully completed the project and turned the units over to individual owners. Completed a 198-unit, $22M, apartment complex in 38 weeks (from ground breaking to completion). The project was under budget, two weeks ahead of schedule, and a high-quality product. (May '97 to Nov. '99)

Facility Engineer, US Army Corps of Engineers, Captain -- Responsible for developing long-range construction programs; reviewing plans and specifications for all new construction, and the allocation, utilization, and maintenance of over 2.4M square feet of existing facilities. Developed and gained approval for a construction program involving over $50M worth of new construction; planned a successful reorganization of commercial and residential facilities to accommodate the needs of a newly formed unit consisting of 1,000 soldiers. (March '95 to May '97)

Support Platoon Leader, US Army, 8th Engineer Bn. -- Supervisor of 40 soldiers, responsible for the utilization and maintenance of over $35M worth of heavy engineer equipment and mobile bridging. Heavy weapons training officer responsible for running integrated multi-weapon live firing exercises. (May '94 to March '95)

Company Executive Officer, US Army, 2nd Engineer Bn. (Korea) -- Responsible for the maintenance, training, mess, and supply operations of a 160-man combat engineer company deployed along the DMZ in the Republic of Korea. Developed and implemented a maintenance program which led to a 9% increase in on-line operating time and won a Maintenance Excellence Award. (Nov. '93 to May '94)

Platoon Leader, US Army, 2nd Engineer Bn. (Korea) -- Responsible for maintaining the combat readiness of a platoon of 35 construction and demolition specialists in the Republic of Korea. Unit explosives officer responsible for training and safety on live explosive ranges and missions. (Dec. '92 to Nov. '93)

HONORS AND ACTIVITIES

- Teaching Assistant, Finance Department, Louisiana Tech University, -- I teach a finance problem-solving lab to undergraduate Junior level business majors.
- Licensed Professional Engineer (Louisiana - Mechanical)
- Distinguished graduate, US Army Engineer School

GRADUATION   August 2001

Jeremy Spillane

LOCAL ADDRESS
8 Farmville Road, #8
Murray, KY 54503
(721) 381-9841

PERMANENT ADDRESS
322 Concord Road
Chicago, IL 33413
(312) 648-4773

EDUCATION

Murray State, Masters in Business Administration, emphasis in telecommunications management, expected December 1999; current GPA 4.0.

Murray State, Bachelor of Science in Electrical Engineering, May 1998; overall GPA 3.25.

EXPERIENCE

Associate Electrical Engineer, Morgan Products, Inc, Lincolnshire, IL -- programming in turbo basic and turbo C; Printed Circuit Board (PCB) Electrical Analyses; R&D in microwave Triple and microstrip transmission lines; PCB testing (Summer '93, Spring and Fall '96 -- total one year, full-time, as part of the cooperative engineering program).

Associate Telecommunications Engineer, Dynatech Corporation, Murray, KY -- cost allocation program development for double-ring fiber-optic network in Lexington, KY; database development and management for "Fiesta Kentucky" telecommunications project in Lexington, KY; engineering support (July '97 to July '98, part-time).

HONORS AND ACTIVITIES

Murray State: member of the Freshmen Honor Society ('94), National Honor Society ('94), International Honor Society ('95), Golden Key Honor Society ('95); on the Electrical Engineering Honor Roll for Spring '94, Dean's List ('93-'94).

Murray State: member of the MBA/MS association, active participant in the "Europe Club" student organization.

OTHER POTENTIALLY APPLICABLE INFORMATION

- Passed the Engineer-In-Training Examination (EIT).
- Will graduate at age 22.
- Tri-lingual (French, Hebrew, and English) / Cross-cultural background.
- Familiar with many spreadsheet, word processing, database, and programming software for both the MAC and PC (DOS, Lotus 123, Excel, Quattro Pro, DBase3, MS Word, WordPerfect, MacWrite, Sprint, PSPICE, MathCad, Turbo Basic, Turbo C, Pascal, Fortran).

GRADUATION   December 1999.

Thomas L. Edwards

LOCAL ADDRESS
35 Wylie Road, Apt. E-3
Haverford, PA 19324
(610) 793-2684

PERMANENT ADDRESS
77 Manor Drive
Dover, DE 19788
(302) 747-6454

EDUCATION

Villanova University, Masters in Business Administration, emphasis in Business Analysis/MIS, expected May 2000; current GPA 3.50

Villanova University, Bachelor of Science in Aerospace Engineering, August 1996; Overall GPA 2.9

EXPERIENCE

Engineer, GE Aerospace, Philadelphia, PA, F-16 Stress Analysis Airframe --
Determined structural integrity of F-16 fighter; proposed a repair for the test aircraft; approved design modifications for future airplanes; communicated structural requirements to the design group; automated production of stress reports using the CAD/CAM graphics system (August 1996 to January 1998)

Co-op Engineer, GE Aerospace, Philadelphia, PA, CAD/CAM Engineering --
Coordinated specifications between departments in development of a data base; organized and presented quarterly status report to the planning office (August 1994 to January 1994)

Co-op Engineer, GE Aerospace, Philadelphia, PA, Propulsion Analysis --
Acted as liaison between GE Aerospace and the engine manufacturer; produced and submitted engine performance data to airplane customers; coordinated progress of engine modifications to U.S. Air Force (January 1994 to May 1994)

HONORS AND ACTIVITIES

MBA/MS Association
Villanova University Corps of Cadets, August 1991 to May 1995
Distinguished Student 1992

COMPUTER SKILLS

MS DOS: Lotus 123, dBase, Harvard Graphics, Wordperfect, MS Word
MACINTOSH: Excel, MS Word, MacWrite
LANGUAGES: Fortran, C, BASIC

GRADUATION   May 2000

Stephen Evans

LOCAL ADDRESS	PERMANENT ADDRESS
5056 East Parker Road	Fair Meadow Farm
Bryan, TX 75430	Lake Charles, LA 78438
(713) 952-1834	(572) 532-6753

EDUCATION

Texas A&M University, Masters in Business Administration: emphasis in management information systems, degree expected May 2001; current GPA 4.0 (as of March 2000).

Texas A&M University, Bachelor of Science in Aerospace Engineering: focus in control systems and astrodynamics; degree received May 1990; Magna Cum Laude; GPA 3.83.

EXPERIENCE

Manager, Titan 11 Guidance Analysis & Software Validation Group, Dalfort Aviation, Dallas, TX Supervised the software engineering group, whose charter was to validate computer programs which guide unmanned rockets carrying various satellites into space. Composed detailed work plans, schedules, and developed labor estimates for new contracts. Managed the department's cost accounts in accordance with Cost/Schedule Control Systems criteria. Achieved a 20% cost reduction for analyses which were conducted to support the launch of a defense satellite mission. Interfaced with customer representatives from the United States Air Force, other contractor firms, and internal departments regarding the design, development, and flight readiness of the guidance software. (November 1993 to August 1999).

Engineer 11, Advanced Projects Flight Controls Group, Cooper Industries, Aircraft Division, Houston, TX -- Responsible for development of software for advanced aircraft simulations. Tasks included flight control algorithm design, analysis, testing, and mathematical modelling of various aircraft systems. Communicated with government and company test pilots in the simulators, obtaining evaluations of the flying qualities of fighter aircraft. (June 1990 to October 1993).

HONORS AND ACTIVITIES

Received three commendations for exemplary job performance at Dalfort Aviation. Member of Phi Kappa Phi, Sigma Gamma Tau, and Tau Beta Pi honor societies. Member of American Institute of Aeronautics & Astronautics; served as committee chairman at Texas A&MUniversity Student Chapter 1989-90. Lake Charles High School Valedictorian 1986. Elected National Honor Society President 1985-86. Named in Who's Who Among American High School Students, National Register of Commended Scholars, and Society of Distinguished American High School Students 1986.

COMPUTER SKILLS

Mainframe: CDC Network Operating System, UNIX Workstations, IBM TSO.
Macintosh: Microsoft Word, Excel, MacDraw, CricketGraph, NCSA Telnet, SmartForm Assistant, Microphone II, SoftPC.
PC DOS: Lotus 123, WordPerfect, dBase III Plus.

GRADUATION May 2001.

Larry Ellis

LOCAL ADDRESS
333 Logan Avenue South, #1-A
Boston, MA 02211
(617) 292-3389

PERMANENT ADDRESS
82 Slope Road
Killington, VT 03382
(234) 773-8912

EDUCATION

Massachusetts Institute of Technology, Masters of Business Administration, Expected degree date: August, 2000. Graduate School Specialty Electives: Total Quality Process, Engineering Economics and TQM, Polymer Engineering Computer Aided Design and Engineering.

Massachusetts Institute of Technology, B.S. Mechanical Engineering, GPA: 3.3, Degree date: August 11, 1998.

EXPERIENCE

Graduate Assistant; MIT, Technology Licensing Office, College Station, TX. Research Assistant: Interface with University inventors; conduct patent and literature searches, application and market research, and pursue industries which could benefit from the technology (Fall 1999 - present).

Camp Counselor; Killington Camp, Killington, VT. Christian Athletic Camp; top rated in America; Cabin Counselor for 13 and 16 yr. age kids; Instructor for tennis, volleyball, wind surfing and soccer; led Bible studies and counseled kids (Summer 1999).

Co-op Engineer; GTE Government Systems, Waltham, MA. Liaison Engineer: Resolved manufacturing and engineering problems, coordinated between production and design engineers, completed required design, drafting and document changes (Fall 1997).

Co-op Engineer; GTE Government Systems, Waltham, MA. Assistant Design Engineer: Worked on advanced test project. Involved mechanical design, CAD/CAM, composites technology, aircraft structures and coordination between project groups (Spring 1997).

Co-op Engineer; GTE Government Systems, Waltham, MA. Engineering Assistant: Delivered electronic hardware and documentation to and coordinated with people throughout plant. Performed mechanical design on CAD/CAM for manufacturing problems (Summer 1996).

Summer Intern; Northeast Research Institute, Emissions Control Department, Boston, MA. Engineering Assistant: Assisted in experimental and literature research, prepared figures and data for technical papers, computed engineering calculations (Summer 1995).

HONORS AND ACTIVITIES

MIT- Distinguished Student Award - Spring '94, '95; M.E. Dept. Scholarship '94, '95; Tau Beta Pi, Engineering Honor Society; Pi Tau Sigma, Mechanical Engineering Honor Society; Memorial Student Center Council - Operations Committee '94; Opera and Performing Arts Society '95-'96; Campus Crusade for Christ; ASME; MBA Association; MIT Intramural Sports; Tennis singles and doubles, Flag Football, Soccer, Softball and Basketball.

GRADUATION August 2000

Paula Cole

333 Michigan Avenue, Apt. C
East Lansing, MI 66432
(342) 841-8934

EDUCATION

Michigan State University, Masters of Science in Human Resources Management, expected December 2000; current GPA 3.81

Duke University, Bachelor of Arts in Management, May 1995; Overall GPA 3.2. Major GPA 3.9

EXPERIENCE

Human Resources Assistant, Rockwell International Corporation, Automotive Division, Troy, MI; Professional Summer internship -- Assisting labor relations staff in preparation for December 2000, contract negotiations; preparing summations of labor arbitration cases; assisting staff with various needs related to employees at the Troy Automotive Division (Summer 2000).

Graduate Assistant, Department of Management, Graduate School for Business, Michigan State University, East Lansing, MI -- Assisting several faculty in the Department of Management with research and class preparation for graduate and undergraduate level courses in management (Fall 1998 - present); Interviewing 76 undergraduate applicants for the College of Business administration's "CBA Fellows" Program (Fall 1999); Working with faculty from the Departments of Management, Urban Planning, Family Medicine, and Statistics on a project funded by the National Institutes of Health, investigating the effects of health facility design on patients' compliance with treatment and on staff's absenteeism/turnover behavior -- leading a four-person research team, coordinating data collection and entry, budgeting/expense management of a $150,000 research grant (Fall 1998 to Summer 1999).

Senior Banking Representative, Teller Supervisor, Consumer Lender, National Bank of Michigan, Detroit, MI -- Supervising six tellers at a branch office, including quarterly performance appraisals and annual salary reviews, developing programs to enhance teamwork, with a special emphasis on group efforts to improve customer service; Consumer Lending authority level two of five: authority to independently lend up to $15,000 secured and $5,000 unsecured per customer; responsible for 25% of monthly sales for the branch (January 1996 to August 1998).

HONORS AND ACTIVITIES

President, Graduate Women's Business Network, Michigan State University, 1999-2000
Member, Society for Human Resource Management, Michigan State University and National Member, MBA/MS Association, Michigan State University, 1998-present
Catcher, MBA/MS Co-Rec Softball team, "The Masters," Spring 2000
Member, American Institute of Banking, Detroit, MI, 1996-1998

GRADUATION   December 2000

Martha P. Lane

LOCAL ADDRESS
35 Columbus Avenue, Apt. C-3
New York, NY 10322
(212) 645-8348

PERMANENT ADDRESS
812 Baxter Street
Downingtown, PA 19458
(610) 358-7843

EDUCATION

New York University, Master of Science in Management with a concentration in Human Resource Management Candidate, May 2000.

Duke University, Bachelor of Science, Major: Psychology, May 1997.

Duke University Studies Abroad Program, Cortona, Italy, Marble sculpting and drawing, June-August 1996.

EXPERIENCE

Graduate Assistant, Department of Management, New York University (September 1998 to present) -- assist two professors, including the Department Head of Management, in research.

Intern, Gartner Group, Inc., New York, NY, HR management consulting firm (Spring 1997-Summer 1997) -- organization of job satisfaction surveys and result, compiling self-help packets for feedback, marketing research (Christmas 1998) -- co-wrote report on HR strategies for Workforce 2000.

Assistant in Operations, Hemisphere Graphics., Durham, NC (Spring 1996, Fall 1996) -- graphic design, training documentation development, software testing, electronic forms design (Christmas 1994, Fall 1995) -- receptionist.

Tutor, Duke University (Fall 1994, Spring 1995) -- tutored students in software use, computer hardware installation, troubleshooting.

HONORS AND ACTIVITIES

Graduate Women's Business Network, Treasurer
MBA/MS Association Member
Dean's Honor List, Honor List
Allison Meyers Scholarship, 4 years
USSR Friendship Force Exchange
Catalyst Committee Chair
Intramural Association, board member,
Artwork selected for 25th Annual Mostra, Cortona, Italy

COMPUTER SKILLS

PC DOS: Lotus 123, dBase, WordPerfect, MSWord, Wordstar
MACINTOSH: PageMaker, Microsoft Word, MacWrite, MacDraw

GRADUATION   May 2000

Kelly Ann Franklin

LOCAL ADDRESS
103 Rosewood Drive
Richmond, VA 14583
(303) 943-8374

PERMANENT ADDRESS
3567 Spanish Bay Road
Albuquerque, NM 89343
(852) 234-3454

EDUCATION

University of Virginia, Master of Science in Human Resource Management, expected May 2000; current GPA 3.75

University of New Mexico, Bachelor of Arts in English and Spanish, May 1998; Graduated with Honors -- completed 36 hours of Honors Courses; GPA 3.4

EXPERIENCE

Summer Intern, Human Resources, James River Corporation, Richmond, VA -- Worked on Equal Employment Opportunity and Team Effectiveness projects (Summer 1999).

Graduate Assistant, Department of Management, University of Virginia -- Compiled a mailing list of Human Resource Executives to be used in a department research project; reviewed textbook galleys; assisted in grading tests (September 1998 to present).

Summer Intern, Human Resources, Microdyne Corporation, Alexandria, VA -- Developed and moderated a New Employee Orientation Program; identified issues and impacts of the current disability reporting process and made recommendations to improve the process; coordinated tours, activities, and weekly lunch speakers for summer interns (May 1998 to August 1998).

Tour Guide and Desk Worker, Visitor Center, University of New Mexico -- Scheduled visitor appointments; showed prospective students around campus (September 1996 - May 1998).

Summer Intern, Human Resources, Public Service Company of New Mexico, Albuquerque, NM -- Coordinated the summer intern program including tours and activities and compiled a manual for the coordination of this program; developed supervisor guidelines outlining pre-arrival steps and a summer timetable for supervisors of summer interns; interpreted data from recruiting surveys (May 1997 to August 1997).

HONORS AND ACTIVITIES

- Honors Graduate, University of New Mexico, 1998
- Who's Who Among Students in American Universities and Colleges
- Student Government: Freshman Programs (Outstanding Freshman Aide)
- Parents' Weekend Committee Programming Sub-Chairman for 2 years
- Mortar Board, Inc./Cap & Gown (Publicity Chairman) - National Senior Honor Society
- Cardinal Key/Tau Kappa Chapter - National Junior Honor Society
- Freshman Program - planned activities to assist incoming freshmen with their transition from high school to college

GRADUATION   May 2000

Rebecca Sommers

LOCAL ADDRESS	PERMANENT ADDRESS
345 College Lane, Apt. D-3	1753 Westheimer Road
Durham, NC 23345	Houston, TX 75703
(342) 874-8934	(713) 954-7867

EDUCATION

Duke University, Master in Business Administration, emphasis in marketing, expected December 2000; current GPA 3.63

Texas A&M University, Bachelor of Journalism, emphasis in public relations and marketing, December 1998; Overall GPA 3.75

EXPERIENCE

Public Relations Intern, ARCO Oil and Gas Company, Houston, TX -- compiled a HAZWOPER cross-reference list and researched all MSDS sheets for the area. Described the routing of ARCO pipelines through communities for inclusion in ARCO's Environmental Response Plan. Attended community meetings in which the plan was presented to fire and police personnel as well as community members (May 1998 to August 1998).

Advertising Intern, ProSports Designs, Inc., Raleigh, NC -- wrote copy and designed graphics promoting celebrity golf tournament and professional tennis event. Oversaw all stages of production for both projects. Used Macintosh computers (January 1998 to May 1998).

HONORS AND ACTIVITIES

- Graduate Assistant to Dr. Conrad Reicher, Journalism Department Head
- Recipient, Minority Merit Fellowship ($10,000 per year)
- MBA/MS Association-Mentors Program
- Graduate Women's Business Network
- American Marketing Association Student Chapter-Publications
- Member, Women in Communications, Inc.
- Public Relations Student Society of America-Attended the 1997 PRSSA National Convention
- Kappa Tau Alpha Honor Society
- Bloomingdale Retailing Communications Competition - Outstanding Performance Award, January 1999

RELEVANT COURSE WORK

Consumer Behavior	Analyzing Consumer Behavior	Retail Concepts & Policies
Services Marketing	Research Marketing Decisions	Advertising Principles
Marketing Management	International Marketing	Media and the Community

GRADUATION   December 2000